Stuart Blofeld was born in 1915.

As a new boy at Bromsgrove school he was warned by his housemaster to stop keeping the other boys awake by recounting adventure stories. Years later he lived through his own personal one, journeying through a minefield of events as a P.O.W. in Austria until, helped by the Austrian girl whom he later married, he escaped and saw at first hand the horrifying occupation of Eastern Austria by the Russians.

Later, he became the Creative Director of a Dublin Advertising Agency, finally retiring to Bath where he and his wife live with their unforgettable memories. They have two sons and one grandson.

Journey Through
A Minefield

Stuart Blofeld

Journey Through A Minefield

Vanguard Press

VANGUARD PAPERBACK

© Copyright 2004
Stuart Blofeld

The right of Stuart Blofeld to be identified as author of
this work has been asserted by him in accordance with the
Copyright, Designs and Patents Act 1988

All Rights Reserved

No reproduction, copy or transmission of this publication
may be made without written permission.
No paragraph of this publication may be reproduced,
copied or transmitted save with the written permission of the
publisher, or in accordance with the provisions
of the Copyright Act 1956 (as amended).

Any person who does any unauthorised act in relation to
this publication may be liable to criminal
prosecution and civil claims for damage.

Although the characters in this publication are drawn
from the author's wide experience, any precise
resemblance to any real person, living or dead, is purely coincidental.

A CIP catalogue record for this title is
available from the British Library
ISBN 1 84386 110 0

*Vanguard Press is an imprint of
Pegasus Elliot MacKenzie Publishers Ltd.*
www.pegasuspublishers.com

First Published in 2004

**Vanguard Press
Sheraton House Castle Park
Cambridge England**

Printed & Bound in Great Britain

To Hilde

Chapter 1

By the end of October 1939, when it dawned on me that I was the right age to get killed by a German, I decided that there were more sensible things to do. Becoming a 'conchie' was out of the question: I was far too much of a coward to be cast out by my friends and banish myself from society for the sake of some remote principle. There were simpler ways of getting as far away from a bayonet as possible. The Auxiliary Fire Squad, for instance. I could have a go at joining that. But what about the other two men in the family? How would they take it? My father, a patriotic, conservative canon in the Church of England, made of the stuff that was going to win the war for the Motherland, and my brother, previously in the Territorial Army, and now a chaplain in an infantry regiment, ready to be shipped out to the slaughter in Europe, where he would be mentioned in dispatches for distributing unholy cigarettes and gramophone records, under fire, to the living, and administering holy communion to the dying.

Expecting my call-up papers to arrive any day, I happened to have come back home from London, where I'd worked for four years in advertising, to spend a weekend with my family in Birmingham. Nothing had been said about my plans until my father called me into his study. Like the big gun that he was he opened fire without warning.

"You'll be going for a commission, of course."

There seemed to be no need to answer such a positive statement, almost an order; but he had always taught me to be polite, so I replied, understandingly:

"Not really, father. I don't like the idea."

Once more I was the erring youngest son as he glared at me over his spectacles, a habit which had had me shaking with terror until I had found my feet away from the apron strings.

"It's not a matter of likes and dislikes, young fellow-mi-lad." (He always called me this, accompanied by an uncontrollable shaking of his unusually large head, when he was extremely annoyed with me.) "England needs men to lead; men with qualifications. Why have I lived a life of self-denial to pay for your education? You have your Certificate 'A'. I do not see what possible excuse you would have for joining the ranks."

This was obviously not the time to mention the Auxiliary Fire Squad. There would be plenty of occasions for the vicarage roof to get blown off when the bombs landed.

True, as a compulsory member of the O.T.C. at one of the country's lesser known public schools I had, after many attempts at the age of nineteen-and-a-half, managed to lead my platoon of totally disinterested school mates, armed with twelve-year-old service rifles loaded with blanks, to victory against a non-existent enemy with an audience of several giggling rabbits and a bored adjudicating brigadier until, apparently, we had won the battle. After this they had given me my Cert. 'A' which would enable me to get a commission, should the need ever arise, without any string-pulling.

But the time had come to face up to my father.

"If I am told to shoot somebody, I suppose I shall," I said. "That's quite a different matter from ordering some other chap to kill his fellow human beings and shooting him in the back if he prefers to run away, especially if I feel like doing the same myself."

He seemed puzzled.

"I don't expect a son of mine to talk like that. Duty is duty."

You could almost hear the turmoil in his mind. The whole idea of war, I knew, was detestable to him. But it was there. We were up to our eyes in it; and we were in the right. Hadn't the Times been plugging it for months? And to my father the Times was the fifth gospel. Chamberlain had said we would be fighting against 'brute force' and 'bad faith'. If these evil things were represented by innocent men with hats shaped like jeremiahs, it was their bad luck. But whenever I had dared to get into an argument with my father he had beaten me as soundly as he always beat my mother at chess, (mainly because she preferred a peaceful atmosphere to winning), so I decided not to continue the subject at this stage; instead, I just shrugged my shoulders and turned to go. At this, he started to point out how superior my brother was to me, until his conscience got at him and he began to relent.

"Of course you are entitled to your convictions. I understand what you say about killing people. But remember: we must have faith. We must fight for the right — for a better world. God moves in mysterious ways. We must not question Him."

A hell of a sight too mysterious for me, I thought, more determined than ever to join the A.F.S. If necessary, putting out fires in air raids would be the job for me. But so far there had been no air raids: why should things change? As soon as I could, I'd get away back to London. I had to beat those call-up papers - volunteer for something before they got me.

My mother, hating her own indecision, flung her arms round my neck, kissing me, and said:

"You should do as your father says." Then she hesitated. "But then again, perhaps you should do as God tells you. I will pray that He does that."

She looked thoroughly miserable, and a bit doubtful, at the prospect of bringing the Almighty into it, so I didn't tell her that He'd done that already.

In London again, I had to get down to business, but I hadn't reckoned on there being so many others taking the sixth commandment (Thou shalt do no murder) seriously. Snaking round side roads to the main entrance and finally into the converted dining hall of the Paddington Hospital for Venereal Diseases was a queue at least half a mile long. Undaunted, I bought myself two magazines and a paper, shuffling along inch by inch, reading, for three hours before I eventually got through the door into the hall. When I saw the uniformed member of the London Fire Brigade at the table, taking down particulars, my feet were aching. Two hours later they were itching to kick him and the rest of his staff in the rear.

As I had arrived at the table he had taken a look first at me, then at his watch and had gone off for his lunch. Such was the lure of the A.F.S. that, even when someone had asked, "How long will you be?" and he had answered: "About an hour and a half: with my job I have to eat well, you know–not hang around like you lot of layabouts," nobody had complained. But it had been enough for me. I had already had my fill. I gave my magazine, paper and my sympathy to the man behind me, and left; the wiser by three short stories and an article on planting mustard and cress in inverted steel helmets when the war would be over.

The next morning my call-up papers arrived and I was doomed to one of the services. It seemed the Royal Navy was out, unless you were at least related to an admiral. There was the R.A.F., of course, but when I arrived at Brixton to find the queue being dispersed, a notice on the door of the recruitment centre, FULL UP -- NO MORE APPLICANTS WANTED, was the answer to that little flash in the pan.

So I was to become a member of the ground forces; which could mean anything safe, dangerous or suicidal, as long as you were in some way connected with the ground before you got blown off it. Now was the time to play the little card tucked up my sleeve - the H.A. (Heavy Artillery). With any luck I would be in a dugout when the missiles arrived, using my bayonet to open a tin of McConochie's stewed steak between salvos. This would suit me. With this in mind I went out and found what I hoped was the right queue. But, with God moving in his mysterious ways, like my father had said, I was fated for something entirely different. Being in no hurry, and hoping the queue would get shorter, I went to a local pub with a peace-loving friend to celebrate his total failure to pass his medical, arriving back in a slightly overconfident and facetious mood.

The recruiting officer who interviewed me looked grim-faced and bored.

"Why do you want to join the H.A., man?" he asked. Perhaps it was my imagination which told he was sneering or perhaps a guilty conscience, or the beer. Whatever the reason, I immediately disliked him intensely. To hell with the H.A.

"Because my father is a canon!" I said.

Not even the tiniest trace of a smile broke the sardonic line of his tight lips. Nor did he even oblige me by looking annoyed.

"Good! There is a nice big cannon in a 'Matilda Two'."

"What's a 'Matilda Two', sir?"

"Good God, man.......!", He turned to his clerk, "Tell him, Corporal Higgins. Tell this clever fellow what a 'Matilda Two' is."

"The 'Matilda Two' is Britain's latest thirty ton tank," said the clerk sympathetically.

"Sorry, I didn't know that, sir."

Still with nostalgic visions of the H.A., I had managed to sound completely ignorant, hoping the officer would change his mind and get me as far behind the lines as possible.

"You'll know a lot more than that soon," he said. "Corporal, put this man down for the R.A.C.–heavy tanks. The lead in his head may slow the tank down but at least it will put him where all clever dicks should be, right up in the front line with the least possible distance between him and the nearest German."

This was the prelude to my introduction to the British armed forces, with plenty more surprises to come. There was no question about the mysterious ways in which they moved. Square-bashing until the feet, surviving the blisters stage, had become like reinforced concrete, learning everything a 'Matilda Two' gunner should know–and more; being taught that we were the cream of the Royal Armoured Corps and that light tanks and Bren gun carriers were 'crap'. Keeping up my determination not to 'get out there and kill the bastards,' I worked harder than I'd ever worked to pass out and qualify as a gunnery instructor. When I failed, my fate was sealed. It was no good trying any more. If the politicians could do it, I would. With my future in the wobbly hands of the war office I did a complete 'U' turn.

When we were all called out on parade at the end of our training, for what we thought would be a good send off by the C.O. of the training regiment, standing at ease and waiting, I finally convinced myself that I was actually looking forward to getting into action; with one reservation; there would have to be nine or ten inches of armour plating between me and the enemy. Yes, our Matilda Twos, if I was in one of them, would beat hell out of the Jerries.

The points on the ends of the regimental sergeant-major's waxed moustache vibrated as he called us all up to attention at the approach of the glum–looking C.O. Having cleared his throat almost guiltily the colonel launched into the speech that must have been keeping him awake at night for weeks.

"First of all," he said, "I have to congratulate you men on your performance over the past nine weeks and the speed with which you have become so efficient". He cleared his throat again. "And now I have to tell you something which, I am sure, will be a disappointment to most of you. You have been trained for heavy tanks but you are being drafted to light tanks and Bren gun carrier outfits." (In other words, to the 'crap' of the R.A.C.)

Like an approaching tornado the moan of disbelief grew louder until the men were shouting in anger. The sergeant–major's moustachioes double-twitched and the colonel raised his hand.

"Yes, I know," he said when the noise had died down. I understand your feelings. I would feel the same way myself, but I have my orders which I must obey. I am sure you men will do as well under these unexpected circumstances as you have been doing recently, once you get used to the idea."

While the men growled with discontent he beckoned in the direction of the moustache:

"Sergeant-Major, would you take over?"

Then, obviously glad to leave it all to someone else, he walked away. The sergeant–major, together with two or three unsympathetic corporals, began the demoralising process of splitting us up. Cursing the army and not really knowing what we were in for, we followed our orders obediently. "Even numbers on the right, odd numbers on the left. O.K., mi' lucky lads, we'ain't got all day."

With these simple words everyone's fate was sealed. The lucky lads might stay alive. The others - well....

Late in the morning of April 23rd 1941 thirty Stukas screamed down out of the sun, dropped their bombs and came back with machine-guns firing at eleven hundred rounds a minute, while I crouched behind a boulder in Southern Greece.

In spite of my efforts to keep away from it all, here I was (with teeth chattering on the hottest day of summer so far), waiting for the next order from our company commander, who was full of enthusiasm after winning an M.C. for conspicuous bravery in the face of the enemy; losing a whole squadron of chaps like me in the process. Unlike the rest of us, Captain Michael St. John Blakeley-Forbes had not even bothered to take cover.

"The idiot thinks he can hide behind that fuckin' great 'tache of his," said the chap next to me. "Beside that load of fungus old Kitchener's would have looked like a bleedin' worn-out toothbrush."

But our company commander was really no laughing matter, though his tin hat was supported on his ears, sticking out like a couple of bat's wings, and his moustache was fortunately big enough to hide the rest of his face. The disturbing fact was that his 'Sam Brown' leather belt was shining and his brasses were glittering in the sunlight so much that he had become an easy target for even a half-blind German.

"Nobby Clarke was pissed last night on the bottle of whisky he pinched from Forbes's kitbag," said the chap next to me, chuckling. (Nobby was the captain's batman). "If the git knew that Nobby'd had a hangover and forgotten to khaki-blanco them brasses, he'd have 'im castrated."

I wasn't listening. Searching the distance, nothing but woods and olive groves with not a human in sight, the captain had just swung his arm over his shoulder, like a fast bowler. He must have spotted something, and was going in for the 'kill'. Whether it was to be 'them' or 'us' didn't seem to worry him.

"Come on chaps, let's get at 'em," he shouted.

It was a matter of running away or following. There was no alternative. If you ran away you got shot in the back: if you followed you got shot in the front. It didn't much matter, except that being shot in the back would be a bit like an 'own goal' and I wasn't keen on this idea. Just then, the captain sprang into the air with a yell, and landed on his back in a ditch.

Quickly, my platoon sergeant, Bob Crabbe, ran over and dragged him to cover, soothing him tenderly.

"Nasty one, this. Right in the arse, sir. But not to worry. In one cheek and out the other, clean as a whistle. sir. Never mind, you never was one for sitting around much, sir, was you?"

As, by this time the captain was unconscious the sergeant's friendly little joke was lost on him.

"Who the hell shall I leave him with?" shouted the sergeant. "Come on you lousy lot: make up your minds. We've got to get those bastards before they get us."

"I'll s-stay, Sarge," a terrified Trooper Crawley called in a quaking voice from behind a bush.

"Why you?"

"I'm colour blind, Sarge. Everything looks the same to me: k-khaki, field-grey, the lot. I'd be dangerous to have around any more, Sarge. Don't know how I passed my m-medical."

He had my respect. Here really was a man who was going to keep the sixth commandment, at all costs.

There was no time to waste. The Jerries were firing a few random shots again. So we left Trooper Crawley with Captain Blakeley-Forbes and waited for orders from the sergeant. We supposed the captain had been leading us towards the woods where he had thought the Germans were when he had 'copped' it in the rear. But nobody was quite sure, and the best thing to do seemed to be to get behind something solid, hope there were no Jerries behind you and put up with the tingling in the back of your neck. Now that Sergeant Crabbe had taken over we let him do the thinking.

"O.K., lads, follow me. We're surrounded, but we'll make a fight for it."

We began to crawl like caterpillars through a field of scrub right into the welcoming beak of the German eagle.

"Keep yer fuckin' 'eads down."

With ten years of regular service behind him the sergeant had decided that this was the way to keep a chap's morale up. If only I could bury my head in the ground and join the ostriches, I thought. But Trooper 'Baldy' Ferguson didn't share my sentiments. 'Baldy' was the sort of fellow every good 'lover of life' dreads having around. Apart from the fact that he simply invited misfortune, he was usually quite harmless, but this time he had left his steel helmet in the truck and, to crown everything, had decided that the only way to find out where he was supposed to be going was to stick his head up and see for himself.

This was just what four Jerry machine-gunners were waiting for - a glistening, inviting, brightly sunburnt, red target, the top of 'Baldy's' egg-shaped head. Within seconds they had started target practice, missing Baldy but adding yet another to the list of his enemies by hitting the chap next to him in the arm. While the sergeant, who had stopped crawling, was accusing 'Baldy' of having no legitimate father I watched from a distance one of the others helping the wounded man with his field dressing, and during this brief respite suddenly realised that at that moment I was about as much use to Great Britain as a bee without a proboscis. Where the hell was Frankie Ball? Frankie was carrying a Bren gun that was supposed to have my bullets in it: I was carrying two magazines of ammunition which were supposed to be for Frankie's Bren gun. The organisation had collapsed when the horror of the whole situation had liquidised Frankie's bowels without warning and, after a grim battle with nature, he had disappeared behind a bush. Shouting to him that he should catch me up when he had finished I had gone on with the rest, leaving him doing his bit for Greece by fertilising a disgusted-looking cactus. And now he had disappeared. Chucking the magazines at the Jerries would not have done much good so I stuffed them into my haversack beside two hand grenades and gripped my rifle extra tightly. One bullet in the wrong place and I was all set to go up like Vesuvius.

With 'Baldy's' head out of sight, the machine gunners had stopped firing in our direction and, encouraged by this, Sergeant Crabbe led us on towards our doom. With great trust in him we clambered down from the field into a dusty lane, following him blindly and asking no questions. Years before, this same regiment had charged at Balaclava and if they had had our Mark VI light tanks instead of horses, they might have taken longer to get annihilated. As if that had not been enough, here they were doing much the same thing again. We had started off with these 1926 Mark VI's, reconnoitring successfully behind the German lines up north but, when it had come to a fight, the tanks had had to move so fast that half of them had lost their tracks and been abandoned. In the retreat south nearly all the rest had suffered the same fate. Before I had seen any action the tracks on my tank had disintegrated and as a result I had spent most of the time since the attack up north bashing radios and gun breeches to bits with a sledge hammer or helping to push useless tanks off the roads into the valleys below where the peasants, who still had any roofs left on their cottages, were probably dismantling the remains and selling the scrap metal on the black market. This had left most of us, drivers, gunners and wireless operators with nothing to do but stand in for the casualties. Quickly, we had been issued with a couple of grenades each, with a Bren gun to a platoon, and told to stop cleaning our rifles and get ready to use them.

Trooper Crawley, staring at his grenades as if they had been red scorpions, asked Sergeant Crabbe:

"Hey, Sarge! What do we do with these bloody things?"

Sergeant Crabbe was never very patient with conscripts.

"I could say 'stuff them where they might hurt, Crawley, but you're so pig-ignorant you'd probably do it, and I might lose my stripes. Just pull out the pin, count five and throw it at the bastards."

"How quickly am I supposed to count?"

The sergeant was beginning to look rattled.

"In your case slowly, mate. It'll be a good way of getting rid of you...'Ere, you," he called to Frankie Ball who had turned up and was leaning on his Bren gun as if it was a walking stick, "If that thing jams, they won't give you nuffin' to lean on in 'eaven.'

Within two weeks, helped by the Australian infantry who by now had earned the respect of the whole world, we had retreated past Athens and over the Corinth Canal to Kalamata, in the south-west, where we waited on a beach during three nights, hoping to be evacuated by one of our Sunderland flying-boats. Eight miles inland after the third unsuccessful attempt to get away we waited, hiding in the olive groves, to try again; but this time the Germans had got in first and we were surrounded by a parachute division. Sergeant Crabbe had led us as near the enemy as I hoped I would ever get, when I suddenly saw my first German. His square tin-hatted head was sticking up above the top of a wall two hundred yards away. Before I realised it I was aiming at him - to hell with the sixth commandment. The others hadn't seen him because he was so still. The whole situation was unreal - like someone else's dream. The fact that I might kill him didn't really come into it. I just knew I mustn't miss. For a moment I was back at school in the shooting 'eight', listening to the sneering voice of the instructor, a latent homosexual, who took it out on us because we were so unattainable.

"Legs well apart at angle to the body." (We were so innocent that we didn't realise why he took so long to push us into that position.) Now ... squeeze gently. Don't pull the trigger, boy. Hold your breath if you like, but not for long. Your school fees don't cover the cost of a wreath. Ha! Ha!...Squeeze....Wait, you stupid boy. You've shifted your position. (Another excuse for a fumble.) Take your time, boy. Now ... hold it... Hold it a bit longer."...(the sadist)...BANG!

The quick fantasy faded away. I had fired for the first time in the war and was thoroughly back in the present. The steel helmet was slumped forward. I had done my duty to King and Country and was now a qualified murderer - at last understanding just how mysterious the ways of God really were.

As everyone was trying to get behind something I chose the wheel of a three-ton truck. Good solid rubber, this. With luck the bullets would bounce. Considering the number of prayers that were arriving in heaven from just this section of the battle front alone, whoever was on duty up there must have been very busy and at his wits end trying to understand all the stuttering languages and dialects. Just then, hoping I had a guardian angel somewhere, I seemed to be the most important fellow I knew.

We had spread out, each man hoping that his own little bit of protection would save his life. Hopefully guarded by my truck wheel I felt like a mouse trying to hide behind a matchbox in the middle of the floor with a cat licking its lips a yard away. How long would I have to wait before I got killed outright or, worse still, had to face some six-foot-four German with a blunt bayonet and die slowly? I hadn't given a thought to any other form of death-dealer like, for instance, the metal ball twizzling in the dust, as small as a grey egg, where I could almost have reached it. Its innocent look completely mesmerised me; but luckily for me, someone else had seen it. Who he was I shall never know, but the yell he gave is still with me:

"Quick! Quick! Look out - oh, Christ!" The voice was screaming now. "BUGGER OFF OUT OF IT."

And I did, but it was too late.

The explosion seemed to be in my head. The Stuka bombs, landing only a few yards away, had sounded like mild plops compared with this one. I was half way up from the ground when the flash came and a split second later was sailing through the air like a bird, so numb that I could have left a leg behind without knowing it. Instinctively, I ran zigzagging up the road with at least one poor marksman missing several times. Round the corner I flung myself into a ditch. Still very close, the Germans were shouting meaningless numbers like a robot opera chorus. "Ein ...Zwei...Drei...Ochtafufzig ....." (If this was what made them such good soldiers, why didn't we try it? "One....Two.....Three ....Fifty-eight.") If war had anything to do with mathematics, I'd had it. It seemed as if the whole German army was concentrating on getting rid of me, personally. As I lay in the ditch, I waited for the bayonet that was going to finish me off. Two minutes later I was unconscious.

When I came to, the noise was much further down the road. Both the sleeves of my jacket were crimson and saturated, but I could move my arms. What's a bit of blood, I tried to think? I put my hand up to my face, sticky all over. But my eyes would blink all right!! I could move them from side to side. My nose was still there: my ears not hanging off. Then, where was the blood coming from? Hell! Surely not from the top of my head? Of course not, I had my tin hat on. ("A marble'd go through that lump of scrap metal if it was thrown hard enough. A lot of 'em don't never wear 'em - too bleedin' 'eavy".) Perhaps the Q.M. stores orderly who had said this had been joking, but that hand grenade had not just chucked out marbles. I felt round the front of the helmet until I located it, a nice neat little hole right in the middle. Then I stared at my crimson fingers and passed out once more.

When I opened my eyes and remembered everything it was early evening. The fighting sounded miles away and I was being bitten by a regiment of anti-British mosquitoes. Straightaway I thought, 'that hole in my helmet means there's a hole in my head......Keep calm! Keep calm!'

I got the helmet off somehow and, true enough my fingers found the hole in my forehead, as big as the hole in a putting green, or so it seemed. I felt the back of my head, expecting a handful of brains, but everything was quite normal. So, with awful finality, I decided that the splinter had stuck somewhere in the middle. Then I knew it, a silly thought but so definite: 'You can't have a metal splinter in your brain and remain sane, That bayonet I could see, for instance, ten yards away, sticking through the hedge above the ditch, was a madman's hallucination. I shut my eyes and opened them again. The bayonet was being drawn slowly out of sight. 'I can't be mad', I thought. That was a bayonet!' I got a hand grenade out of my haversack and, sweating with fear, screwed myself up and waited.

Now, I could hear the heavy breathing on the other side of the hedge above my head; almost smell the dirty socks inside the jackboots. What a nice chap; he must be wishing the fellow he was about to kill goodbye with a friendly fart. All the prayers I had ever sent up to heaven came out in one long, silent....'PLEASE!' and generously, up there, they sent me back into oblivion.

Once more I was conscious again when the red ball of the sun was disappearing below the horizon of cactus bushes and olive groves, and waited for half an hour to see whether the Jerry with the bayonet was still around. But there was silence, apart from the far off noises of the machine-guns and exploding shells. At last, feeling sure he wasn't there, I began to drag myself up. When I found I could stand, I slung my useless rifle into the ditch, together with the two Bren-gun magazines, my helmet and my couple of hand grenades to keep them company, and emerged, like a bright red butterfly from a chrysalis; then I lurched out into the open and started to shuffle down the road at the end of the dust track.

Almost immediately, a German dispatch rider roared up from behind, slowed down, staring, then shrugged his shoulders and rode on. The road seemed to stretch straight out into space; dusty and primitive, skirted by olive groves and high walls, concealing the silently terrified Greek peasants, crouched in their farmhouses, behind them. After another two minutes I looked round at the sound of a truck coming from behind and saw an open German infantry lorry. Like the despatch rider, it slowed down, almost stopping alongside. Seated in it were twenty tough, obedient soldiers, facing each other from opposite sides: every man with a long sphinx-like expression, as if he had just been given an order to shoot himself by midnight. No sign of humanity amongst this lot, I thought, but though they appeared to be made of granite, there was one joke all of them were going to enjoy immensely. One of them had put his rifle to his shoulder and was taking careful aim at my crotch. I wanted to scream, fall down and grovel, but just as I thought I was praying for the last time the German lowered his rifle and gave me an exaggerated Nazi salute. It was then that I decided perhaps a bit late, that if ever I was going to die in this war I would take as many of their practical jokers with me as possible.

Half a mile further along the road, after the laughter from the granite faces in the truck had faded in the distance, an old woman was standing at a farm entrance ringing her hands, wailing and staring at a bare orange tree. I understood Greek well enough to know that the look of hatred she gave me was one specially reserved for all thieving German bastards. To her, everyone in uniform was a German. She spat at me viciously.

"I'm not a German ... Oichi Germanski!" I protested; which only brought another torrent of abuse, as she waved her thin arms in the direction of the orange tree. I thought, perhaps, she couldn't see that I was covered in blood, so I tried out one of the only Greek words I knew. Water was not a popular commodity round these parts, judging by the empty bottles of Ouzo lying around and the manure caked all over her hands and arms. But I chanced it.

"Aqua," I croaked, hopefully.

It did the trick. She had at last seen what was wrong. With

all her rags wrapped around her the white-haired old woman went off and came back with a bucketful of water, rubbing her hands together and indicating that I should wash.

"No," I said, deciding it was better to keep up the 'bloody' appearance, but managed to drink about a quarter of the bucketful, while she looked on, amazed and almost forgetting her orange tree. Then, I thanked her and walked off into the dusk.

But soon everything began to get blurred. I had the feeling of being drunk, without the carefree enjoyment. Dizzy, I sat down on the pavement and leant against a high white wall, knowing I had to get some help from somewhere. The grunting of pigs behind the wall was reassuring. In Greece, where there were pigs there were people. I began to drag myself along the wall until I got to a small green door, and, without thinking about the noise, crashed my fists against it. Engulfed in the midst of a mass of black and grey shadows, surrounded by the drone of noisy voices and warning 'Sh-r-rrrrs,' I knew vaguely that something was happening to me. I got the impression of blurred figures, first almost on top of me and then drifting into little specks a million miles away. Out of the blackness, two great black and white balloons were coming at me, squashing me. Right above them was a woman's voice, cooing. The big woman in the black lacy dress hanging open at the front kept on engulfing me, stroking my hair. Staring at the mass of white flesh I wanted to push her away, to be able to breath. I heard my voice shouting,

"For God's sake, I'm suffocating."

They must have called the local doctor, because suddenly there was silence and everyone had drawn back. The unshaven doctor used a carving knife to cut away my battle-dress jacket. The woman, bending over me again, wrapped pieces of torn sheeting round my arms and head.

Then came a competition as to who would carry me upstairs. All half dozen entrants had different ideas, some suggesting 'feet-first', others insisting that 'head-first' would be more practical. As a result, while they were turning me round my head got stuck between two of the iron rails in the staircase and left me staring at the ceiling while they had a conference about getting me out with my ears attached. After what seemed hours, they came back with a rolling pin which they used to force the rails apart; propelling me once more into heavenly oblivion.

CHAPTER TWO

I woke up lying on an iron bedstead in a room with a clear shadeless bulb hanging from the ceiling a foot away from my face, flooding the inside of my head, when I shut my eyes, with a red searing light. The walls were daubed with Eau-de-Nil enamel paint running in behind the torn poster of General Metaxas admonishing the Greeks to fight. A hand covered with dried manure was holding a salami sandwich against my lips. At the other end of the hand was a voice:

"Eat," it said. "Eat." The hand was prodding the lump against my mouth.

I shook my head, violently retching: words wouldn't come. I opened my eyes aching in the brilliant light, and now I could see him; a small dark, kind-looking fellow in overalls, sitting on a chair by the bed; a plate piled high with more sandwiches on his lap.

"Salami O.K. for the brain," he was saying, with a rasping American accent. "Refreshes it. Makes it goddam lively. All the best professors eat salami."

Was he joking? Had they discovered I was mad? Were they saying stupid things just to make me feel better about it? My arms were hurting. My head was clamped in a vice being slowly tightened. I had been lowered into a furnace of white hot ashes. Above all, I wanted to talk to the ceiling and the walls, just talk. Whether I 'said' anything was unimportant.

"They're fighting ...... fighting in the hedges." (That's not me. Somebody else is saying it.) "Bayonets ..... ten foot bloody bayonets .... just right for carving the Sunday joint. Buzz, buzz, little mosquitoes. Buzz, buzz ..... zzzzzzzzzz Mosqui......Oh, hell!...... toes. They're hiding between my toes.

The cowardly little bastards. Shoot them. SHOOT THEM! But be careful......don't shoot my toes off.....!"

The man looked scared, his hands shaking as he nervously ate the sandwiches, one after the other, sitting on the edge of his chair. Ready to make a quick getaway, he relaxed only when I quietened down.

All night he sat by my bed, dozing, looking at me anxiously or reading a Greek newspaper. Once or twice I heard a female voice, whispering, and smelt some sort of musty scent. Through the night I slept fitfully, waking over and over again in a sea of pain, all my nerves alive and throbbing where the numbness had worn off. Long after the sun had come up my watchdog, sitting with his head lolling down on his chest, the grunts coming from his half-opened mouth competing with the pigs outside, woke up too. Looking at me anxiously he seemed relieved.

"You said some funny goddam things last night," he said, "but you seem O.K. now. Here, you must be hungry. Eat ..."

He offered me the last two sad-looking sandwiches and, shutting my eyes, I pushed them into my mouth rather than hurt his feelings. Then he helped me off the bed and down the stairs, upright this time. In the yard about a dozen men and women, together with three or four children, had arrived to have a look at me. Some of them gave me presents of bread and more salami. One girl, flinging her olive-brown arms, beginning to get fat like her mother's, round my neck and kissing me squarely on the lips, pushed a bottle of wine into my haversack before I could warn her that there was a hole in the corner. With a crash it shattered on the floor, leaving her in tears, my feet soaking wet and some of the people laughing for the first time in weeks. My watchdog gave me one of his old leather jackets, first emptying a handful of mouldy black olives out of one of the pockets.

The time had come to say goodbye. The men shook me by the hand; the women smothered me with kisses. My watchdog beckoned me to follow him down the road.

"I'm going to get you to a goddam hospital. But look out," he warned me. "If you see a goddam smelly German son-of-a-bitch, get out of sight, quick. Every day they are shooting people like me, who sympathise with the British."

I followed him at a safe distance, ready to take cover. After a mile, and several scares which came to nothing, he stopped a Greek civilian ambulance, said something to the driver, pushed some money into his hand and called back to me:

"Hurry, Mr. Englishman. He will take you to the hospital in Kalamata. They will look after you there." With genuine gratitude I grasped him by the hand: and with tears rolling down his face he took me by the shoulders, pressing his stubble-covered cheek against mine.

"Come back to Greece when the war is over and all the German son-of-a-bitches are frizzling in goddam hell," he shouted.

In the ambulance was a man, just alive by the looks of it, who had had his leg blown off by a bomb; and a pregnant woman with a nurse who was warning her that if she had the baby in the ambulance she would upset the hospital curriculum. Ten minutes later we arrived at the hospital, where I was put straight into the cleanest bed I had seen for six months. Soon I realized that with the bed went a nurse, well-built plump and dark, and by the time she had brought me the second bowl of sour milk, I had fallen in love with her. Without anything being said, it was easy to see that looking after an Englishman was so novel that she had almost forgotten the civilian casualties, who really deserved a lot more attention as, after all, they had not been trying to kill anybody. A Greek doctor spent half an hour looking for the splinters in my arms with no success; then, after he had examined my head, told me that there was a splinter between the skin and the bone. I could tell he was hungry. For one thing, with my ear pressed against his stomach I could hear it rumbling and, for another, he was continually looking at his black market watch, which told him it was lunchtime.

"It won't do any harm to leave it there," he said, with a hollow rumble, like a clapped-out 'Matilda Two'.

That was all right with me - I couldn't have stood much more of the digging, anyway.

Regularly, every four hours, Melanie (my nurse) brought a boiled lamb chop and sat on the bed watching every mouthful hopefully to cure me, her brown eyes brimming over with maternal concern. Her eyes were so magnetic that once, gazing into them, I missed my mouth and jabbed the forkload of lamb into the pillow.

"You poor boy," she murmured. "That splinter must have given you a small bit of 'otitis media'. I will see the doctor".

Then she spoilt all the good she had done, following the meal up by giving me the nearest thing to a ticket to heaven - a Greek cigarette, which doubled me up coughing. I was just getting through my fifteenth bowl of sour milk, while she pinched me to see whether I could eat it without laughing, when the peace of the hospital was shattered by the arrival of several top-brass German officers. A moment later in came the matron, an ugly, square-jawed woman, following the safe course, with the Germans about, of keeping severe and impersonal. She was at the head of an entourage of six of them of various ranks, plus a general.

"That's him", she said in German, pointing an accusing finger at me, as if I had just tried to blow up the Acropolis.

"Good, "said one of the colonels". Get him out and lined up with the others in the main hall in ten minutes."

Whether I had any legs to take me there obviously didn't worry him.

The 'others' were five Allied wounded who, like myself, had found their way into the hospital. The sad wet eyes of my nurse were doing more to boost my morale than the lamb chops and sour milk until she gave me a hug. When I cried out in pain she thought it was with rapture and did it again. Then she pressed two packets of Greek cigarettes into my hand and said:

"It's only a little present, but perhaps you will see me again in the how-you-say rings of smoke, and will think of me and get better quick."

She should have said: "I am doing you a favour; these will keep you in hospital a bit longer, away from the prison camp. Unless you're lucky, you won't even get camel dung to smoke there."

The German military ambulance took five minutes to get to the town hall, which had been turned into a makeshift hospital, housing about five hundred Allied wounded plus the bits that were left of the crew of an ammunition boat, blown up in Pyreus harbour by the Greek Fifth Column, collaborating with the Germans. When I saw some of the battered results of the war in Greece lying around I felt lucky to be in one piece, though my right arm was beginning to swell. Nowhere was there more than a foot between the beds. I was put into one near the 'gangrene' ward, where the smell was so bad that, with my head under the blankets, I went straight off to sleep for lack of oxygen. Two M.O.s, a New Zealander and an Englishman, both of them prisoners, were doing their best with the help of a few R.A.M.C. orderlies and three Quaker non-combatants from the Field Ambulance Unit, to keep three hundred men alive with a few bandages, a quarter-full oxygen cylinder, two bottles of iodine and a pair of forceps. They soon tried to lose the forceps, searching for the splinters in my arm and, as they had no anaesthetic and wouldn't stop when I begged them to, I did them the favour of going unconscious without any. But, after what seemed like hours, they still couldn't find the splinters. The M.O.s had asked the Germans if it was possible to get an x-ray apparatus (in order to save some lives, they had said), but the Germans were not particularly interested in that aspect. Just the same, they had agreed to ask the only local doctor who had one, for a loan of it.

"My dear gentlemen," the doctor had said. "The British, Australians and the New Zealanders ran away from you. Now, you are my masters and it is my turn to do the same to them. Simple philosophy, do you not agree. They must do without my x-ray." (The thought struck me that, if we were to win the war, he might have a bit of time to study philosophy in a prison cell.....before they got round to hanging him.)

My arm was now as thick as my leg. The M.O.s examined it together, told me everything would be all right and moved away to a place which they thought was out of earshot, relying on the noise coming from a Cypriot in the next bed - with a hole in his chest - begging for air as if someone could give him a box of it. But I overheard all right. It was a simple statement, like someone back home commenting on the weather.

"If we can only get some anaesthetic by tomorrow, we can take that arm off. If not, the lad will die."

"I entirely agree, Harry."

That was my fate fixed. I had been relying on my left arm for a couple of days; if they took the right one off it shouldn't take long to get used to losing it altogether. That was, if the anaesthetic turned up. They were having a look at the Cypriot. I had never seen such a wound. If he had been standing with his back to the light I could have seen right through his chest. As he stared, with glazing eyes, at the two M.O.s, he appeared to think he was looking at two gods who were going to save him, if he prayed hard enough.

"Please, I want air. I WANT AIR ..."

Someone had wound up the gramophone on a windowsill three yards away and 'A sentimental journey' was blaring out in deadly scratching monotony for the twentieth time, cutting out any chance of hearing what else he had to say. It only took one look to see that the M.O.'s had given him up. I saw them shaking their heads and saying something to the orderly with the oxygen-cylinder, who came over to the Cypriot, still trying to drown the music with his pleading.

"Shut your fucking mouth," he said, "and let some of these men die in peace."

But the Cypriot didn't understand much English. He thought he was wishing him 'peace', poor chap.

"I have peace, if I have air," he gasped. "PLEASE..."

His eyes rolled back, fixed on one spot on the ceiling; his mouth stayed open. Nobody ever knew how much English he spoke, but at least he was polite. At the same time the record finished abruptly and I saw the doctors looking sympathetically at me.

"If we don't get the anaesthetic and we can't take that arm off, he's going to end up in the gangrene ward..."

"It's the luck of the draw, Harry," the other answered. "A hundred years ago you'd have given him a stiff rum and lopped it off with a kitchen knife, and then you'd have gone back to your job as a blacksmith. One of the sad things about progress, old boy."

It was easy enough to hear: yet, the one called Harry came over to me and said:

"Don't worry, old chap. Your arm's fine. You'll be as right as rain in the morning. Now try and get some sleep."

Someone had just wound up the gramophone again, and now it was Gigli, normally at his best in the second act of Aida; but this time very seasick, riding up and down on a record as uneven as the Irish Sea in a force nine gale. But, in spite of the chaotic sound, no amount of noise or terror would have kept me awake.

I was dreaming that I was being tortured by the Gestapo, shouting at me to tell them where they would find my grandmother who, they insisted, was somewhere in the Albanian mountains, spying against Mussolini. As I couldn't tell them, they were hanging me by my ankles on a pulley, with a hundredweight bag of cement tied to my right arm, and slowly lowering me into boiling oil. I woke up screaming, to find that a member of the Field Ambulance Unit was pressing a scalding poultice onto the wound. In his eyes, as he stared at the wall, was the pale, far-away look of a monk, constantly praying. He seemed to be used to screams and, when he had calmed me down, spent the rest of the night changing poultices until by morning I was left with an arm more or less normal size, a blister on it the size of a saucer, much less of a temperature and a firm decision to become a Quaker. Here was a true Christian, with no inhibitions; and nothing like a monk, as he soon showed.

"You're lucky, mate," he said." They used up the last bit of ether last night whipping off what was left of Nobby Clarke's balls after they stopped a shell splinter, poor chap. A regular rascal he was, so I've heard. Never mind, I expect a few randy Greek tarts made the best of them while they lasted." Then he looked serious. "If they had been able to get more ether, this arm would have been in the incinerator with Nobby's treasured possessions by now, or chopped up more like in some Greek pig trough," He gave me a friendly pat, "It'll be O.K. now I've finished with it. So keep your pecker up."

I liked his easy confidence and went back to sleep. A week later my temperature was normal and I was getting well.

The six foot four German sergeant-major in charge of the hospital kept us amused by goose-stepping behind any officers who happened to drop in and making faces at them behind their backs.

"Heil Hitler!" he would say to their faces and, when they had gone: "Zum Scheissen mit dem Kerl!" (In to the shit with the idiot.)

When a colonel, weighed down with medals and spurs, arrived to inspect the hospital, the sergeant major showed him round with the cringing deference common to most sergeant majors on both sides. But we soon found he was shamming. To him everyone, German or ally, was a human being and, in this place, might not be for much longer. With this in mind, he had decided to keep as many of us as possible laughing until the end. When the colonel turned to go, his handkerchief held over his nose after visiting the gangrene ward, the sergeant-major followed him, his hand outstretched in a Nazi salute and goose-stepping to the blaring rhythm of 'Colonel Bogey', which someone had put on the gramophone, especially for the occasion.

When Maria, a Greek auxiliary nurse, arrived one day she was given half a dozen beds to look after. For the past few days the sergeant-major had been allowing in some of these nurses to help our overworked orderlies but, as they couldn't speak English and we couldn't speak Greek, the result was usually a matter of sitting on the bed and smiling at the fellows in turn for half an hour or more or perhaps looking at photographs of their wives and families. But even the sight of a girl smiling was enough to give some of them a bigger urge to get better. Fat girls had never appealed to me, but a girl as fat as Maria was so uncommon that I simply was hypnotized, not being able to take my eyes off the vast expanse of her, especially when I heard her speaking near-perfect English. It was lucky that my leg had not been hit instead of my arm because, when she came and sat on it by mistake, she nearly broke it. The profuse apologies and the "Oh, it doesn't matter at all"s cemented a friendship which, but for certain facts which I found out later, could have ended up with a brick wall and a firing squad. As she sat again on my leg, holding my hand, she saw me wincing and asked me if the doctors had given me any tablets for the nervous complaint I had of screwing up my face. When I couldn't help laughing, she became annoyed.

"Do you know who you are laughing at?" she asked.

"No", I said. "I'm sorry."

"The daughter of General Metaxas," she said.

It was my turn to apologise.

"I had no idea you were so important," I said.

"Never mind," she said graciously.

At this stage I noticed that the 'bun' on top of her head, surrounded by the white nurse's cap like the castle wall round a 'keep', had slipped to one side.

"Now listen," she said. As she leant forward the 'bun' slipped more to the front. I could see that she was very serious. "My secret connections, with the help of my father, have arranged that a submarine will be waiting off the coast at Kiparissa a week from today. There, I shall be picked up and taken to Alexandria. I do not wish to remain in Greece under the rule of the Germans. Will you come with me?"

When I started to open my mouth she put her hand over it. "Good", she said, beaming at me. "You will be the nicest Englishman who ever decided to be an Orthodox priest."

"Orthodox priest?" I was amazed.

By this time the fellows in the two beds next to mine were craning their necks to hear more. The 'more' was worth listening to. When the time came I was to slip into the lavatory, dress up as a Greek priest with a jungle of false hair to hide my face, a long cassock and an elongated mortarboard on my head; all of which she would provide; and then I was to leave with her past the guards. Very simple. With so many Greek Cypriots attached to the British army dying, priests were in and out all day. When she put her hands on my shoulders and bent down to kiss me her 'bun' fell off and hit me square on the forehead, bouncing onto the floor. With a flourish, she picked it up and, saying goodbye, promised to be back the next day. My mouth was still open when one of the nuns, who had been let in with a tray of cakes and who spoke English, came over and asked me politely:

"Has she been talking of escape and did she tell you she was the daughter of General Metaxas?"

I felt embarrassed, still not sure what it was all about, but the nun didn't wait for an answer.

"She has been asking you to escape with her in a submarine?"

It was no good stalling.

"Yes," I said, "As a matter of fact she has."

The nun shook her head sadly.

"You are the sixth in a fortnight: the others have all gone to the convalescent camp," she said, "I'm afraid the poor creature will have to be put away again."

"Put away?" I said, remembering a sick guinea pig I had once taken to the vet.

"Yes," said the nun, peering at me kindly through rimless spectacles from under her black and white crimped headdress, "Yes. She will have to be kept somewhere, as before. We have tried giving her nursing to do as a therapy, but it has not worked. The Germans have cleared the asylum, which they want to use for barracks. There were no really dangerous patients you see, and now they are all let loose on the streets: she is one of them. We have been trying to help her but, poor girl, she has become schizophrenic."

"But I don't understand. She seems intelligent and speaks perfect English.

"That is so. She was a clever university student, until her parents were both killed in the bombing. Now... well... you have seen her for yourself- what she has become."

So much for my ego. I had thought she picked me as the perfect escaping companion.

Next day, when she came again, I decided to play along with her, asking my two neighbours not to give the game away.

Looking at her more closely I saw that, after all, she was quite pretty. She could not have been more than nineteen, and seemed very happy with the adventure in her imagination.

"I have made all the arrangements," she said. There was a dimple, which I hadn't noticed, in one cheek as she smiled, which made her face pleasantly lop-sided. "We shall go next

Tuesday at three in the afternoon. I shall put a parcel of clothes at the door of the toilet when the sergeant-major is not looking". She gave me a searching gaze. "Aren't you getting excited about it?"

"Very," I said. Very excited, Maria. I can't wait."

What a pity this delightfully romantic girl was off her rocker, especially looking as she did: she had left her 'bun' behind and had combed her hair, and the two remaining curlers were almost out of sight.

"It will be a great adventure," she said, grabbing my hand and pressing it against her cheek.

It was then that I saw the sergeant-major standing behind, imitating her, pressing his ammo' pouch against his own cheek and winking at the others. My two neighbours were trying hard not to laugh, while I was wondering whether she had done exactly the same with the other five prospective escapees.

Waiting for her each day helped the time to pass, instead of thinking of nothing else but pain and death and an empty stomach. Also, it helped me not to concentrate too much on the Cypriot in the opposite bed. When they changed his dressing he never stopped laughing and joking, while I watched fascinated as they uncovered the red-raw stump of his leg, amputated above the knee.

The day before the escape plan should have been put into operation, after I had asked the nun to try to get rid of Maria before she stirred up too much trouble, my problems were solved for me. In the midst of all the moaning and shouting for help which couldn't be given, the sergeant-major stood on the platform of the town hall, surrounded by beds, and made an announcement, interpreted by one of the nuns.

"Tomorrow, fifty of you will go from here," he said. "Your doctors have pronounced you fit to travel. As you are no longer invalids, you will go away to a convalescent camp."

The names were posted on the notice board and mine was amongst them. We were taken, stifled by the blazing heat, through the countryside of olive groves, Cyprus trees and lush vineyards, along the dusty road north to Athens and from there to Piraeus, across the harbour, where we were driven past a group of grim-faced guards, and an eight-foot surrounding fence of rolled barbed wire, into another commandeered building: a four-storeyed, clean white cube of tasteful Greek architecture which had once been a reformatory for girls. Perhaps they had all been pushed out into the streets like the schizophrenic. My bed, in a corner four feet away from the next one, was on the fourth floor: a few steps, and I was on the roof, with a better view of the Parthenon, standing aloof on its mound above the city, than most pre-war tourists, who had paid to see it, would have had. While I stood there, blistering in the relentless sunshine, my mind was dazed by the whole unexpected trauma. Surely things were going too well for somebody who had tried so hard to keep out of it. I was mistaken. Within two days I realized that now I had become part of the German 'prisoner demoralising plan' -a chunk of bread, a quarter inch thick slice of our own captured corned beef, a piece of goat-milk cheese (no respectable goat would have admitted having anything to do with it) and a mug of coffee, made from roasted acorns. On this meagre diet, we were all supposed to get well again, and under these conditions I lost interest in the view from the roof as quickly as I lost weight and, not being able to lie on my sides, stayed on my back developing bed sores.

The Scotsman in the next bed was so silent, as he lay with his eyes fixed on the ceiling, that I felt I had to draw him into conversation.

"What are those tags on your mug and plate?" I asked him, pointing to the curious circles of metal fixed through the enamel with wire.

When I saw the look he gave me I knew that this tough little Glaswegian was frightened. He kept silent about the reason until two days later, when he turned to me and said out of the blue:

"If ye will know the truth, Aa have syphilis: and that's ma trouble. Wi' syphilis Aa dinna feel like doing a lot o' talking."

"Oh, God! I'm sorry," I said.

"So am Aa, too," he said, desperately. "The fockin' Jerry quacks dinna care too much. They dinna gi' me much treatment, nay matter how much Aa beg them. Gi me a wee spot potassium,

Aa ask, and Aa'll do it myself."

"Where did you pick it up?" I said.

"Och, in fokin' Cairo, doon Berker Street fri' a filthy mulatto lass. Aye, Jimmy, Aa shid a' listened to ma wee ma. She wa a gid Presbyterian, ma wee ma. She always told me Aa should pray ti' God afore Aa ever took a dig at a lass Aa wouldna marry. Bless her wee soul, which the Lord took awa say soon."

He was crying. What could I say? It was just a pity that I was beginning to get the feelings about the Germans that I should have had long before.

"Och, it kanna be helped. Aa suppose, I'll..." he stopped, looking across at a man who had just been led in by an orderly to the spare bed opposite. He was grinning at the Scotsman, repeatedly nodding his head and putting out his tongue.

"Hey you!" shouted the Scotsman when the orderly had gone. "Dinna stare at me like a crazy man."

But the man went on grinning.

With a grunt of anger the Scotsman leapt out of bed, ran over and grasped the other fellow by the lapels of his pyjama jacket. With his fist raised high he was just about to hit him when he suddenly stopped. Patting him on the shoulder, he turned and came back.

"The poor lad's gone off his wee lid. Och, Aa shouldna be so hasty. Ma nairves are nay so gid." His eyes filled with tears again.

I looked over. The man had turned sideways, still grinning, but this time at the wall. Right across the side of his head, above the ear, was a half-inch deep bright red gash. The bullet that had hit him had left him alive but simple. He was still grinning when the R.A.M.C. elderly came and bandaged his head.

"Don't disappear like that again," said the orderly, giving him a friendly punch. The man stopped grinning, gave a vicious snarl and lashed out with his fist, missing the orderly who was quick enough to jump out of the way. Soon he was grinning again.

After a fortnight while stomachs got smaller and bedsores bigger, it was a relief to be declared totally cured and told to get ready with about twenty-five others, for transport. This time we were taken away in an army truck. With us went the lice we had picked up, which were beginning to grow up; and lucky for them too, because when we arrived at the transit camp near Corinth they had plenty of little dysentery germs to make friends with.

Similar to a handful of currants being emptied into a hundredweight of pastry, we were let loose in the middle of ten thousand hardened P.O.W.s and within half an hour had lost all sight of each other. The camp, a vast compound surrounded by two-storyed red Greek army barrack buildings, was a quarter of a mile in diameter. Like a football crowd, the P.O.W.s were spread out over the dusty area. Here and there a queue, sometimes twenty yards long, waited outside a latrine. A longer queue waited for their ration of uncontaminated water for washing, shaving and drinking – about one litre per day. Above the only row of taps in the camp was a notice with six inch high red letters:

DANGER ... BACTERIA ... DO NOT DRINK.

I soon found out that the fellows who were drinking the water would probably, before long, be heading for heaven, giving their dysentery to others on the way.

The only shade was under the walls of the barrack buildings. Most of the men chose to defy the blistering heat of the morning sitting against the walls where they would be in the shade in the afternoons. The heat inside the barrack buildings was stifling. Many of the Aussies didn't bother to find shade, but rather sat in twos or threes in the sun picking the crawling lice off each other's backs. You had to learn never to catch hold of the inviting bodies sticking out from under the skin because their heads would stay where they were, causing soreness and sometimes going septic.

In the morning, after 'Appel' (Roll call), the men queued for a mug of ersatz coffee, made from roasted acorns: at midday, dripping with sweat, they queued for the main meal, a dixy of mashed potatoes slushing about in water (half a pound of butter to every thirty gallons of it). In the evening, cooling down, they queued for a chunk of bread and more coffee, putting the cold coffee grounds from the morning in between two slices to give the meagre ration more bulk. If you were in a syndicate of six men, you got a sixth of a loaf: if not, a separate, and usually smaller, piece. The P.O.W.s had spilt themselves into hundreds of these six-man syndicates, sharing their official food, together with anything they could get from the black market and cooking, if they were lucky enough to find anything to make a fire with. As the guards kept an eye on everything made of timber there was no chance to break anything up for firewood. According to your capacity for wolfing or nibbling you had some bread left over every day, from the day before, to eat with the midday potato slush. The men in the syndicates just about bore each other's company, with no interest in anybody's troubles, and as there was no chance of getting into a syndicate, I soon found it would be a matter of fending for myself. After a day of nibbling and enviously watching the various syndicates in action, I was wandering about the compound when I met Geoff Parker. Geoff owed me a favour for wheeling him in a wheelbarrow through a torrential downpour in North Greece before the German attack, with a bottle of ouzo in his pocket and another in his bladder and dumping him in the back of the quarter master's truck, with the officer's spare linen, just as the regiment was moving off at half-past-five in the morning.

"How the devil did you get here?" he asked, in the Hayleybury accent you could never imagine him losing. "We saw you cop that damned grenade and disappear. We were trying to get to you, old boy, but the Jerry crossfire was terrific. Licked us completely."

He pushed his fingers through his thick matted hair. Through the 'V' of his shirtfront I could see two lice copulating joyfully. The dirt from everywhere seemed to have picked him out to cling to.

"Good heavens, old man, you look in a bad state," he said.

"I'm all right: just bloody hungry," I said.

At that point I noticed the tin he was carrying and felt embarrassed to have said it.

"Contact the black market, old man," said Geoff. "It's run by Cypriots, with the Australians a head and shoulders behind.... That is, if you've got any money or valuables," he added through his matted beard; his Michaelangelo eyes beginning to look sympathetic. "You're obviously not in a syndicate and, if you had been in mine, that watch you've got on would have been forfeit straightaway, or you'd have got your throat slit." Once more his fingers, with their long dirty nails, were trying to push their way through his matted hair. "But, I tell you what I can do without them finding out." He tightened his grip on the tin, as if it might fly away. "I don't suppose they would notice if I gave you a slice of my Chinese rice biscuit cake."

My resolutions of being happily self-sufficient, after I hadn't been able to join a syndicate, had been flying away with every look at the tin. Inside, when Geoff opened it, I could see a solid brownish lump, so beautiful at that moment that, beside it, the crown jewels would have looked like a pile of lead. Getting out a rusty knife, he cut off a slice, closing the lid with a sigh of relief.

"Hide it, old man, for heaven's sake. If they knew, they'd kill me. I'll bring you a bit of something now and then if I can," he said. "In the meantime the only way to produce this stuff is to get your oil from the black market. If you're lucky, the Jerry looking after the incinerator will let you shove it on his fire for ten minutes. If it's a bit underdone you'll have to put up with it."

"What about the biscuit?" I asked.

He gave me a sad look.

"You'll be getting those occasionally, as a present, from the Jerries," he said. "And I assure you, old man, after you've hammered two or three Chinese rice biscuits to bits, you'll be wishing you were fighting the Chinks instead of the Germans."

For the next week Geoff kept me from starving. Nothing I could get with my few drachmas in the black market was much good. The Jerry at the incinerator had been warned by the camp commandant, and had clamped down on the cooking; I couldn't use olive oil or raisins without a fire and, as I wasn't in a syndicate, I couldn't get the closely guarded wood or even a match to light one. Besides I was spending valuable hours in the latrine — where I was getting all the latest news from other squatters but no offers of help — emerging to stand in the grub queue, and then going back to share the grub with the flies in the latrine queue.

Each latrine must have been modelled on the sort of thing used by the ancient Greek slaves - a room, about ten feet square, with a five inch diameter hole - in the middle of a floor which sloped towards it from all directions. The only time of the week when it was possible to use the latrine as it should be used was during the half hour after it had been cleaned out by a group of Greek workers on a Friday. As everyone in the latrine queue was in a hurry, it was a matter of getting in quickly. Once there, you performed where you could, hopefully as near the hole as possible. Consequently, after an hour or two, there was no chance of getting within two yards of the bull's eye, unless you felt like a paddle: by the end of the day, half the floor was covered with excrement and, within a week, with no floor left to see, the worst cases were unable even to get as far as the door. Their latrine then became the dusty compound, as near to the door as possible, in full view of a lot of men, all hoping they would not find themselves in the same boat.

My first Chinese rice biscuit was the most beautifully moulded golden brown delicacy I had ever seen — and the least edible. Six inches in diameter and snow white inside, it was rock-hard and completely tasteless.

"Soak it in water, mate, until tomorrow morning," said one helpful fellow, seeing me staring at the tooth marks I had just made in it, "Add a sprinkle of salt and, I kid you not, it'll be the best bit of roofing felt you've ever tasted."

I gave up trying to bite it and went round in search of something to break it with, passing several syndicates, avidly guarding their bread rations with suspicious glances at each other in case the next man's was bigger, until I found someone with a stone.

"May I borrow that?" I asked and, as he hesitated, picked it up and began to wrap my biscuit in the vest I was carrying, while he watched me suspiciously. The biscuit took some breaking but, by repeatedly hammering it, I managed to turn it into a sludge by pouring it into a dixie of cold coffee - making the sort of brown, slushy mess which would have given any pig a nightmare. After a day or two of this, I was giving my rice biscuits to Geoff, who secretly fried them, soaked in the syndicate pan. The inevitable happened: one of the others caught him and he was thrown out of the group. From then on we had to look after ourselves.

With the aid of my watch and his signet ring, both somewhere in the black market, we got together a large stock of oil, raisins, salt, jam and German salami, bribing our way into various fires where we did our cooking, making sure we always carried everything about with us, until, with their usual lack of warning, the Germans started to clear the camp.

CHAPTER THREE

As the dawn of an early June day was breaking, the ten thousand P.O.W.s of the Corinth transit camp, carrying their few belongings in haversacks and kitbags, began shuffling out onto the main road heading north and flanked by several hundred guards. Geoff and I kept together, watching the magnificent orange circle of the sun appearing over the horizon to the east — a beautiful friend that, within two hours, would become a fierce enemy. At the start it was a matter of plodding, with nothing to hold our attention and nothing to talk about. By the time our section of the line reached a farm or village, most of the people had tired of watching the endless procession and were back at work. The guards had soon put a stop to any acts of sympathy, such as throwing loaves of bread or packets of cigarettes, obeying orders and threatening the people with fixed bayonets.

Geoff, who at that time had dysentery worse than I had, soon tired, as we pulled our feet along for mile after mile up the incline towards Thebes and Lamia. After five hours, about fifty of us were allowed to wash, with one piece of soap between us, under a farm pump, using a well-worn vest as a towel. As one Aussie passed a grey, heavy-as-lead piece of soap around, he exclaimed:

"What the bloody hell's this crap?"

One of the Cypriots gave a short, dry laugh. "It's made from Jew-fat, digger. You might still have a bit of Einstein at the back of your ears, unless he got away before they grabbed him.

"What yer talkin' about, Bruce?"

"I've told you. The Nazis exterminate Jews: they don't waste them. They get more out of dead Jews than live ones —

"Balls! You've been reading fairy tales."

So we went on happily washing ourselves with Jew-fat (the Cypriot was right: later the world would find out the truth). By this time the blisters on Geoff's feet were so bad that he hung his boots round his neck by the laces and limped along in his socks, his toes sticking out like wet strawberries through the holes in the front. Several of the others followed suit. As we neared the top of the incline he decided to throw everything except the toothbrush we were sharing into a ravine.

"The damned Greeks can do what they like with that lot," he said, as his kitbag went sailing through the air. "I'm travelling light." I knew this was just his way of saying that he felt faint, and was prepared to catch him when he fell. Two of us carried him until he came round and then, though he objected, got each side of him and helped him along. In the longest procession since Moses and the Israelites we dragged ourselves over the passes on the way to Lamia; through Larisa, a town which had been flattened, first by German bombs and then by an earthquake, on above the coast, high up overlooking the brilliant blue Aegean, and towards Katarini; passing under Mount Olympus, where the terrified Gods had jumped out of sight into the shell-holes: a journey on foot of about a hundred and sixty miles. At night, we were herded into groups, while the guards walked round or, if it was more convenient, over us.

The Germans gave us a generous ration of mint tea, but no water to drink it with. The only way to have a drink was to lie on your back, when you got a chance to fill your mouth with tea leaves and brew your own with saliva, if you had any. On the second day we were issued with a piece of raw fish and a chunk of black bread, to keep it down. If there were any guardian angels watching us, they were holding their noses. The fish arrived in wooden tubs, quite harmless until the lids were prized off; but even then, the stench could not put us off eating it. Few men carried more than one mug or dixie. As there was so little water, we drank as much of the coffee ration poured on top of the remains of the fish as we could, leaving enough in the bottom for swilling round and rinsing. From the top of a pass we could see the long snake of limping men stretching into the mist fifteen miles away.

Geoff, still plodding on, had his feet wrapped up in all the pairs of cloth socks I could lay my hands on, tied round them with string. Some of the guards, carrying rifles and full kit, and fainting in the heat, were left to be picked up, and court martialled for failing in their duty.

At last, at Katarini, the journey came to an end, and the German propaganda machine took over. Here, on the main line to Salonika, five trains, each with ten corridored coaches, waited for us, clean and inviting, insulting our intelligence. Some men refused to realise that here was Nazi trickery at its lowest. To step from misery into luxury of this sort was part of an obvious hypocrisy; especially when we caught sight of a cine-camera being held by the most German-looking Greek in the country; with bull-neck, cropped hair and wide-brimmed hat, turned down at the back: getting us onto film for the benefit of his propaganda-soaked 'Heimland'. His camera, and no doubt others out of sight, were being kept far enough away to make sure that the scowls on our suspicious faces would not be seen. We guessed that German actors in British uniforms were being used for the close-ups.

As the trains moved off, we were allowed to stand in the corridors, with unbarred windows open and a fresh breeze making a valiant attempt to blow away the B.O. The Germans saw to it that the trains would be going so fast that nobody could jump out and stay alive; until they reached more film units, posted along the line at intervals, when the guards would suddenly appear from nowhere, with friendly smiles on their faces, apparently very worried about our welfare. The bonus of extra rations which we got before leaving Katarini was too much for the high-principled fellows who had decided to keep scowling. Before long the freedom and fresh air had dulled any noble intentions as, laughing and joking as if we had just come out of a comic review, with the barrels of several machine guns pointing at us from various vantage points, we glided into the station; disembarking to the floundering music from a terrified local brass band, trying to play 'Pack up your troubles' and 'It's a long way to Tipperary'. Several German actors were throwing their British berets and side hats into the air near the news cameras. The fact that they were all shouting 'Hurrah!' in a way that only the girls of Cheltenham Ladies' College had ever been known to shout it would hopefully go unnoticed in their cinemas.

When the newsmen, with their red hot cameras, had gone, we had something more important to worry about as, back under our previous conditions, we were butted around by rifles until we had formed up again into a snake a mile long, ready for the 'grand finale', the victory procession through Salonika.

As the seemingly unending stream of beaten men who, not long ago had been 'heroes to the rescue', shuffled through the town, the Greeks were shown how they would be treated by their conquerors if they should start getting funny. The few courageous ones who threw food and cigarettes to us were 'helped', at bayonet point, to the back of the procession, where they stayed, marching into the compound at the other end of the town with us, on their way to concentration camps. In temperatures nearly high enough to roast the Sunday joint the three thousand of us who had been separated and herded onto the parade ground of a vacated Greek army barracks were kept waiting for three hours, while the civilian prisoners filed past tables, answering the cursory questions of several Wehrmacht officers.

As no man was allowed to move from his standing position on the parade ground, for those whose dysentery was out of control, the results were disastrous. When we eventually began to file past the tables, the colonel and his clerical staff kept their handkerchiefs to their noses, while they noted the answers to their questions, with the aid of interpreters. In this way, during the next two and a half hours, they obtained a record of every man's name, rank, number, occupation in 'civvy street', how many languages he spoke and whether, given the opportunity, he would be willing to work...'for extra rations',...the clerk interrogating me added, with a wink: and with the thought of food uppermost in my mind, I said 'Yes'. With this over, it was a matter of following the man in front of you into a three-floored red brick barrack building, helped on, as usual, by a prodding bayonet. There was no question of choice: everyone just got whatever area of floor he was given: in my case it was 'three square yards on Floor Two.'

Geoff had disappeared. I felt upset about this: he had been a good companion but, as I spread two pairs of ragged underpants, three off-white vests and an extra wood-pulp shirt on the floor, to lie on, and laid our toothbrush and a thumbed copy of Samuel Butler's 'Erehwon', the last fifty pages of which had been desecrated in the latrine at Corinth, the cavity in my stomach took over, and he was forgotten.

In this camp, near the Albanian border, the grim reality of the situation really began to sink in. As stifling days ground by, our stomachs shrunk and the lice grew bigger, burrowing into our skins like pneumatic drills. Here, it seemed, was every species of bug placed in this world to tantalise humans. At first, some of the 'toughs' were still managing to keep a small section of their minds for sex, but the few half-hearted jokes, coming from a couple of Australians who were getting extra rations from the black market, went unheeded by men who, only a month before, would have guffawed with laughter. Slowly, the jokes died out, to be replaced by a heavy silence: the silence of hundreds of men with only one thought between them - FOOD. Images of wives and mothers were there because they represented food and cooking: sentiment had been wiped out of men's minds by the gnawing emptiness in their stomachs.

Within a week, the friendship I had struck up with a fellow five yards away was blossoming under the spell cast by a competition between us of concocting hideous mental recipes. For hours we would lie silently staring at the ceiling and then, with no warning, would crawl over, I to him or he to me, to divulge in a whisper, like passing on a vital political secret, the method of somehow mixing, cooking and eating a spherical Yorkshire pudding, the size of a football, filled with chopped liver and exotic vegetables — the whole thing rolling about in an inch of Y.R. sauce: or something which would start off as a strawberry flan but would be completely disguised by layers of mashed pear, passion fruit, pomegranates, orange segments, raspberries, gooseberries and banana slices; crowned in glory by a tin of Nestle's sweetened condensed milk poured, with abandon, over the top. When the time came, losing all control, we hugged our little chunks of stale black bread in ecstasy, either eating them lovingly then and there or perhaps just licking them occasionally until the glorious moment arrived when they could be dunked in the daily dixie of 'potato slush'. Now, it was every man for himself: there was no alternative to self-torture. Either you wolfed everything down like a dog and lay, unsatisfied, watching the sippers and nibblers enjoying themselves, or you went through the agony of sipping and nibbling, plagued by a craving to wolf the lot.

The black marketeers were doing a roaring trade with those fortunates who still had something left to trade with. The black market even took its toll in lives. One R.O.A.C. corporal, swapping his gold wedding ring for three newly baked, almost white loaves, killed himself so effectively by eating the lot at one sitting that Australian Sergeant Perry, self-appointed head of the market, closed it for a day in his memory – and, of course, to relieve his conscience. After a week or two, we found that it did us much less harm to sit outside in the blistering heat, picking the lice off each other's backs, than to stagger up and down the stairs, resting several times on the way. Besides, we were nearer the latrine. The P.O.W.s had gradually sorted themselves out into the 'haves' and the 'have nots'. Geoff seemed to have disappeared into one of the other camps, leaving me as a 'have not'. Under these conditions it was easy to go under. Lack of energy was already there but, when this was followed by a lack of enthusiasm to think out new recipes, to queue up for the daily 'slush', or even a chunk of bread, I had become really ill and, to save a whole lot of energy, was content to lie on the bug-ridden floor boards and wait to pass away peacefully into oblivion. But, St. Peter, who (unless I was due for Hell Fire) must have had the register open and ready to enter my name, probably gave a sigh of relief when I spotted the object which was to make life worth hanging onto — a totally shapeless uninteresting pot of raspberry jam. Like a beacon light shining on a derelict coal pit, it stood there, swathed in its sticky glory; brought by an Australian from the black market and placed on a convenient shelf above his area of floor. Watching this fellow continually bringing in extras, which others couldn't usually obtain, had become a mental torture until I had managed to cut him out of my mind; but the sight of the jam was too much. After another day and a half, seeing the jam gradually disappearing, I threw in the sponge. The fight to retain a little bit of self-respect was over. He was there, gorging again and reading a tatty paperback.

"Hey! Aussie," I croaked. "Please, just a tiny lick at that jam of yours."

Like a confirmation bishop who had just been asked for another sip of communion wine, he came over and stood glowering down at me.

"That pot of jam cost me my silver cigarette case, sport. Go and buy your own fucking jam!"

He could not have put it plainer: but it was too late. By now I had been K.O.'d and carried out of the ring. In for a penny, in for a pound. To hell with morals and resolutions. I might as well lose all my pride.

"Please," I said. "Either give me some or get it out of my sight".

"Get off your arse!"

That was enough. The jam had become a 'must.' Somehow, I would get it. My friend, who had given me up and had found somebody else to swap recipes with (and was certainly destined for Heaven at some later date), offered me his ration of 'potato slush', which I had to refuse. But a spoonful, a ladleful, a bucketful of sweet jam had become a fixation. There was no plan to work out. Straightforward thieving was the only answer. While the Aussie was standing in the queue for the chunk of bread he was going to spread the jam over, I hoisted myself up, crawled over to the shelf, reached up and, grabbing the pot, with its spoon sticking out, with utter abandon, began to wolf it down: one, two, three large spoonfuls...After that, I couldn't stop.

The gates of hell rocked when the Aussie, nursing his bread like a baby, and with a dixie of coffee to wash it down, arrived back and saw what was happening. With all the extra vitality gained from a full stomach, he leapt across the floor like one of the kangaroos 'back in the bush'. Reaching down and trying to tear the pot from my hand he screamed:

"You fucking bastard. You dirty, thieving rat!"

But, by this time, most of the jam was slopping down the side and the pot had become slippery. With a sickening crash it fell to the floor, where it broke in pieces, spreading out in a beautiful, delectable mess. With no hesitation the six-foot two Aussie began to kick me around the floor. By this time, the hatred I had developed for him gave me the strength I must have had in reserve somewhere and, grabbing his legs in a tight squeezing tackle-hold, I turned the game from football into rugby and brought him thumping to the floor. Eyes blazing, he launched himself on top of me, gripping my throat, and would probably have solved my problems for good if one of the Cypriots hadn't crawled over and started spooning as much of the jam as he could off the boards into his mouth, licking up what was left with a tongue full of splinters. With a bound, the Aussie was on top of him, but it was too late: the rest of the jam and half the pot were in the Cypriot's belly.

Yet, the taste of the jam, in spite of the repercussions, had done something to me. Through the mists of illness I had seen that there were still some good things in life, even if a bit sticky. I was in the right mood to find some help in the rasping voice of a guard, trying to speak English, with an American accent, from a position he had found amongst the prone figures in the middle of the floor; with one jackbooted foot in somebody's dixie and the other in the pool of coffee which had spilt out of it:

"O.K., gentle-guys," he was shouting. "Herr Doktor arrives camp tomorrow. O.K.? Not eat. Not drink, ja? O.K. You obey....shit-runs go."

In other words, a miracle man was coming to get rid of our dysentery.

"Sod off," growled the Aussie, licking his fingers, covered with jam from a second pot that had appeared on the shelf, from nowhere.

For me, it was easy, at that time, to go on not eating, but only about three quarters of the others managed it. When the doctor, an M.O. in the uniform of a captain, with an iron cross second-class on his breast pocket, arrived, another chap (who should have had a halo) helped me down to the queue and held me up while we passed the medical table. From a bowl piled high with a black, soot-like powder, each man was given enough to fill the palm of the hand.

Our English-speaking guard was there.

"Eat. Eat. Not drink. If drink...shit-runs not go. ja?"

With the temperature at about a hundred degrees in the barrack buildings, I had completely run out of saliva and, lying on my back, spent the next two hours swallowing the powder in little bits, to the delight of the Aussie, as he smeared more jam over his already sticky face.

After rigidly following the German doctor's orders for two days, I was so much better that I was able to start a new occupation. Unexpectedly, I was called into the commandant's office.

"We haf you as a commercial artist in our records," said the clerk. The commandant kept his distance; he didn't want his uniform to smell. Seeing him for the first time, I marvelled at the way a German uniform could make any person, however insignificant, look important; as he glared sideways at me through gold-rimmed glasses, balanced on his hawk-like nose above a small black moustache, creating an image as near to that of his Fuhrer as he dared.

"Yes," I said, surprised.

"You will please paint the names of your dead comrades on the crosses which the Wehrmacht haf kindly provided."

I had to obey. It was a depressing task, but one I could not get out of. In any case, I felt I was doing them some last service. Very carefully I copied what had been given to me onto twenty or thirty crosses, made from deal, while the days and weeks went by. When I had finished them the crosses were taken away to some small patch of ground, acting as a cemetery, which would sink under the dust and disappear quietly into the annals of forgotten history.

My dysentery better, I was very careful to keep away from the tap water. When I ran out of paint, a chance came to fight off the bacteria with even more certainty. Explaining to the guard who spoke English about the paint, I was surprised when he asked me to paint his name inside his kitbag....."In case I blow to pieces for the Fatherland, and nobody not recognise the bits," he chuckled, with a wink.

"I will," I said. "On one condition. You get something for me."

"Vot do you vant, Mein Herr?" he asked.

"A bottle of disinfectant."

Unexpectedly, he brought it almost immediately and, from then onwards, until I was one of the two thousand moved to another camp two months later, I put a drop into everything I ate and drank, finally becoming immune from every ailment except a perforated stomach and severe halitosis.

The new camp was ruled over by quite a different sort of commandant; known as 'The Bull', because of his typically stetonic bristling short hair and neck like a pier support. With the aid of a revolver and a gift for performing sadistic tricks he reigned supreme. We got a taste of him on the first day, as we formed into a line, winding like a crippled snake around the compound, dixies ready, waiting for the inevitable 'potato slush'. To collect this we had to file past three giant steaming copper urns, British, Australians, New Zealanders and Cypriots, with no distinctions. From a distance the 'Bull' watched, his hand caressing the butt of his revolver in its belt holster. Because there was always the chance, however remote, of a second helping for those who had enough energy to queue again, some of the men carried their ration straight round to the back, where they shuffled along, eating it and licking the last remnants off their fingers. A guard was posted to see that there was a distance of a few yards between the first and second queues. But when the leading members of queue two were advancing hopefully, empty dixies at the ready, the commandant suddenly sprang to life, dashing in, waving his revolver and shouting: "Zuruck! Zuruck!" (Back! Back!), and splitting up the queue as the men moved away, mixing with the others, until there was a wide circle, with the urns, still steaming gently as the 'slush' cooled down in the middle.

Now it was time for the 'Bull' to start in on his little game; turning his back on one half of the circle and advancing, head lowered and gun pointing menacingly towards the other side, which drew back as one man. In the meantime, the men behind him advanced on the urns: but, with deft timing, the 'Bull' suddenly turned on them as they were about to fill their dixies with leftovers; pushing them back at gunpoint, while the others closed in behind. With a schoolboy's delight, he repeated the performance several times, until he seemed to have had enough of the game, returning his gun to its holster and strolling off. Gradually the men, regaining confidence at the sight of his back and the smell from the urns, began to close in from all sides but, before the men at the front could reach the target, standing on the platform outside his office and drawing his gun again, legs apart like a quick-firing cowboy, he was once again the master, driving everyone back to a safe distance.

When, eventually, he disappeared through his office door, some of the enthusiasm had gone from the hungry mob, which hesitated uncertainly, until one man, whose tormented stomach had made him suicidal, ran and dived head first into the nearest urn. Following his example, more imitated him, filling their dixies and trying to get away, but were pushed back where they had come from by others clamouring from behind; creating the grand finale: three urns with legs sticking out like aspidistra leaves, as the men scraped and shovelled the slush into their mouths, finally squirming out with heads covered in a gooey yellow mess. We soon learnt what a German's idea of washing out an urn was when a New Zealander, the next day, was lucky enough to get one of the lenses of a pair of glasses ladled into his dixie. Straightaway he flogged it in the black market, where the original owner had to trade in his midday 'slush' to get it back.

We soon got used to this daily game and took no notice of the 'Bull', who was really quite harmless, sneaking round and waving his revolver, hoping to intimidate somebody, with no success. In fact, afraid of him at first, we were now openly laughing at him; joined by one or two of the guards, when he wasn't looking. But such understanding guards, all paratroopers having a break from active service, were not to remain for long. At the other end of the swinging pendulum were the S.S. and, when the paratroopers left, we got them. Within minutes they were indulging in various demoralising sports. Two of them, pretending to move an urn, overturned it on purpose, so that they could watch some of the prisoners scraping the steaming yellow mess off the dusty ground. They liked to 'fix' any light bulb still on one minute after the 'lights out' order, with a bullet fired from out in the compound; but had to stop this form of entertainment when there were no more spare bulbs and some barrack buildings were in darkness. The commandant, delighted to see real bullets being fired, as long as he wasn't the target, had shown no objection.

Under these circumstances, nobody was sorry when the day of our removal from Greece towards some unknown destination inevitably arrived and, with no warning, we were packed into cattle trucks, the doors were rolled shut and, in almost complete darkness, we left the country.

(Back in the 1880's, when a certain young Adolf Schikelgruber had been chewing the heads off toy soldiers in his playpen, someone in Germany had designed a mobile oven - air tight, lightproof and capable of raising its temperature from lOO to 120 degrees Fahrenheit in five agonising minutes.

Though they were for carrying the bodies of cows, pigs, sheep and other livestock, Adolf Hitler, now fully matured and playing with real soldiers, decided to use them to deliver all those who seemed to threaten the master race, to Auschwitz, Dachau, Treblinka and various P.O.W. camps.)

In the sizzling heat of mid-July fifty of us were roasting in one of these ovens, grinding and snorting its way through Yugoslavia, like a mechanical slug. During the night, when the train had slowed down, twelve of the men in the rear truck had managed to cut a hole and roll out onto the track without being spotted. In the Wehrmacht, one of the worst blackmails in history was being practised on the faithful German soldiers ... "If you don't behave yourself and do what you are told or, for that matter, make any mistakes in doing what you are told, you will almost certainly be sent to the Russian front..." Nearly every soldier realised what this would mean, that the Russians would be ruthless and that their winter would be even worse, and it was with this punishment in mind that the stocky little train commandant, with a 'bad liver' complexion, made every man get out and line up, when the train next reached a siding. Grasping onto the English he had learnt years before at school, and trying to look taller by standing on an ammunition box, he gave us all the Nazi salute. Those guards who were not sitting on their uncomfortable wooden seats at the front of each carriage roof, covering us with machine-guns, were standing rigidly at attention in a row facing us. After drawing himself up to his full height of five foot two, the commandant shouted through a megaphone:

"It is mit zees salute zat I your bloody fate seal. Zwolf of your kamerads have zuring zee night tru zee floor descended. ja? For zees you vill all be punished. No one vill be allowed from zee trucks out. In your drawing rooms (a smile twitched on his stony face as he came out with these long-forgotten words), you vill eat, sleep and die. Zee guards, zay vill not zee door open make, for all I don't bloody care. Your stupid kamerads zay vill be caught. Zat is my last vords, ja?... Heil Hitler!"

Under the glowering eye of the commandant the guards, pushing us back into the trucks, gave us an extra prod with their rifle barrels. Geoff and I had unexpectedly met up again and were squashed into a corner, unluckily under one of the two nine by eighteen inch ventilator-slits in the sides of the truck. Judging by the amount of barbed wire covering these, the Germans weren't letting any of the cockroaches keeping us company out and, in order to get rid of the contents of several dixies being used as latrines, we had to force a hole through ours. Emptying the dixies kept us going most of the day and night but any fresh air which did get through got to us first. As we continually waited in sidings, we had plenty of time to peer through the slits at the victorious German army on its way along the main line to Russia. Practically the only conversation took the form of one fellow cursing another, either for relieving himself too close to the other's face, or hogging the middle of the floor and lying there while the others had to lean against the side.

At the end of four days, apart from two men who were ill with high fevers, everyone had eaten his two-days ration of bread and German sausage. The monotonous bumping of the wheels had become part of our lives. Occasionally either Geoff or I would struggle up to have a look through the slit as the train jerked and wrenched its way through the panoramic mountains of eastern Yugoslavia out onto the plains, where the endless golden fields of wheat and maize and the fir tree woods sunned themselves under a cloudless blue sky. The expression on the faces of the peasants, who usually stopped working and stared, leaning on their rakes and hoes, were blank and slightly wary. Occasionally they would wave at the guards perched on the carriages but not at us, yet it was easy to see that they were more frightened than unfriendly. As the scenery became more industrial Geoff was first to shout some welcome news across the darkness. He had seen the name high up on a board over the railway - BELGRADE. There was a scramble for the ventilation-slits and Geoff and I slid down into our corner, listening to the reports as the train came into the station.

"Christ! Look at them bleedin' buns. Look at them urns: must be tea or summat."

"Hey, digger!" shouted one over-sexed Aussie, who had been stuffing himself with black market bierwurst, to another. "Take a gander at them nurses."

Pinned in our corner by a mass of legs, boots and clogs, Geoff and I picked up the gist of what was going on outside. The Red Cross were there, on the station, ready with food for the allied prisoners from Greece. The train commandant, arguing with a Red Cross official, was gesticulating and shouting 'NO!' The official, backed up by the nurses in their trim blue uniforms was pleading; but the commandant was adamant. What had happened was obvious; as obvious as the boos and whistles from the slits in the trucks along the entire train. For a moment the commandant turned and scowled: then he sauntered off to his carriage at the rear. But he had left his orders that the guards would have to obey if they wanted to stay alive.

"Tea only — No buns."

While we drank the watery tea passed back through the slit to the fifty men in the truck, we had to imagine the taste of the hundreds of wasted buns. No feelings could match the hatred we felt for the five-foot-two commandant. Geoff's face was pale and expressionless as he held one arm round the shoulders of the fellow next to him, who was crying like a baby. By the time the train left the station the commandant had learnt a few adjectives not in his school dictionary, all describing him and usually followed by 'bastard'.

The next day was the hottest since the journey had begun. As it was impossible to lean against the truck walls without getting blisters, the men were piling on top of each other towards the centre, and rapidly dehydrating. Hunger we had got used to, but this was a different matter. As the train crawled out into the country again the peasants must have seen the steam pouring through the ventilation-slits. Within a few hours an insatiable thirst had gripped everyone. Tongues were beginning to swell and fill the mouth like lumps of rubber. Hunger was forgotten as thirst took over. One of the men with a fever was staring with fear, his mouth blocked open by his tongue as he struggled for breath. Praying seemed quite useless, as no prayers seemed to have been answered so far: and who could blame them up there, with their hands so full? The only thing to do was to sit and hope for a miracle... and, unlikely though it was, the miracle came.

Slowly, the inside of the truck was getting darker: night seemed to be coming early. But this was no night. As the first flash of lightening lit us up for a split second, the scene inside the truck could have been taken straight out of the Chamber of Horrors. Down came the rain in a solid sheet, trying to batter the roof in and wash the guards off the top. Within seconds every available dixie and mug, whether being used as a latrine or not, was handed to Geoff and me, and the two in the other corner. One after another we filled all the receptacles, passing them back through the darkness. The water, streaming off the roof past the slits, was black with soot and, though hot at first, tasted like all the welcome pints ever drunk rolled into one. The truckload of men was like a wilting plant brought back to life.

The rain stopped as quickly as it started, the clouds disappeared and the sun seemed to be calling to us:

"You thought you'd seen the last of me, didn't you? No such luck, chums, I'm here to stay."

And it kept its word, until the end of that day when the train stopped and the nightmare journey was over. In the early mists of the next morning we found that the ovens had pulled up right inside our next holiday camp. Through listening to some of the guards talking, we learnt that we had arrived at Marburg-am-Drau near the Austro-Yugoslavian border.

In the Marburg camp the dust didn't seem so dusty, there were no stairs to climb and the potato slush smelt that little bit less like an Egyptian sewer. Within an hour we were queuing for 'slush' and then going round again for rice pudding, but any idea of this sort of treatment continuing was soon shattered when we realised that, as we had been expected the day before, we were only getting two days rations in one go.

When those who, back in Greece, had volunteered for work were sent out in working parties, the larger ration of food now helped to increase their energy, however slightly. Mine was one of the numbers called to make up a group of forty. With three guards, we were marched through the town, across the bridge over the torrential waters of the river Drau and along the main street, buried in a red white and black ocean of Swastika flags. From every window on every floor of every building at least one flag was thrust proudly out towards the centre of the street, forming a victorious archway. All this ceremony for one man, not even the Fuhrer himself, but a fairly remote gauleiter, Dr. Ley, who would be arriving during the day to make a quick speech before passing on somewhere else. With an emptiness in my stomach, not caused this time by lack of food, I realised what the allies were up against - a patriotism and trust in their leaders of a people not even German; yet who must represent the feelings of the public throughout Germany. What was ever going to beat them into the ground? Certainly not anything we had done so far.

"Let's face it. We've lost the war," said the chap next to me and, as I was no clairvoyant, I agreed.

After leaving the town and marching another four miles, we arrived at an officer's training barracks; a large red brick building with four floors. Within minutes I was assigned a job which was to last me a week and to bore me beyond all description; at the end of a flat four foot square wooden tray, nailed to two poles protruding at each end and wide enough apart for a man to stand between. At the other end was an Australian, as bored as I was. It was our job to shovel onto the tray and carry about ten tons of earth from a cellar, which was being constructed under the barracks, down a path to a dump a quarter of a mile away, at opposite ends, with a pole in each hand.

With such a monotonous job, we were glad to get some relieving moments. The first real laugh we had had for weeks was to be provided by the Aussie who had kicked me around the floor. Some of the officer cadets, a stage more intelligent than the O.R.s, showed a certain amount of sympathy towards us. But, when giving away some of their rations, they didn't bother who they gave them to and, if possible, preferred trading. Consequently, the opportunists, including the Aussie with the jam, jumped in and grabbed whatever it was for the black market. He would trade three loaves to us for a watch, ring or wallet, and then trade these items with certain of the guards for ten. But his luck was not to last. As he was plodding along in front of us with an armful of shovels, a whistle from a fourth floor window while no guard was in sight, was the signal for him to put down the shovels and catch a loaf. This was quickly followed by another. The first one he caught but, getting his timing wrong while stuffing it out of sight under his loose shirt, exclaiming: "Cripes! That's the stalest bastard so far," the other had hurtled down, hitting him on the head and knocking him unconscious with an inch-long gash in his scalp. That was the last I saw of the Aussie, who was taken away to the sick bay on the ground floor. As far as I was concerned, I had been lucky enough to view a bit of poetic justice.

As the ration hadn't, after all, been increased, within three days we were hungrier than the others left in the camp. Under these conditions someone had sniffed out the refuse bins at the barracks and this area, in spite of its variety of un-appetizing smells, had become a happy hunting ground for some. On the fifth day 'Fatso' Lewis, hungrier than most of us though still too fat to see his toes three months after being rescued from one of the rafts of a cruiser sunk in the Mediterranean, provided some light entertainment by fighting with a skinny R.A.S.C. private nicknamed the 'Ferret', over a four inch mouldy German sausage.

"It's mine," screamed the 'Ferret', holding the limp greasy pink piece of flab high above his head with the stocky sailor, his face purple with rage, jumping for it like a puppy.

"I found the bugger, didn't I?" shouted 'Fatso'. "Give it to me."

But no demon from hell would have had the power to get that sausage from the 'Ferret' because, as he had been shouting he had been cramming it, wrapped in its jacket of green mould, into his mouth. This was too much for 'Fatso' who barged into him, hurling him to the ground and pressing the top of his head and the bottom of his lower jaw together so that he couldn't chew. In an effort to swallow it the 'Ferret' choked and out flew the sausage, an inch and a half shorter, into the dust. Letting go, 'Fatso' dived, falling onto it as the winner of a posthumous V.C. might have fallen onto a grenade to save his friend's life – though all 'Fatso' had in mind was to get something in his belly. Before the skinny private had recovered, 'Fatso' had crammed it into his mouth; but not before one of the guards, hearing the commotion, had arrived on the scene.

"Schpuk aus! (Spit that out...!)" he shouted at 'Fatso', pointing his gun menacingly.

'Fatso' hesitated, but spat the miserable looking sausage out into his hand when the guard jerked his rifle as if he meant business.

"Put it on the ground," shouted the guard in German.

'Fatso' had enough sense to obey immediately.

The guard drew his bayonet and, bringing it down on the sausage like an executioner, cut it clean in two.

"Now, eat!" he said.

The two men looked doubtful and slightly crestfallen.

"EAT!" shouted the guard.

By this time about twenty of us stood in a circle, eyes fixed half approvingly on the semi-chewed sausage, which had lost its green jacket in the fracas and now had a delightful fresh pink colour, as inviting to us as it was unappetizing to the guard.

'Fatso' and the 'Ferret', their problem solved, needed no persuasion. With the guard's rifle pointing at them they made short work of what was left of the tortured sausage.

"Gut!" said the guard, followed by something else which one of the Australians seemed to have understood.

"Great jumping kangaroos!" he gasped, staring wide-eyed at the two men. "Do you jokers know where that sausage came from?"

"Where?" both asked at once, looking scared.

"Off the plate of one of those Kraut bastards. Up there....Room 117. He was carried off last week with bubonic plague!" But, before the remark had sunk in, he was doubled up laughing.

"Shit! did you see their faces?" he kept on blurting, the tears streaming down his sallow cheeks.

"ARBEIT! (Back to work)!" screamed the guard, brandishing the bayonet and, within a split second, round him was an empty space.

As the weeks passed it became obvious that Marburg was a transit camp, and it was not long before I was once more leaning against a blistering oven wall, listening to the rusty protest of unoiled wheels and waiting for the next turn of events.

CHAPTER FOUR

The continuous grinding and scraping had drowned most of the noises coming from inside the trucks. There seemed to be more purpose in the attitude of the guards, who gave the impression that they were glad because they would soon be rid of us. Every time the train stopped, to the guards perched on their crippling little seats high up on the truck roofs we must have sounded like wailing mourners at a biblical funeral. Forgetting to put up a good show for King and Country in front of them, we were arguing, grousing, cursing each other and generally acting, now that our morale was up, with a bit more liveliness and enthusiasm. We knew that, being in Austria, wherever we were going could not be very far away. After two hours we pulled into a siding to let a trainload of self-confident men on their way to further victories at the Russian front roll past, and at this point the train commandant took advantage of the opportunity to let us out to relieve ourselves. One of the guards, a red faced friendly fellow with a heaven-sent squint keeping him away from the front line, called out to us in English, when we seemed to be taking too long:

"Quickly! Quickly! Gentlemen. We are getting rid of zee Ruskis quicker than you are getting rid of your vorter. If you do not piss a little faster zee vor vill be ofer before you vinnish."

In the commandant's coach at the front, the wireless had been turned on full throttle so that we couldn't miss Dr. Goebbels forcing his latest propaganda down the National Socialist throats. The Germans were paying us the compliment of assuming that we understood their over-zealous newscaster.

"You don't believe that crap, do you?" Corporal 'Shorty' Rowlands called disgustedly to the English-speaking guard who, with eyes shining, had just breathed reverently,

"Listen! Our Propaganda Minister."

But luckily for 'Shorty', the private, only hearing the word 'crap', had not associated it with his ranting idol.

"Gentlemen," he said, with a touch of sympathy. "My orders zay only allow for zee pissing, not zee crapping. Please to get back and crap in zee trucks. Schnell (Quickly)!".

The raspberries the Propaganda Minister got from us, to show our opinion of the optimistic promises he had been making to his gullible countryman, would have put the massed bands of the Aldershot Tattoo to shame; but as the trucks grew hotter the men became more silent. Travelling inland, we could see through the ventilation slits the rectangular fields of Austria, shoulder to shoulder like a patchwork quilt; dotted here and there the farmers, mostly women and old men, stopping to look at us as we clanged past.

Half an hour after the train had left the siding and was travelling inland again, it jolted to a halt once more. At first there was silence, except for the noisy hissing of the steam from the overheated engine; but it was quickly followed by the muffled sound of voices and laughter outside; for once, not those of the guards urinating with carefree abandon against our truck wheels. Sensing a more civilised atmosphere, we stopped talking and listened, trying to distinguish the sounds coming from further down the train, where it seemed that one of the trucks was being opened and that the men were being let out.

"Schnell! Schnell!" the guards were shouting together, as if any dawdling would mean a bullet in the back of the neck for them. We could hear the scraping shuffle of boots and wooden clogs as they brought the men up and halted them outside our truck. Except for Big Tom, an Australian infantryman and former fruit farmer (a character who we all knew would have cracked a joke under torture), everyone seemed to be silent and doing what he was told. A fragile-looking chap they called 'Brummie', packed like an anaemic sardine next to me, must have been a mate of his.

"What they dowin' to yer, Aussie?" he shouted from the darkness, his mouth against the two inch thick side of the truck.

"Cripes!" shouted the Australian, "If it ain't that there Pommie from Bairmingam. Still aloive, mite?" He imitated the accent.

"Joost abaht," shouted Brummie.

The Aussie lapsed into his usual semi-cockney.

"Good on yer. You want to know what they're doing to us. Well I'll tell yer. The natives here have got us all lined up like they're waiting to chuck us in the boiling pot. Such a right lot of cannibals like this lot, you ain't never seen. They could be turkey cocks, the way they're cackling. Thank the Lord my eyeballs have seized up. I can't even see their ugly faces."

"If yer gowin bloind, mite, yow sh'd lie off it a bit. Din' yer dad never tell yer abaht them things?" Brummie, who by now was annoying everyone with his bull-like voice, would have doubled up laughing at his own joke, if there had been room.

"Give them Jerry bastards a birrof yer charm an' tell 'em to lerrus aht," he managed to splutter between giggles. "Yer never now, 'Itler moit not 'ave castrited all them 'owmowsexuals yet. There moit be one as'd stroik a bargain wiv yer".

"Oh! Get lost, you stupid Bairmingham ..."

The Aussie stopped and, judging by the grunts of pain, was being kicked about by the guards who were probably enjoying the only exercise they had had all day. Soon after, we heard Big Tom and his group being marched away and our row of ovens was clanging and rasping like a suit of armour being dragged over an iron grating, out into the country again. Trying to get through the ventilation slits a little of the sweet smell of summer hay from the fields was battling against our almost solid B.O.

For the next four hours the arthritic train crawled on, stopping at intervals to unload more of the men, until our turn came. Outside, the steady hissing of the steam from our faithful engine was joined by staccato shouts, the door was slid open and, at an order from the guards, we crawled and rolled out through the great square of blinding sunlight onto the platform of a small station.

"Schnell! Schnell!" The guards shouted, like a Wagnerian opera chorus.

Everyone was laughing at Brummie, who had ripped the

seat of his pants while getting out and stood immobile exactly where he had landed, the cheeks of his lilywhite rump shining proudly, like two neatly shelled hard-boiled eggs at a picnic. (With Brummie around, who wanted ENSA to entertain the troops?)

"Bist ruhig (Be quiet)!" screamed a guard whose beady eyes and scraggy hair would have won him a booby prize at Cruft's. Some of the civilians near us nudged each other and giggled.

Corporal Taffy Llewellyn tore the air apart with one of his cunningly camouflaged raspberries and the guard's rifle came up to the ready as if he had been a clockwork toy. With eyes shining like black buttons and eyebrows meeting in a terrifying scowl he seemed to be wondering whether shooting one of us would get him an Iron Cross; but he hesitated. After all, if the commandant's digestion was as bad as usual it could well mean the Russian front instead, where he would probably have to get blown up to get one. So, with a sneer, he shot a streak of saliva in the direction of the raspberry through a gap in his front teeth. A murmur of approval from someone in the crowd seemed to give him back self-esteem.

When the commandant arrived, weighed down with medals and swastikas and trying to catch up with his fingers stretched out in a Nazi salute, he looked at the townspeople as if to say:

"Sorry we've landed you with this bunch."

By this time, a New Zealand corporal called Willis, who spoke German fairly well, had become our unofficial interpreter and, with his qualities as a leader and conscientious nature, had automatically taken over command. After a word with the German corporal he turned to us and called hopefully:

"O.K., you jokers. They want us to line up and march off. Try and look a bit smart, lads. We haven't lost the war yet."

A few stifled grunts showed that his optimism wasn't shared by all. He looked anything but the 'man in charge'. In fact, a rusty safety-pin, doubtfully holding a tatty corporal's stripe to one of the sleeves of his pre-war Croatian cavalry officer's jacket, was the only thing to give him any claim to this title. But we liked him as much as we felt like liking anyone and were prepared to do what he asked.

As my eyes grew accustomed to the light, I began to take in my surroundings. We were standing on the platform of a station that looked as if a large puff of smoke from our engine would blow it away. A fellow in a tatty uniform, who seemed to be the stationmaster, was anxiously hopping round the guards, while only yards away stood about fifteen people staring at us like children at a Punch and Judy show. With my small knowledge of German, I was beginning to pick out words here and there and to understand roughly what was being said. A couple who might have been a farmer and his wife were passing judgement on us as they might on a bunch of pigs at a market. For a moment, as their eyes rested on me, I felt as if my three-sizes-too-large French Poileau's trousers and 'ersatz' woollen shirt had been snatched away.

"Ach ja! Maria", the man was saying, weighing up my value in kilograms, as if I had been a bullock. "Big and strong. But I wouldn't trust him with Lisl and Mitzi. They can't bear strangers pinching their tits." He half turned to the two girls standing near him, who nodded solemnly. "You know what a fuss Lisl makes when you get the brush anywhere near hers." (I quickly realised he was talking about his cows.) "Look at his hands. Not used to hard work — the hands of a schreiber (office worker)." The last two words were accompanied by a slight sneer.

His wife was more sympathetic.

"The poor fellow needs lots of food," she said. "To make his hair grow." I caught her eye as my hand went to the thinning patch on top of my head, and she half smiled.

By now, her husband's gaze was resting on Harry Duke standing next to me, as thin as a beanpole, with his feet floating about inside size thirteen wooden clogs. The boils he had developed from guzzling raw potatoes had decided to concentrate on the white flesh showing between the top of his clogs and the bottom of his Czecho-Slovakian sergeant's trousers, which only reached half way down his thin calves. Wherever else he had them he wouldn't say — though I did notice he seemed to be standing up most of the time.

The sight of Harry was enough for the farmer.

"Come," he said to his wife. "With soldiers like that to fight against, we have no need to worry about winning the war. Don't let's waste any more time."

Then he turned and walked smartly away, calling to his wife impatiently, without looking round: "Schnell! Maria, schnell (Quick, Maria, Quick!")

Without a murmur, she ran after him.

The steady rhythm of the stationmaster's arm, swinging up and down in endless Nazi salutes, was beginning to slow down, and his 'Heil Hitlers' had already lost their edge.

"I-ee-ya," he kept on gasping unenthusiastically as he faced each new German sergeant, corporal and private, as if chewing a quinine tablet. He was obviously thankful when all the guards were back in their positions on top of the trucks and, while everyone's eyes were on the train as it pulled out, leant over to Willis and, with lips semi-closed like a ventriloquist, muttered from the corner of his mouth:

"Hitler... no good! Churchill... good!"

To those of us who had been near enough to hear, the stationmaster, in his scraggy uniform, was now as good as a model in a Burton shop window, and a friend forever.

As we marched off, two girls, arm in arm, were giggling and nudging each other. Jack the 'Stoat', one of the Aussies was so thin that the wink he gave them, a hangover from the days when s-e-x had meant something, nearly put him off balance. Looking from the station down into the town, we saw a small cluster of clean buildings, offices and shops with a main road running through the centre. As we dragged our worn out boots and clogs along the road, the curious semi-pitying gaze of some of the people might have been demoralising to men who had not already kicked pride through the back door, and most of us returned the stares of the office workers, lined up in their windows, without even a scowl.

The sight of the town was an unforgettable introduction to Burgenland; this quaint part of Austria where the cows, pulling cartloads of hay piled up nearly as high as double-decker buses, governed the movements of the traffic. With udders swinging hypnotically and tails fighting an endless battle with the flies, they took no notice of either staff cars or army trucks, 'honking' at them to get out of the way. Apart from giving their animals an occasional flick with the whips the farmers, in league with them against the military, took little notice. The monopoly of the highway was theirs in spite of the Nazis; and now we were there to make the congestion even worse.

A friendly colonel, reclining pompously in the back of an open Mercedes, took away the handkerchief he was holding to his nose to protect it against the smell from a wagonload of steaming manure, long enough to call to the farmer's wife, sitting at the front of the wagon:

"Heil Hitler, gnadige Frau."

"Gruss Gott (God's greetings)," she answered with not even a smile. At the same time, one of her cows, knowing which side it was on, decorated the road with a distinguished-looking anti-Nazi cowpat.

We passed the barracks and the town hall, almost smothered by a swastika flag big enough to carpet two rooms; then several more buildings, until we were nearing the outskirts where the farms, with their skilfully carved wooden gates set into twelve foot high whitewashed walls, took the place of the shops. Through one or two of the gates that were open we could see the farmyards, with busy hens pecking around the manure heaps, old women carrying buckets and children covered in dust and straw. Now and then the delicious smell of food tortured our nostrils. Stopping us at a point where a narrow lane disappeared off the road between more farms, shut away behind their high gates and louvered windows, Willis, who had been talking to one of the guards, a sallow man in his early forties with corporal's stripes, shouted:

"O.K. you jokers. This is where we get split up,"

Acting on the orders of their corporal, the guards began to separate us into two groups, twenty of us remaining on the road while the other thirty formed up at the head of the lane. We asked Willis what was happening.

"I don't know," he said. "Just do what the silly buggers tell you. One of them looks as if he could turn nasty."

"You're wrong," said the 'Stoat'. "They all look nasty already."

We did what we were told and soon I was one of twenty marching away from the town along the straight tarred road running through a patchwork of rectangular fields. Here and there the farmers waved to us. Sitting high up on top of a cartload of hay drawn by two cows, which seemed to know their own way home, a girl, bulging in all the wrong places, was smiling at Jack the Stoat.

"Cripes! I wouldn't mind having that one", he moaned. With 'sex' taking a back seat, nobody paid any attention, until he added... "barbecued." Somebody laughed: then we all had a look, frustrated, trying to imagine her sizzling on a spit. Rather scared, she flicked the cows, which took no notice but plodded on, chewing the cud disinterestedly. Still staring at her over my shoulder, I was an easy target for the prodding end of the nastiest-looking guard's rifle.

"Gehma! Gehma! (Hurry! Hurry!)" he hissed. "Our Austrian girls can do without the attention of you degenerate idiots."

With a blank expression I tricked him into thinking I didn't understand his German.

"If I had my way," he went on excitedly. "All your measly testicles would be lopped off and fed to the Russian prisoners. That would soon kill them off and save us a lot of trouble."

That settled it. Imagining his short, stocky body with four legs, as far as I was concerned, from that day onwards his name would be 'Pig'; and I was gratified to hear the rest of them taking up the nickname. After we had marched for a couple of miles I edged my way up near Willis and the corporal.

"I have my orders in my pocket," the corporal was pleading. "A fixed time for arriving at certain places along our route. We are behind time, my friend."

"The fellow who worked out the times must have been a lot healthier than us, with a lot more in his belly," said Willis.

The corporal took no notice.

"Please," he said. "If you can get your comrades to walk a little faster, we can all have a rest later."

Another one with a 'Russian front' fixation, I thought. But by this time Willis had become quite popular with us and we did what we could to smarten up the pace. Enviously watching the 'Pig' at the front munching bread and bierwurst, we forgot our blisters until we arrived at a point fifteen kilometres further on, where a neat little signpost, marked Shaffendorf, pointed up a cart track. But Willis's admirable 'Chins up for King and Country' idea had soon died a natural death and, swinging round mechanically between the two guards, we looked like a lump of black pudding between two neatly cut slices of bread. Along the track, which sloped slowly upwards towards the top of a hill, where it disappeared between two walls of tall pine trees, Brummie was walking contentedly in his sleep, with one foot on the bottom and the other at the top of a cart rut. There he remained, supported by a long-suffering mate, until a punch in the back from the 'Pig' woke him up with a start.

"Fookinell!" He exclaimed in astonishment, looking as near angry as he ever would, and went on trudging with one eye half open. In the fields each side of us the piles of hay dried themselves luxuriously, the thick maize stretched towards the cloudless sky, and the eyes of the few workers, mostly women and old men, followed us curiously, giving us the feeling that we were expected. The corporal, either because he was tired himself or because we had beaten our correct-to-the-minute schedule, with his eyes fixed on his watch like a football referee, ordered a halt at the top of the hill under the shade of the trees and we all sank gladly to the ground. Within a split second I had fallen asleep and was in a kitchen neatly arranged with all the food and utensils a one-track subconscious could think of. I was just about to gulp down the first mouthful of a Mars Bar, Devonshire cream and Glace Cherry pudding after drinking a cup full of neat Maple Syrup, when the stubby toe of the 'Pig's' jackboot made an easy dent in my stomach. With a yell I jumped to my feet, to find his moonlike face, with its two sore little eyes, just in the right position for an uppercut. Yet, though I was filled with a primitive instinct to screw the small bulbous nose round like the stopper in a beer-bottle, there was no mistaking the two and a half foot of polished rifle barrel again poking into my ribs.

Better a live coward than a dead hero: I had never felt more positive of this.

"Gehma! Gehma! Schnell! Schnell!" he shouted, and Brummie, who had woken up, seeing me still a bit dazed, helped me to understand.

"I think he means get a fookin' move on," he explained, without a trace of humour.

Jock McFinlay, from somewhere in the back streets of Glasgow, was glaring at the 'Pig'; his eyes, usually as placid as the Sound of Mull on an August afternoon, full of hatred.

"Get stuffed!" he growled from the back of his tonsils. Like an angry cur, the 'Pig' turned on Willis.

"What is that 'Get stuffed'?" he demanded plaintively.

Of course this was no time for the truth. Willis thought quickly and covered up with the first excuse that came into his head.

"Oh ... er ... yes. 'G-get stuffed' ...This is an expression we use in the army. It's a friendly one, actually: a friendly way of putting things if you like. It means .. er ... roughly: 'Come along, lads. let's go!'

The look of suspicion twisting the rounded pink features slowly gave way to one of pride and satisfaction, as the guard voiced his first two words of English.

"Get stuffed!" he kept on repeating softly, smiling to himself, until he was confident that he had mastered the phrase perfectly.

Now was the time to show us how really clever he was; to warn us how easily he could pick up English. Raising his head in triumph and stretching all his Michelin tyres up to their full five-foot three, he shouted at the top of his voice:

"GET STUFFED!"

Even in our unfunny condition we couldn't help laughing, trying not to show it for Willis's sake, as we followed the 'Pig' up the road hiding our faces. But he was far too pleased with himself to notice, repeating quietly in rhythm with his feet,

"Right-left-right-left-get-stuffed-get-stuffed."

I noticed the corporal smiling to himself as if he knew that this time the joke was on the Germans.

Once over the top of the hill we might easily have been in a dream, such was the soft beauty of the countryside, spreading itself out like the unfurling petals of a great green and yellow sunflower. A mile beyond us, at the end of a steady downward slope, a village was nestling neatly round the willows of a stream flowing through it. If we were, as it seemed, heading towards this unexpected place, now was the time to be thankful that we had volunteered for work — no matter what it would be. As we marched down towards the cluster of farms, dominated by the slender red steeple of a whitewashed church, some excited children were running up to greet us. But their laughter and shouting suddenly died out only yards away, as if they had hit an invisible brick wall, such was the ferocity of the 'Pig's' glare.

"Geweg! (Clear off!)" he shouted at them.

The corporal looked at his subordinate and shrugged his shoulders. The most daring of the children, a boy of about eight with a mop of curly hair and eyes full of the cheek of being free, stuck out his tongue before heading the rush back to announce our arrival. As their laughter faded we could hear music and the corporal said sarcastically to the 'Pig':

"The Fuhrer would be very angry if he knew this was going on. People laughing and enjoying themselves in wartime."

By the look on the 'Pig's' face he was planning to report the remark to the next officer he could find.

When we rounded the corner into the village we could see what was happening. The villagers were gathering round a variety of stalls displaying pottery, clothes, bags, boots, hats, aprons; all the paraphernalia of a country market. Two white-bearded old men were playing gypsy-type music on their fiddles, accompanied by a young crippled boy with an accordion. The whole lively scene became a tableau, as they all stopped what they were doing and stood still, watching the arrival of the strange 'Gefangenen' (prisoners). A group of geese, their peace shattered by the unusual noise of twenty pairs of shuffling feet bearing down on them, waddled in all directions, heads held high disdainfully, with the 'Pig's' well-aimed jackboot picking out the slow-coach at the rear. Automatically, we straightened ourselves and fell into step, as the people, still staring, smiled and greeted the guards with a chorus of 'Gruss Gott's! Almost immediately their friendly greetings faded to a reverent murmur as someone called out:

"Guten Tag (Good-day), Herr Burgomeister".

Dressed in a dark suit, with an open shirt collar and a clean blue apron tied under his jacket and reaching halfway between his knees and his polished boots, the man they all seemed to respect was coming up the road. Everybody waited for the dark, opulent-looking farmer in his mid-fifties, who didn't seem worried that his well-filled paunch was preventing him doing up his jacket, to speak — except the corporal who, raising his hand in a Nazi salute called out: "Heil Hitler," with the superior confident tone developed from plenty of practice.

The Burgomeister stopped looking at us and turned to the corporal.

"Gruss Gott!" he said with a patronising smile, leaving his arm where it was.

Final proof. The Fuhrer was obviously not getting his quota of respect from these parts. Though by now it was difficult to think rationally, we could still see our future blossoming out a little more rosily.

We left the crowds behind, and passed through the village. The novelty of the surroundings, with the thatched roofs peeping above the tops of the white walls, the high wooden gates, the geese and ducks and the familiar cows lazily plodding in front of the wagons, still couldn't compensate for the emptiness of shrunken stomachs. Secretly I had made up my mind that sometime in the future, even if I had to live like a pauper, as long as I had a mouth and a stomach I would concentrate on filling them day and night with something, it didn't matter what. My thoughts were already beginning to wander. I imagined the ducks were cackling personally at me:

"Waddle-loddle-uck! Waddle-loddle-uck."

Yes, I thought, what a lot of luck. By rights, I should have been dead, instead of some other people with less reason to be. But here I was, shuffling through the peaceful Burgenland countryside, without the thought of being killed within the next five minutes. Of course the 'Pig', another lucky one who could well have been on his way to heaven or hell via the Russian front, had to put an end to these pleasant daydreams.

"Schnell! Schnell!" he roared, three inches from my right ear, luckily still deaf from the explosion in Greece. Because he had tripped over a goose he was taking it out on the nearest prisoner. But it had woken me up in time to hear the news rippling through from Willis, who had just been told by the corporal that this indeed was the end of the journey: here on the farms, working to help with rural production. The reason ... all the young farmers were at the front keeping alive as long as the Russians would let them, with the food we would be helping to grow.

There was an exception. He stood, supporting himself on crutches, in the centre of a group of people; a boy of about eighteen, dressed in field-grey, the careful creases in his trousers wasted on the side with no leg in it. Chatting with the villagers and conscious of the Iron Cross 'second-class' on his breast pocket, he wore a proud expression, as if the reality had not yet sunk in. Perhaps, this lover of the land with the hopeless life ahead of him, might have been better off in heaven with a 'first-class'.

It was an awkward situation. His gaze, when he suddenly saw his unarmed enemies, was cold as twilight in the Arctic. But at least this child in uniform was safe until the Fuhrer he worshipped would start calling up the cripples, even if he would have to hobble around. For a moment, with one of their own sons back with them in this condition, some of the villagers seemed antagonistic but their inborn capacity for sympathy soon took over and they were smiling at us; even calling after us "Good luck!" I was neither glad nor sorry. There, but for the grace of God, might I have gone, I thought, and was back with my exciting gastronomic images: a stupid waste of time, when just then a bowl of cold porridge or even a plate of week-old tripe would have been welcome.

The unpleasant little episode of the wounded 'privaat' was soon forgotten by all as we shuffled along a road flanked on one side by farmhouses, glimpsed through half-open doors and cracks in the high walls, and, on the other, by the willow-clad stream, where the unmolested ducks swam slowly or displayed fluffy under-bellies searching the bottom for food; more fortunate than their brother geese on the road at the mercy of the 'Pig's' jackboot.

Somehow I had to stop these hideous mental images, I thought. What about the only verse I could remember from school, a verse from Sir Walter Scott:

> Breathes there a man with soul so dead,
> Who never to himself hath said,
> This is my own, my native land?
> Whose heart hath ne'er within him burned,
>
> As home his footsteps he hath turned
> From wandering in a foreign strand?
> If such there breath...

At this point the whole fairy-tale image collapsed like a badly built house of cards. Above the gentle gurgling of the stream, the irritated cackle of the geese and the shuffle of boots and clogs, a high-pitched semi-scream pierced through the still air...

"Chroist! I'm boostin'. Where's a bog? Quick!"

The corporal acted speedily. Perhaps he had found himself in the same situation at the interview to decide whether to send him to the front or to guard P.O.Ws; but in his case it would have been abject funk, not uncontrollable dysentery. With a firm grip, he led the red-faced Brummie, almost beaten by nature, through the nearest farm gate and pushed him through the door of a wooden privy. Even Brummie deserved our sympathy, wedged into a space the size of a telephone box, leaning at an angle of ten degrees. When the corporal eventually sent the 'Pig' to investigate, the sadistic little fellow opened the door so unexpectedly that Brummie fell out with his trousers at half mast and his shirt round his neck. A cheer went up as he joined us again, deflated but happy.

At a point two hundred yards past the end of the village we were herded through a gate and into a field. Brummie, who had got himself this far with no more mishaps, straightaway settled himself down in the brand new latrine, constructed from rough timber joists and held together by long slender laths, in the middle of the field, and was soon shouting delightedly that, lucky for our arses, the long pole over the trench provided had no splinters in it. The rest of us followed the guards to the other end of the field where a farmhouse had been specially adapted for P.O.Ws by adding bars to the windows and two-inch strips of studded iron together with padlocks as large as saucers to the doors. A reception committee of fleas and cockroaches was waiting to welcome us on the red brick tiled floor and they were soon trying to beat each other, jumping and crawling up our legs in search of more comfortable accommodation. The pregnant fleas, too fat to jump, were crawling about the floor wondering whether their little mating sprees had been worth it: the ones which reached their goal were disappointed to find squatters there already.

For a home to house the beaten enemy the furniture was not too bad. There were two rooms; one with two-tier bunks lining the walls and one or two chairs, near a wood-burning stove: a pile of logs took up a quarter of the floor space. The other was empty except for two long benches each side of a table, a latrine bucket and a mouse trap invented by a genius whose talent for thinking out 'extermination' processes must already have earned him a good position on the staff of some concentration camp. The number of mice it could get rid of seemed to be limitless, attracting them one after another through a small door, along a precarious strip of wood pivoted at the centre, and finally toppling them into a litre of water, where the fittest was going to push the weakest underneath to prevent itself drowning, until an even fitter one would come along and exterminate it by the same method. It would have to be regularly cleared: otherwise the last ones would merely run about on top of the unfortunates and gambol back up the wood strip to have another go at the cheese, turning the whole contraption into a miniature funfair. I imagined Himmler standing there, scratching his chin thoughtfully ..."If only the damned Jews could be taught to exterminate each other, so many of our best sadists could be spared for the Russian front."

The daylight was making a weak attempt to get through the bars of two small windows, one in each room. The wise chaps had made a dive for the best bunks, staking their claims. Within minutes the 'Pig' had us winding buckets of water from a well outside.

"Get yourselves washed and shaved," he ordered.

Soon the washhouse at the back was resounding with curses as beards were painfully dragged off with the only razor we could find. It had been easy to lift it from Brummie's kit as, by then, he had gone to sleep in the latrine and was far from caring, but the lathers slowly worked up with ice cold water didn't make the pain of using a blade as blunt as a fossil any less unpleasant. When we had finished, somebody dragged Brummie out of the latrine in time for him to shave half his face before we were ordered out on parade. As a hermaphrodite he looked a bit less ugly.

It was obvious why the 'Pig' was in a better temper. Down in the village some near-sighted farm girl with a good sense of humour had kissed him on the cheek.

"A kiss for a brave German soldier," she had cooed. "And a handsome one, too."

This had put him in such a good mood that now he was hopping around like a sparrow, devoting himself to our comforts, his bad liver forgotten, and determined not to be outdone by the corporal, who had been addressing us as 'gentlemen.' Also, since he had learnt the word 'please' he was brimming over with confidence and calling:

"Get stuffed, gentlemen, please. Get stuffed. Schnell. Schnell."

With short, clipped orders, the corporal formed us into a semi-circle. A moment later, the 'Pig' came out carrying a table and chair, which he placed opposite, and a few yards away from the centre. More respectable than we had looked for months, we stood waiting while the villagers, mostly women, began to arrive, taking up their positions behind the table facing us; the whole scene resembling an ancient slave market, with at least fifty of them giving us the 'look over' with an eye to business.

Again the noise faded magically when the Burgomeister arrived, this time with his daughter, a well-built girl of about seventeen, whom any experienced auctioneer would have described as being 'in good condition'. Seeing her robust good looks and obviously amiable disposition, I would have imagined (at any other time and in detail) how quite a few of the village lads had already found this out at first hand? But all that her plump hips were doing to me at the moment was to make me envious of her fat reserve.

The Burgomeister, with a nod here and there, seated his contentedly well-fed body at the table, while his daughter joined the crowd. Losing no time in settling down to business, he plunged his hand into a box filled with slips of paper, which the corporal had brought out. As he pulled out each slip he shouted the number of the farm written on it: a representative of that farm then walked over and picked one of us out. Here was freedom at last, as down the road each man walked with his new employer. While the biggest and strongest went first the rest were left standing like wallflowers at a dance, beginning to look crestfallen and silly.

When my turn came, from the back of the crowd stepped Frau Tagmeier, a small busy-looking woman whose face was almost hidden by a blue head scarf and whose short legs bore her along as if one was always trying to move faster than the other. She bounced straight up to me, smiling wryly, with the corners of her mouth turned slightly downwards, and greeting me with a word I hadn't heard before:

"Servus."

"Servus," I answered, and she gave a hysterical giggle of delight, ordering me, like a sergeant-major, to follow her and stamping across the field, never looking behind, with the self-assurance of the victor over the vanquished.

Frau Tagmeier's farm was almost the first in the village. As she pushed open the nine-foot high wooden gates, the rusty hinges screamed in protest. Grandmother Tagmeier was standing at the farmhouse door, smoking a broken clay pipe, her wrinkled old head almost disappearing into an overhanging vine of luxurious black grapes. Mixed up in her voluminous black skirt were four year old Hans and even younger Judi, thumb in mouth and making sure I couldn't see her by covering her face with her hands and peeping between the fingers.

"Look, Grossmutti (Grandma)." Frau Tagmeier pushed me towards her mother-in-law proudly, as if she had just bought a bargain at a cattle show. "Our new Englander - Stooart."

This was the nearest she could get to my real name. Grossmutti took the broken pipe out of her mouth long enough to look me wisely up and down, showing me her three tobacco-stained teeth in a friendly wrinkled smile. Then, with the two children still clinging to her for protection from this creature they couldn't quite place amongst their fairy tales, she disappeared into the shadows of the front room. As I guessed that she would be responsible for the cooking, my heart immediately went out to her. Drawn, as if by a magnet, towards the tantalising smell, I hardly noticed what Frau Tagmeier was showing me: the well in the corner of the yard, the hay loft, the cart with its slender but tough spoked wheels, the cowshed, flooded and steaming with urine and, most important of all, it seemed, the manure heap, responsible for the quality of everything they grew, standing deserted, except by a few brave hens, in the corner of the yard beyond Grossmutti's own personal vegetable patch, like a Vesuvius full of stink bombs.

Frau Tagmeier was chatting away in a dialect that I found hard to understand, so to keep her happy I nodded after everything she said, realising, at one time, that she was trying to tell me why her husband wasn't there. He wasn't away at the front (I wondered why), but apparently had gone to a neighbouring village market and was expected back soon. Without knowing it, she was having to get her message through the ecstatical closing bars of the Hallelujah Chorus, thundering in my head, as she led me nearer and nearer the smell of the cooking and into the place where it came from.

Inside the whitewashed room with its dark timber panels, everything seemed to be going on at once. By the window was a solid oak table with similar benches round it. It was laid simply with spoons and forks for three, a loaf of Grossmutti's home-baked almost black bread and, in the centre, a large bowl of scalding hot noodle soup; all dimly lit by the sun's rays, battling with the grapevines hanging halfway down the window. Hidden in the shadows was a four-poster bed, so beautifully carved that the bare floorboards underneath insulted it. Putting the temperature up to nearly melting point was a giant stove, white hot inside with blazing logs, and coping with everything at once from cauldrons of hot water down to saucepans and frying pans; with an oven big enough to roast a complete pig. The Waldorf Astoria could not have provided anything more welcome than the meal to come, even if only bread and soup: but I soon realised that Grossmutti was waiting at the stove ready to bring on the second course, vibrating its way past the lid of a cast-iron pot. Terrified that everything would suddenly disappear, I sat down with Frau Tagmeier to start the first proper food I had eaten for three months.

At first I had great difficulty in tackling my steaming soup. As I saw Frau Tagmeier's bowl miraculously empty I was still struggling with my third spoonful, blowing it gently in case it slopped over onto the table, while she stared at me with disappointment and doubt. I noticed that she was constantly glancing over her shoulder at the farm gate. Obviously determined to teach me how to drink my soup before her husband arrived, she told Grossmutti to pour more of the steaming liquid into the bowl and, topping up mine, indicated irritably that I should take a spoonful, still not far from boiling point, and copy her. Following her carefully, I soon found the secret, a simple system but so noisy that, if all the Austrian farmers had been drinking soup at once, the resulting explosion would have wiped Europe off the face of the map and the war would have been over. Blow, suck, swallow! Blow, suck, swallow!

Under the magic spell of this duet the soup in our bowls disappeared unbelievably quickly.

Within two minutes I had finished and was ready for the next course, pleased with myself for having mastered a great art and none the worse except for the blisters on my lips and tongue. From the stove came exultant noises. Raising her arms towards heaven and grinning from ear to ear, Grossmutti was exclaiming softly:

"Jesus, na! Jesus na! What a good boy he is."

Though my stomach was becoming attached to this little Shangri-La I still felt apprehensive. There was a sort of atmosphere here, an indefinable tension. Soon I was to see why; when the great hinges started to squeal as the front gates opened slowly and a man staggered through backwards pulling a thin cow. If it had not been for the gatepost both of them would have fallen over. Though he seemed to be grinning rather viciously, he was really insulting his picturesque surroundings with a loud belch. Still supporting his five foot two of skin, bone and gold teeth against the gatepost, he shouted in broad dialect:

"Mother, I want my food. Schnell!"

As he lurched across the yard to join us, Grossmutti Tagmeier hurried from her corner with his steaming soup, which he dealt with in expert fashion almost before she had got the second course ready. As a learner, I was still admiring him in a sneaking sort of way when he brought out from the breast pocket of his tattered jacket a small mouth organ, which he began to play without a fault, except for one or two belches. So far, he hadn't said another word to any of us but when, finally beaten by lack of breath, he put the instrument away, be stared at me, his watery eyes trying to meet at the back of my neck. With a leer, he leant over and rasped:

"Tell me, boy. How many knodels can you eat in five minutes? A lot, I hope, because in five minutes we are going to start work."

What was happening? I couldn't wait for the next course, but was this going to be a meal, or torture? Before I could reply he turned towards the stove and, in a sinister undertone, as if planning an assassination, whispered:

"Mother, bring on the knodels."

Frau Tagmeier looked scared.

"The guards have warned us not to let the prisoners eat too much to start with," she said timidly." Since her husband had arrived her domineering nature had completely lost its edge. "They say their stomachs have got very small and ... " She finished abruptly as he turned on her, his eyes blazing.

"When I want you to speak, woman, I shall tell you," he hissed. Then he looked at me, relentlessly holding me in his piercing gaze but still addressing her, his voice louder with each word.

"If he is a man, he can EAT KNODELS!" Quickly he calmed down again. "If he can eat knodels, he will become big and strong and a good worker. Then it will be worthwhile having him here." His voice had become almost wheedling.

His mother had been waiting patiently, nursing a massive bowl loaded with a pyramid of what looked like dumplings in breadcrumbs, which she now lowered tenderly into the middle of the table.

Heinrich Tagmeier, his eyes drilling into me, saw immediately that I didn't recognise these delicacies.

"Schwechken Knodels," he explained gently. Don't you eat them in England, Australia, New Zealand?"

Fiercely he dug his fork into the steaming pile of dumplings, squelching out the juice from the large black plums in their centres, and had already spat out fifteen plum stones before he turned to his wife and asked:

"What is he, anyway? English, Australian or New Zealand?"

"English," said Frau Tagneier.

Heinrich peered at me under heavy eyelids, his pointed features twisted in a sly, half guilty smile.

"Churchill good?" he asked, swallowing a plum stone with a frightening hiccough.

What did he expect me to say?

"Of course."

He looked round suspiciously. In his state, even the geese in the yard could have been Gestapo agents.

"Hitler no good." I could only just hear his grating whisper. "The miserable dog takes our pigs, our potatoes, our flour. Before the damned Nazis came it was good here. Now it is terrible, and I am poor — very poor..."

"Moo!" The thin cow in the yard was getting impatient "See, even Mitzi agrees with me."

I looked at the cow. True enough, only a very poor farmer

would have dared to come home with such a pile of skin and bone. At this stage there were twenty plum stones on Heinrich's plate, to his wife's five and my ten.

"I can't eat any more," I said, reluctantly.

Heinrich, with a shrug, spat out his twenty-first, second and third plum stones, together, while he motioned to his mother to clear the table. Then he leant back with another belch and offered me a cigarette, which I accepted. Eyeing me sceptically, he blew clouds of powerfully scented Turkish tobacco at the ceiling.

"You are clever," he said. "Because you speak German." He paused, chuckling. "Funny German, I must say, too. And you are lucky. You English farmers are educated. Here, we are not. Our education is in the sky. We know rain and hail. Our knowledge lies in realising just when to take in the hay before the storms come. We don't know mathematics ..."

"I'm not a farmer," I interrupted. "I'm a schreiber (white collar worker)." With carefree honesty I had plunged into the abyss. The storm clouds gathered in Heinrich's bloodshot eyes as he turned on his wife who was giggling nervously.

"Did you hear that, woman?" he snarled. "He is a schreiber." His voice rose to a choking scream, "How dare you bring back a SCHREIBER!

Frau Tagmeier looked ready to jump out of the way, as her husband's half-inch-long black fingernails tapped the table close to the bread knife.

"He was almost the only one left when it came to my turn," she lied. "Anyway, he is big and strong and can be taught."

"How many potatoes and loaves is it going to take to teach him and how many knodels?" he wailed, staring at my plum stones and forgetting his previous fit of generosity. "He has already had ten. I counted them. By the time he can use a scythe he could have five hundred in his rotten stomach. Mein Gott! As if I hadn't had enough bad luck; and now I am landed with a schreiber."

For a moment he rested his elbows on the table, head in hands; thin strands of black hair protruding through his fingers. Then he suddenly shouted at me:

"Come on out, schnell! Schnell! We'll see what sort of job a schreiber can make of harnessing the cows."

I went to untie the new cow.

"NOT THAT ONE!" he screamed and, turning to his wife, he passed final judgement on me. "Maria," he said gravely. "He is a 'verfluchte trottel.'"

I thought this meant something like a 'bloody donkey'. Anyway, it didn't matter because Frau Tagmeier was doing the job for me far more quickly and skilfully than her husband would have done it. In no time she had disappeared and had come back out of the stable leading two cows, almost as hungry looking as the new one. These she led to the front of the cart and backed up to it, so that they stood with the shaft between them.

"Copy what I do," growled Heinrich, staggering under the weight of two great armfuls of harness.

I watched him carefully and began to fix the halter round the neck of the one called 'Fluki', while she dragged me slowly over to the grapevine where she did her best to let more light into the dining room by sucking the grapes into her dry mouth. I watched fascinated, remembering my own recent hunger and thirst. Heinrich, cursing and swearing, got a pitchfork and prodded her back into position, the effort to keep calm making him shake like a jelly.

"Not like that. Like this," he kept telling me, forcing himself to speak quietly, until his normally flour-white features had turned an unearthly purple. But his temperament, urged on by cheap Burgenland wine, won in the end and, raising his fists towards heaven he shouted as if the Herr Gott was deaf:

Sac-ar-a-ment! Crucifix! Holy Mary and Joseph!" and collapsed like a pricked balloon on the doorstep, sobbing with frustration.

Though I was the cause of it all I wanted to laugh, but luckily, at that moment, the 'Pigs' voice came from the road outside.

"Get stuffed, number three!"

Never, since I had joined the army, had I been happier to obey an order and, nodding goodbye to Grossmutti, I shrugged my shoulders in the direction of Herr and Frau Tagmeier and got out as quickly as I could. Little Judi, who had been watching the comedy fearfully from the folds of Grossmutti's skirt, gave me an angelic smile, while Hans, with his more suspicious nature, stuck out three inches of his velvety white tongue.

The change which had come over all the P.O.W.s, now bloated with food, was remarkable. Fred Bannister, a private in the R.A.S.C. from Bolton, was back in his old form.

"A nice pair of greyhounds your bloke's got," he said. (I guessed he must have glimpsed Herr Tagmeier's cows through the half-open gates.) "I'll lay bets," he called to the others. "Ten to one Stoo's greyhounds beat the rest to t'spud field on Monday."

"Watch it, Fred!" I said. "Or I'll mash the spud you keep between your ears."

This was quite like old times. What wonders a full stomach could achieve... But Fred had come out with the bit of news I hadn't heard.

"What's all this about 'spud fields'?" I asked.

"Potato grubbing; all day, cocker. They've been saving it up for us. My 'Mrs' (referring to the farmer's wife he was working for) told me. At least, she didn't tell me like, because I can't understand the first bleedin' thing she says. We've got a sort of sign language: know what I mean? At first, I thought she wanted me to nurse t'babby while she held potato basket. Bloody 'ell, she keeps babby in 'tater basket, I thought. 'Twas bloody hilarious - like deaf and dumb school. Her old man's fighting the Russians, so I've got to ponce around picking up spuds and choockin' in basket while she hangs onto t' plough, and gets all t' force from t' farts from t' cows. And to think my da used to say: "Never grovel to a woman, lad!""

"That's you," I said. "What about me?"

"Aye. You'll be at it too, lad - unless you work on t' road."

I caught up with Willis, to get a clearer picture. He told me how the Nazis had to use the 'road work' idea to keep the important people in Burgenland happy. After the Anschluss, when German troops had annexed Hitler's historic homeland, Austria, he badly needed as many pigs and potatoes as he could get to help lead his armies to victory. As compensation, in the case of south Burgenland, it had been decided to build a road through the village of Shaffendorf and to pay the farmers for the use of their prisoners. At the same time, the farmers would pay the state for the privilege of having them. The balance was arranged to work slightly in the farmers' favour. Everybody was going to benefit: except, of course, the geese, which were about to lose fifty per cent of the mud they had wallowed in for centuries.

Back at the camp we spent the rest of the day sorting ourselves out - more like human beings. Forgotten photographs of parents wives and girlfriends were produced from nowhere and formed little picture galleries above the bunks; our few belongings, bars of 'Jew' soap, the odd toothbrush, a spare vest or two, or an extra pair of cloth socks, were laid out neatly. Palliasses, packed as tight as pre-war sausages, were bashed into a more comfortable shape to lie on.

At eight o'clock in the evening the guards came in and counted us as we stood by our bunks. The 'Pig' sauntered out, leaving the corporal to ask us a few questions about our farmers. It soon became obvious that I had managed to get landed in the poorest farm in the village: but what did I care — with my belly full of dumplings A quarter of an hour later the door banged shut and the rusty bolt was shot home; the padlock rattled and squeaked and the dungeon effect was complete. Within minutes all the lights except the one controlled from the guardroom next door were out and most of the men were snoring.

Brummie spent a lot of the night sitting on the all-purpose bucket, getting up politely now and then to make way for those who couldn't sleep and were passing the time by annoying him, or occasionally for those who genuinely wanted to relieve themselves. At five-thirty sharp the corporal came in and called:

"Get up, please, gentlemen."

Nobody stirred. Ten minutes later the 'Pig' came in carrying his rifle and shouting at the top of his voice:

"Gehma! Raus, Raus! Los, Los! Schnell, Schnell! GET STUFFED!"

He made his point clear by poking the toe of his jackboot into the middle of Kiwi's back. Kiwi was our only Maori and, like all down-to-earth Maoris, kept a knife under his pillow. But luckily for the 'Pig' he didn't get stuck this time because even Kiwi didn't feel like pigsticking with a temperature of a-hundred-and four.

CHAPTER FIVE

In his own way Kiwi was Satan's John the Baptist, going ahead and paving the way for many abortive attempts by most of us to trick the German doctors, by feigning sickness, self-mutilation anything to get a few days off work. Severely ill with pneumonia, he was rushed off to the hospital at Kurstenfeld, the town where our train had originally stopped. When the corporal arrived back he told us that our dark-skinned friend, with a raving temperature of 105°, had warned one of the doctors who understood English (even Kiwi's), that a member of the nursing staff, a Sister of Mercy of the Order of St. Theresa, with a big white headdress sticking out, severely starched each side of her head, was really a blue and white Junkers 388 and that, if the Germans were hoping for success against our Spitfires, they should have her camouflaged. Also, that under her thick bulging skirt she always kept a machine-gun which, she had told him in confidence, she was going to use on the Fuhrer, if ever he should visit Kurstenfeld.

"Your dark-skinned friend was delirious, of course," he said sympathetically. Then, winking at Willis with a chuckle, he added:

"But I saw the sister myself; and am going to suggest to Reich-Marshall Goering, when I next go to afternoon tea at Karinhall, that he should fit her with wheels and an engine, put her on an airstrip with a bomb in the right place and dispatch her off to London."

He seemed to be less afraid of frizzling in some place in hell reserved for blasphemous Roman Catholics than of the Russian front.

"Never mind", he added seriously. "I am sure your friend

will be better soon and back again with you. They will feed him well in the hospital."

"Like a pet monkey," said the 'Pig' who had just come into the room.

Someone blew a raspberry, but he took no notice. He was learning.

We were going to miss kiwi, lying on his back singing quiet lilting Maori melodies to himself. He was the only one who was genuinely homesick.

At six-thirty in the morning of the first day I arrived at the entrance to the cowshed at Number Three. Heinrich, with a bleary-eyed hangover and not even a "Good morning", handed what looked like a large clothes brush with a strap across the back to put the hand through and told me to clean up Grechi, the queen of his four cows, used for milking except when he had to plough uphill, which would have killed the thin ones quicker than he was starving them. Breakfast was a bowl of ersatz coffee, made from roasted acorns, and two large slices of bread and lard. Heinrich, still glum, left the instructions for the day to his wife, who was wary of saying too much to me in case she got him angry again.

"Follow me," she said and marched me off down the road. Once or twice we passed one of the other P.O.W.s, walking or sitting behind the cows with his farmer, usually an old man or a woman.

"Mein Gott, na!" said one woman to Frau Tagmeier. "That big fellow will take some feeding."

"Look out, he understands," said the other one with her. Then she stared at me with her eyebrows raised and murmured:

"Ooooooooh!"

"He's a schreiber," added Frau Tagmeier, hoping for a consoling opinion.

"Oooooooooooooooooooh!" said the woman. "Schreiber, eh? Oooooooooooh!"

Frau Tagmeier took me down the village to a farm which was being run by a bachelor in his thirties and his old father; and then she was off, with a guarded smile of sympathy for the farmer at being left with such a useless 'Trottel'.

Within ten minutes, I was crawling along in a field behind him like a crippled spider. While he ploughed up and down the rows, I filled basket after basket with potatoes of all sizes, catching up only when he stopped to light his pipe, exclaiming:

"Good! Good! Englishman good! lucky Herr Tagmeier."

After a hard morning's work, we sat down for our lunch which he had brought in a basket: bread, smoked ham, cakes and cider.

"Herr Tagmeier doesn't think I'm good," I said, gradually remembering forgotten German. "He thinks I'm a Trottel".

Whatever the word meant, it made him laugh heartily.

"All legs, big ears and no brains," he chuckled. "Cheeky bugger!" I looked at him, sitting there, his check cap pulled down forwards on his head to make room for the mop of black hair at the back, his thick arms half covered by white rolled up shirt sleeves, his frayed collar and his tatty waistcoat above the inevitable blue apron. Here's some good cannon-fodder going to waste', I thought; but I said:

"You're lucky - not being in the army."

"Ah," he said. "My father and mother ran the farm and I used to help them. But I was ambitious; I wouldn't stay, but went to Vienna, where I got a job as a builder's apprentice. Then I met a girl and we fell in love. She was beautiful, like a Madonna." His eyes filled with tears. "But she was a Jewess and we were not allowed to marry. Her mother had died when she was very young: her father was a jeweller. One day his shop was ransacked and burnt down by the storm troopers, but he had some money hidden and the two of them got away to England, where they were welcomed by your wonderful people. She wrote to me twice, but then the war broke out and her letters stopped. So, perhaps she is now married to an Englishman who has gone to fight against Austria. The world is a stupid place, isn't it? My father was too old to work so I had to come back when my mother died last year. My father said I must find a wife but I didn't like the silly village girls, who are always giggling and have no poise or manners, so I went to church and prayed to the Herr Gott. And he said, "You are married to the land, my son. If you marry a woman as well you will be a bigamist." He looked at me and winked. "So I didn't marry." He clasped his hands together and, looking up at the cloudless sky, called out.

"The Herr Gott is good. If I had married I would be fighting the Ruski, probably without enough to eat, and my wife would be ploughing all the potatoes."

He took a big, solid gold watch on a chain from his waistcoat pocket and looked at the time.

"It is a beautiful memory. Her father gave me this," he said. Then he quickly came down to earth.

Now we must get back to work."

"Just a minute," I said. "Why am I helping you? Who will help Herr Tagmeier?"

He looked at me in astonishment.

"Herr Tagmeier — who will help Herr Tagmeier?" He was holding his sides, laughing. "Listen, my young friend, Herr Tagmeier's wife is as strong as all his four cows put together, so she can help him. Anyway, he will get less sacks of potatoes out of his whole field than we've had out of a couple of rows, because he is so mean with his cow-food."

"Why does he have to be so mean?" I asked, as he started to light his pipe ready for the afternoon's work.

"He's mean with his cows because he can't grow enough turnips to feed them." Now, he was doubled up laughing. "In this village my friend", he spluttered, "the more a cow eats, the more it shits and because of all the manure he spreads around the richer the farmer is. The Burgomeister's cows shit gold blocks, I think. If Heinrich had spent more time at school learning arithmetic instead of flicking bogies at his classmates, he'd have found that out in time. Heinrich thinks he knows better than everyone but, Heilige Maria und Josef, he's the biggest idiot in the village. Come, we must get back to work, or I shall be a bigger one."

By six in the evening I was back at Number. Three eating another hearty meal, mostly potatoes. Heinrich watched me, no doubt wondering how many sacks I would get through before I tipped the balance of his economy in his favour.

All night I dreamt I was grubbing for potatoes, waking up to find my palliass on top of me and the 'Flea Olympics' in full swing on my stomach.

I soon found that Heinrich had taken me on mainly to make money, and that most of the time I would be working on the road. He enjoyed being as lazy as his hard-working wife made him. For a few days, when I arrived at six-thirty, I found him waiting for me in the stable but soon I got used to the routine and was acting as his alarm clock. Before reaching the farm gates I could hear him snoring in the family four-poster, towering up like a mausoleum in the corner of the room where we ate. Under his pillow were the keys to the cowshed. Frau Tagmeier always pretended to be asleep, keeping her head out of sight under the bedclothes, and the number of times I had to shake Heinrich to wake him varied according to how much wine he had drunk the night before. After sometimes as much as a minute of continual thumping he would wake up with a loud grunt and, coughing and spluttering, drag himself out of bed, his Samuel Pepys night cap pulled down over his face. Falling down once or twice, he would then stagger, in his long white nightshirt, across the room to light the oil lamp. (He would not trust me to do this as, being a 'schreiber', I would most likely burn the place down.) Then, he would put on his boots, without lacing them, and lead the way, jangling his keys like a jailor, to the shed where my four cows would be waiting for their morning beauty treatment and breakfast. I would next see him at the table, a yard from where, half an hour before, he had been snoring; dressed this time but still not shaved.

Though the road gang routine was monotonous I preferred it to doing things I had never done before, with Heinrich always watching critically and muttering "Schreiber" disgustedly and with his wife echoing everything he said like a terrified lackey. Grossmutti, being the cook that she was, had remained my friend, always making sure that I got enough to eat, though her bread and cakes, with Heinrich's skimpiness behind them, were always darker than everyone else's. Sometimes when Heinrich was not about, I would play with the children who had grown quite used to me and glad they had found somebody they could be cheeky to without getting their father's hand across their ears.

On the road, we soon found we could laze about in a way

that was impossible on the farms, where the hard-working farmers were setting far too good an example for anyone with a conscience. Between the British and the Australians there was a constant battle, with the British spending more time trying to slow down the naturally hard-working Aussies than they spent doing their own work. At the back of most minds there was still that little voice reminding: 'Every stroke of work you do is a stroke to help the enemy.' Apart from this, we knew that every hour of our work was helping to connect an innocent little village with the harsh world outside. As soon as he had got me conveniently onto regular work Heinrich was in a better mood, constantly tucking away the Reichmarks I was making for him.

The idea of escape from here had so far not entered the men's minds. At night we were locked up: in the daytime any one of us would have been recognised for miles around. The borders of pro-Nazi Hungary, twenty miles away, were mined and closely guarded by police with tracker dogs. Living almost like civilians we had not, as yet, caught the 'Big Camp' disease of "Let's get out of here, or bust". On the rare occasions when Heinrich could keep the crinkle of bank notes out of his head and would keep me on the farm, it was usually a day to be remembered. One morning in mid-September, at breakfast, he stopped his usual habit of sucking scalding coffee out of a soup bowl long enough to say, without looking up:

"You! Today you will stay on the farm and help us."

Tapping a tattoo on the table with his long finger nails, his coffee finished, he glanced nervously at his intricately carved pocket watch (worth at least two of his cows) and, getting up, walked across the yard towards the pig-sty where Blumchen, the one and only pig, was grunting good morning to the world. When half way across, he stopped uncertainly and came back, again looking at his watch. At seven o'clock to the second he went to the cupboard and pulled out an air rifle. As if he had given a signal, at the same moment the farm gate squeaked and growled as five village women arrived wearing blue aprons and looking ready for work. I had been watching Frau Tagmeier and Grossmutti, who had both been on the move for sometime, like two feathers blown about in a breeze, occasionally running into each other. The logs were glowing white hot inside the range under several cauldrons of water, with sinister billowing clouds of steam rising from the biggest and disappearing into the shadows of the ceiling. Straightaway the new arrivals, who had been joined by four men, got to work carrying a five foot long trough out into the yard and placing it in the centre, surrounded by spoons, knives and scrubbing brushes. Completely at a loss, I tried to stop Frau Tagmeier as she sailed past with an armful of straw, feet hardly touching the ground. Joan of Arc reviewing her troops could not have looked more inspired and triumphant than she did, as she gave orders to her five woman helpers. After she had dumped the straw near the trough I caught her on the rebound.

"What's happening — please?" I asked as she flew past. "What am I supposed to be doing?"

With a nervous giggle she called back over her shoulder. "We're going to stick Blumchen. Heinrich has his own special methods." At that moment there was no mistaking the pride she had in her husband. "He will tell you what to do."

What was this, then? Heinrich was actually going to trust me with a job on such an important occasion. I felt as nervous as he looked, and more and more sorry for the pig. Surely he wasn't going to shoot it — but, if not, why the air rifle? With all these vultures around, what sort of a chance did a thing of her size stand? A sudden shame came over me: I had come away from England to kill armed Germans; not defenceless, underfed pigs — especially pigs I had made friends with. Heinrich handed me a juicy-looking carrot, as if paying me in advance for my services.

"You! Put that in your pocket and follow me. Keep your head down: we don't want her seeing you."

As we advanced on the pigsty I felt I was in Greece again, creeping through the field of scrub behind Sergeant Crabbe. But the Germans had stood more chance of living than this pig. All the onlookers seemed to be holding their breath as we neared the door. Heinrich, his hand stretched out behind him towards me, waving me down, raised his head very slowly so that he could see what Blumchen was doing. As he was not watching me, I looked too. On the dirty thin straw stood the pig, head down and facing the door as she nosed about for any stray bits she could find to eat. Luckily I had lowered my head again, when Heinrich, turning to me and, raising his gun slowly to his shoulder, pointed it at the door. With his other hand he pointed at his forehead, leaning back and whispering in my ear:

"Everything is going well. She is in the right position. I shall hit her between the eyes and stun her. You will see. You will be able to go home after the war and tell them what a clever man you worked for."

"Won't you slit her throat?" I asked, amazed.

For the first time Heinrich admitted his shortcoming.

"I can't do that," he whispered. "The Herr Janush will stick her with a knife before she can come round. He never misses."

He directed a streak of tobacco juice at the manure heap, muttering:

"That's why the bastard charges twenty marks."

Now my turn came to join in the merciless game. Speaking so softly I could hardly hear him, he looked up again to make sure the pig was still in the right position.

"When I give the signal, I want you to kick the door open, and keep your foot out of the way, because I shall fire immediately." Though I felt sure there were other better methods, Heinrich's word was law:

"Blumchen doesn't know it," he said, "but this morning I fixed the latch open. She is far too stupid to try to get out."

So I waited for the signal. His rifle was in position pointing exactly where Blumchen's head was supposed to be. He took careful aim:

"NOW!"

My foot kicked the door, which swung inwards with a crash.

"Sac-a-ra-ment! The little bastard." Heinrich screamed. Somehow, in the short time that had elapsed, the pig had turned completely round. Heinrich had only just managed to stop himself shooting the wrong end.

"You nearly made a pig's arse of that!" shouted Herr Janush, and everyone laughed.

Heinrich turned to me, snarling like an angry dog.

"You — give me the carrot, schnell!"

I handed it to him. Looking at us suspiciously, the frightened Blumchen had almost recovered from the shock. The villagers, still sniggering, watched from the background sceptically. Frau Tagmeier looked on, deflated. Heinrich called to the pig, his voice full of rasping sweetness:

"Here, a special breakfast, mein Schertzel (my pretty one)." And he threw the carrot into the sty so that the pig had to put her head down to reach the unexpected treat.

Quickly, his confidence back, Heinrich whispered to me:

"Now, we've got her. Watch this."

Again be was aiming: but by this time my metal was up. It was all too cruel and sadistic...I looked across at all the expectant faces...Too unfair and one-sided. As Heinrich's fingers squeezed the trigger once more, I coughed. Blumchen moved her head a fraction to one side and dead-eyed Heinrich missed. I made room for the terrified pig, as she charged through the open door, knocking Heinrich flat on his back and tearing up the yard into the orchard beyond the farm. In a second, she disappeared amongst the apple trees.

"'Fix (short for Crucifix)!" shouted Heinrich, jumping up and dashing after her, followed by two of the farmers, stumbling over each other with laughter. Barging into the apple trees and bumping off onto the farmers, darting everywhere like a rocket let off along the ground by mistake, Heinriech was yelling: 'Crucifix! Herr Gott! Heilige (Holy) Maria und Josef!"... And a whole lot more profanities I had never heard —enough to undermine the gates of heaven.

Up in the orchard the farmers followed the grunts amongst the thick trees, leaving their hats stuck on branches and tearing their aprons. But Blumchen was fighting a losing battle. Nothing could save her now and, when she was running past Herr Miklos, he fell on top of her, hanging onto her ears, bouncing up and down like a cowboy at a rodeo until she threw him off and they both lay panting on the grass, their noses only two inches apart. Finally overpowered she was dragged to the execution yard. Heinrich snarled at me, showing his eight glistening gold teeth (one bit of wealth he couldn't spend on wine) and shouting at me to help. As the game was up for Blumchen the kindest thing now was to get it over quickly and, putting a knee on her back leg, as she lay on the dusty ground panting pathetically, I held her down with three farmers, as Herr Janush, sharpening his long knife (every stroke an extra few pfennigs in his purse,) manoeuvred himself into position in the middle of the blaspheming, writhing mass. Frau Tagmeier waiting to scrape off the hairs with a kitchen spoon, was poised with her troop of women over the trough full of scalding water, watching indifferently as the knife slid cleanly into her pet pig's neck on its sure way to the heart on the opposite side.

Blumchen's squeals subsided into a gurgle and it was all over. While we all bounced rhythmically up and down on top of her, the blood was caught in a bowl by another nerveless woman, who finally rushed it off to Grossmutti waiting at the cooking stove. Straightaway, she poured it into a pan, stirring it well over the heat and, within two minutes, was out filling up our bowls, one for each executioner. While Blumchen was being carved into little bits I had to pretend I was enjoying my share of the 'fun'.

Within half an hour the whole lot of us were sitting at a long trestle table in the September sunshine, sharing pork and Sauerkraut with the flies from the manure heap. Heinrich, who had made sure he got well over his share of the wine, had his arm round the waist and hand cupped greasily over the breast of one of the women and was suggesting as many erotic variations as he could think of before going unconscious. His wife, trying to pull her teeth out with a pork bone, took no notice. Over our heads, drying on the clothes line, together with a few other personal parts, hung Blumchen's vagina, a tip for her chief executioner, who would be out in the fields that afternoon with it hanging from his belt, stuffed full of tobacco. One and a half hours after they had arrived the villagers had all gone, Heinrich was snoring in the hayloft and Frau Tagmeier and I, on good terms until the effects of the wine would wear off, were clearing up the yard. Before passing out, Heinrich had shot a streak of saliva in my direction, hitting the farm cat in the eye.

Towards the end of September I noticed that the number of geese seemed to be getting less and discovered that, like the Jews, they were being systematically exterminated; but not before they had been turned into obese, waddling lumps by the farmers, who were putting them through an age-old form of torture. One morning I arrived to find Grossmutti sitting in the yard, pipe in mouth and an overweight goose held firmly between her knees while she ladled spoonfuls of un-ground maize into its mouth like one of Bismark's gunners ramming powder into a cannon. As the goose swallowed, she would form her thumb and first finger into a tight ring round its neck and force the lump in its gizzard down into its stomach.

"Isn't that a bit cruel?" I said.

Her mouth opened and the pipe, usually held firmly wedged between her gums, fell out.

"Cruel?" she said, amazed. "How do you think we can sell thin geese? If Heinrich was going to sell his cows he would fatten them up, I can tell you, even if he had to beat them into eating. But he wouldn't have to, of course: they're so hungry they'll eat him one of these days, in spite of all his gristle." She began to laugh, giving the goose a chance to get its breath and try to get away: but there was no chance of that. She shrugged:

"Ach! Anyway, it can't be helped."

I had heard the expression so many times that I was beginning to fall under the spell of this simple Austrian peasent philosophy. Later in the afternoon I heard it again, when Herr Feiler, an old Hungarian farmer who had to do everything himself because his farm was too small to warrant a P.O.W., was coming towards us, as we worked on the road. Sitting on top of a wagonload of turnips, he was fast asleep. His two cows were finding their own way home. Fred Douglas, looking for a 'bit of a laugh', got as close as he could and shouted in the old man's ear, "Servus, Herr Feiler", giving him such a fright that he slid off his cart onto the road, where he sat just in the right position for a nine inch turnip to land on his head with a nasty crack. Willis turned on Fred:

"You rotten bastard. That's taking it a bit far, isn't it?"

Fred grinned stupidly, while some of us went to lift the old man up to his wobbly feet and help him back onto the wagon: but there was really no need. Pushing us away, though he was shaken, he staggered up onto his feet.

"Shouldn't have been asleep," he said, taking it all in good part.

"Your head's bleeding a bit: get to the doctor," said Willis.

"Jesus,na!" said the farmer. "I've got far too much to do. I'll get better. Never mind. It can't be helped."

Heinrich was the next one to say it, in the evening, as I sat drinking coffee and eating Grossmutti's cakes.

"Do you know," he said, "your troops are being driven back in North Africa? Field Marshall Rommel is too good for them. You seem to be losing the war." Though he was sneering, he seemed worried.

"You don't believe everything Doktor Goebbels bleats over the wireless, do you?" I said, far less confident than I sounded. Heinrich looked doubtful.

"If you lose," he said, "we farmers will have even less than we've got now. Hitler will have no mercy." He looked resigned. "Ah well," he said, "It can't be helped."

And so I was beginning to wonder: did anything really matter? After all, however nasty it was, could it really be helped?

There was a subtle change taking place in the attitude of the guards. The corporal, for instance, was not really joking as he said one evening when the 'Pig' was out and he was handing out our Red Cross food:

"If only I could write to Churchill, gentlemen, I would suggest that the only way for your countries to start a civil war in Germany would be to send every available bomber over, loaded with bars of Cadbury's Dairy Milk chocolate and packets of State Express 555, instead of bombs." The present of six bars of chocolate which we had seen him hide under his mattress must have done a lot towards making him see the truth at last.

As the winter drew nearer, most of us were being released from our farms to work on the road that was now nearing the top of the hill above the village. The war seemed a thousand miles away and discipline was lax. Working on the road was gradually driving us to a state of indescribable boredom. After breaking up the rocks we had quarried we had to lean the big ones against each other like dominoes and fill in the gaps with the smaller ones, finally hammering the whole lot into fragments. Standing with two pound hammers attached to three foot handles we tried to cut down the monotony by sharing our intimate secrets until, by the end of November, couples working together got to know each other like identical twins. Under these conditions everyone's characteristics came out and it was soon easy to place each nationality into a category:

English	75	per cent petty old women
Scottish	75	per cent shrewd old women
Welsh	90	per cent unpredictable old women
Irish	99	per cent crafty old women
Australians	90	per cent tough old women
New Zealanders	90	per cent good chaps
Kiwi	A very good chap if you kept at the handle end of his knife	

The monotony of working on the road was relieved one day by the arrival of some gypsies from a gypsy village six kilometres away. Gypsies had been placed on the Fuhrer's list of unwanted people, just below the Jews, cripples and halfwits. The Jews were being exterminated (though we didn't know this for certain at the time), the cripples were getting no medical assistance and the halfwits were being castrated. What better time than now, with Germany winning the war, to get everything cleaned up nicely, Goebbels preached.

With all this going on, the gypsies could consider themselves lucky as long as they could work. With child-like innocence they brought their accordions, fiddles and mouth organs with them, making fires in the woods at the side of the road where, when the guards let us, we could warm ourselves and listen to their music, which even got the frozen birds singing in the trees and on one occasion forced a noise out of the 'Pig' which was supposed to be a Tyrolean Volk song. The birds stopped twittering and started tittering. When the 'Pig' had finished, his face cracked into a smile and Taffy Llewellyn shouted:

"Don't phone us: we'll phone you, boyo!"

Pleased at the jovial tone of Taffy's remark, the 'Pig' turned to Willis for a translation. Willis, as usual, gave the wrong one. Whatever it was, the 'Pig' grinned from ear to ear and, thanking Taffy for the compliment, gave us another quarter of an hour by the fire.

Most of our Red Cross parcels were arriving at last: the rest had been stolen, en route, by the French. Sitting in the guard room, with food parcels and hundreds of cigarettes only a yard or two away, the 'Pig' was becoming quite a nice chap, and even decided to wake us up without the aid of his rifle butt. The British War Office was concentrating upon the smartness of our appearance, using us as a propaganda weapon. Debunking the bland pessimism of lord Haw-Haw, they were dispatching brand new battle-dresses, shirts and underwear, through the Red Cross. So, at last, I was no longer a Serbian cavalry officer, with an annoying red stripe down each leg and an ill-fitting French forage cap, but an R.A.C. trooper again. We had regained our self-respect. On the other hand, the guards were no shop window for the Wehrmacht, and were constantly asking the farmers' wives to sew patches on the seats of their pants, worn out by their wearers' habit of sitting playing cards, and to darn their wood-pulp socks. The farmers too, naturally enough, were happy to get what they could out of us, wolfing everything we gave them down with fresh praise for the allies and fresh convictions that we would win. To them, Churchill was a Father Christmas tending to their needs. "How could we not win, with all that tea, anyway," they would say, getting drunk by continually topping up their cups of Red Cross tea with schnapps.

"The only packet of tea in the Reich is in the pantry at Berchtesgarten," said Heinrich in one of his rare jovial moods "But the tea is always cold by the time it gets to the Fuhrer past all the poison tasters."

The farmers would stuff the tobacco we brought them into their long hooked pipes, which constantly hung from their necks like saxophones. Heinrich threw away the sardines I gave him. "Phuey!" he said, holding his bony nose. They stink." But he kept the oil and used it to preserve his boots.

"My wife doesn't realise how economical I am," he said. "She thinks I'm mean." As I edged away from the smell, he leant even nearer. "D'you know," he confided. "Sometimes, in bed, she won't even let me get near her." A wicked grin came over his face as he nudged me so hard that I nearly fell off my chair. "But I get what I want in the end," he leered. "Cruci! (short for Crucifix). But Heinrich knows his way around when it comes to women. Ja! Ja!"

The day came when winter, which had been licking its frozen lips round the corner, was unleashed and flung it'self at us. Down came the snow and on went the long skis, chained under the wagon wheels. The farmers slid to and from the fields in a rush to get everything done before the ground froze as hard as concrete.

Though life was dull, we still got a few laughs. One day, at the point where we were working on the road, Herr Miklos, passing Herr Szeged, on the way to the turnip field, flicked an icicle off the end of his nose, and lifted up one of his ear flaps, as the other greeted him.

"Servus, Herr Miklos. Where are you going?"

"Servus Herr Szeged . I'm going to dig up turnips."

Looking at the other's cartload of turnips, Herr Miklos said:

"Where have you been, Herr Szeged?"

"I've been digging up my turnips, Herr Miklos."

On the way back Herr Miklos passed Herr Szeged, unloading turnips twenty yards away from us.

"Servus, Herr Szeged," he shouted over the wall. "What are you doing?"

"I'm unloading my turnips. What are you going to do, Herr Miklos?"..." and so on...... and so on......

They were lovable, harmless people.

Nothing unusual happened to take the edge off a dull winter until, quite suddenly, Heinrich tried to impale me on the end of a hayfork, bringing my days at Number Three to a dramatic end. He had been all smiles that morning, slapping the bottom of one of the village women, squeezing the breasts of another and shouting to the Burgomeister's daughter:

"Come here, and I'll give you a present you'll never forget."

At supper he had decided to terminate the music he produced drinking his soup with something more melodious on his mouth organ. Between a few bars from 'The Merry Widow' and a passage from Mozart's 'Magic Flute', he had sent me out to get down a bundle of hay from the loft. But, saving myself the trouble of using a ladder, I had managed to bring down twenty, some on top of me and the rest headed through the hole onto the manure heap. Throttled in the middle of a bar, the mouth organ recital stopped, and Heinrich rushed out cursing, followed by his terrified wife. Seeing the mess, Heinrich turned on her and began to thump her mercilessly.

"Crucifix (Bash!) You damned idiot woman (Biff!) Herr Gott (Wallop!)! Look what the bloody Trottel has done. I told you (Whack!) not to (Slam!) bring back a damned SCHREIBER."

When he began to chase her round the yard, like a dog after a cat, I jumped down and caught hold of him, to let her get away. After all, though there had been times when I had thought a bit of rough treatment would do her no harm, it was my fault that the happy music recital had come to such a nasty end.

Grossmutti, sitting smoking in a corner was so astonished that her mouth opened and her pipe fell to the floor, losing another valuable half inch. Heinrich, a venomous little mass of hatred and fury, wrenched himself free and, grabbing a hay fork, sticking like the main mast of a windjammer from the middle of the bails of hay on the manure heap, gave a half-throttled squeal and made for me, with the two murderous points in a direct line with my stomach. Luckily my reflexes were quick and before my brain had managed to take in the situation, my body was out in the road and through the gate of the farm next door, leaving Heinrich swearing that, if the guards didn't shoot me, he would shoot them.

From then onwards, apart from one or two encounters in the village or on the way to the fields when, as far as he was concerned, I could have been some other farmer's turnip, I saw little of him.

CHAPTER SIX

My days at Number Three over, I felt sorry that my exit had been so unexpectedly fast that I hadn't been able to say goodbye to Grossmutti and the children. I had nothing really against Frau Tagmeier and hoped that in future she would get less rough treatment from her paranoid husband. After a short session with Hauptnann Bauer, a pleasant military gentleman in charge of the P.O.W.s in the district, I was transferred to another farm. Being an understanding fellow, the Hauptmann passed the whole thing off with a shrug and an admission that they had been doubtful whether Heinrich, with his reputation for bouts of fury, should have a P.O.W. anyway.

My new boss, Johann, was so thin that at any minute he could have disappeared down a rabbit hole without anybody noticing. In total contrast, his mother was enormously fat, with his father a close runner-up. In fact, you only had to look at his wife to see that Johann liked fat things. He owned the fattest cows in the village, ten fat geese, three fat pigs and even a fat owl with a three-and-a-half foot wing span, kept the whole time out of doors, chained to a perch and staring into the sunlight. Its eyes, which were wide open, always seemed to be fixed on me and full of fear or murder — I couldn't decide which, so I kept my distance. At ten o'clock each night she would close her eyes and with a sigh of relief go off to sleep as if she was glad another blinding day was over.

The grandmother, Frau Wagner, used her huge hands to good effect, kneading the dough that made the best bread in the village. Out working in the fields, we spread the lard they called 'schmaltz' on the bread, swilling the result down with homemade cider. Theories about cholesterol were dashed to pieces here, where everybody ate too much fat and nobody ever had a coronary. When I made mistakes, Johann only swore half as much as Heinrich, directing his wrath at the nearest animal, but really intending it for me.

Being a generous man, well organised and better off than most of the farmers, Johann refused to let me work on the road, even when there was nothing to do on the farm.

"Go and sit with Frieda (the owl)," he would say. "She will be happy with your company." And, though I still felt she would be happier to dig her long claws into my neck, I would spend many a morning and afternoon sitting in the yard - at a reasonable distance.

There was a matey atmosphere about Number Thirty-five. Johann, his wife Anna, his mother and I would go out together into the fields or woods, taking plenty of food and cider. Then Johann would go off, smiling and waving, his bushy red moustache dripping with leftovers from the last meal and drooping over his mouth like a weeping willow sprayed with insecticide.

His mother, as she raked up the leaves in the woods, would spend a lot of the time laughing and shaking like a big jelly, her four gold teeth glistening in the sunlight. A lucky person, blessed with no inhibitions, she believed in cutting down time whenever possible. When the urge came to relieve herself, she would never go behind a tree or hedge but would turn her rake upside down, lean on it and manoeuvre herself into a convenient position: then, with legs slightly apart like Napoleon, would smile at me, pretending she didn't know about the ever-widening pool at her feet and holding me in conversation, while her daughter just stood and laughed, nudging me and whispering:

"Don't worry. It's a nice day: she'll dry out."

At Number Thirty-Five the months went by pleasantly but boredom was becoming a disease with apparently no cure. Anna Wagner, to give her her due, tried to lessen it by showing what a powerful healthy woman she was for her thirty-six years. When we were alone in the fields one day, raking up the straw, she stared hard at me with the fixed wooden smile I had grown used to. Though the weather had been fine, her mother-in-law had at last caught a chill from getting too wet (with no rain about) and her father was, as usual, sitting in the yard, struggling to get through an ounce of my Red Cross tobacco; the smoke from his weather-beaten pipe rising in a billowing cloud and causing Frieda to sneeze and shut her eyes, though it was still daylight.

"You're very strong," said Frau Wagner, still smiling, as I lifted a branch that had fallen across the corner of the field. "Poor Johann could not have lifted that."

There was nothing special about the remark, but the way she had said it made me look up. Smiling her fixed wooden smile she was slowly undoing her speckled blue and white apron and taking it off; allowing everything which had been pulled in tight to find its own rolling level. Before I had really got the hang of what was happening, she had taken me by the arm and was guiding me over to a clearing under the willows. Here, she spread her apron out carefully and, gently but firmly, pulled me down beside her. Then, with a series of sighs and grunts she hoisted me up and rolled me about like a sailor in a rough sea as she tried to get her back off two fir cones and a patch of prickly stubble. But, when she noticed she was not getting the response she wanted, being a good sport she whispered:

"This is a good place. Let's eat our lunch. Johann has gone to help Herr Miklos. He won't be back, and there's plenty of time."

As, for the past six months, the only thing as close to me as she was, with anything like her shape, had been a stuffed knodel, I soon began to succumb to the inviting warmth of something more human, especially when she relieved the pressure round the seams of her blouse by unbuttoning the front and allowing everything to burst out with an explosion of tearing cotton. But, being both greedy and versatile, she didn't see why she shouldn't make the most of two pastimes at once and, lifting her fifteen-and-a-half stone into a better position to get the food, rolled back with a lump of bierwurst between her teeth and another in her hand for me, holding me where I was in a grip of iron and insisting that I should eat mine too. Taking no notice of my munching jaws and with her last mouthful still on its way down, she clasped me to her and, with a long greasy kiss, finally took the edge off my ardour, and not even the memory of months of abstinence could bring it back. From that day onwards she was rather bad tempered, not even bothering any more to comb her hair before pinning it all on top of her head in a hurried black bun. But she kept the wooden smile through thick and thin, and nobody suspected.

As one day dragged itself along, trying to catch up with the next, we seemed to be about to settle down to another monotonous winter when, just over a year after we had arrived in Shaffendorf, the 'Pig' woke us up one morning shouting:

"Raus! Raus! Gehma! Gehma! Get stuffed! We are leaving here today, gentlemen." (He had started to call us 'gentlemen' after his third packet of Red Cross cigarettes). "The camp is being closed down."

If this was the way Nazi protocol worked, I was sorrier than ever for the thousands of anti-Nazis in Austria who could do nothing about it but wait, hoping for an allied victory.

We were allowed to say goodbye to our farmers, as surprised as we were, shrugging their shoulders and muttering, "Oh well, it can't be helped." Anna Wagner disappeared from the breakfast table, coming back with her hair done up in a tidy 'bun' for a change, a smile of forgiveness on her face and genuine tears in her eyes. The Red Cross tobacco smoke in the old man's eyes was making him cry too. Frieda, a cloud of smoke enveloping her at the same time, shut her eyes in daylight for once. Grandmother Wagner gave me a foot of Hungarian salami, showing all four glistening gold teeth at once; and Johann, kissing me on both cheeks, cried so much that the tears running through the dust on his face left it looking like the Nile delta.

As we waved a sad goodbye to the villagers and marched past the geese, which had grown so used to us that they had given up waddling away with their heads in the air, the spell of security, cast over us by the friendly peasants, began to recede. At the end of the mud track of high white-washed walls and solid oak gates we reached our special road, which had been just about to bring civilisation to the village. The shuffle of our boots as they reached the smooth tarred surface became a rhythm of "left, right, left ..." The vague tingling at the back of the neck at the sight of a German rifle had come back. We knew again that there was a war on, and we knew that the guards were quite capable of playing cards with us or shooting us, depending on the orders from Berlin. We could imagine the 'Pig', with his new tact produced by the Red Cross, calling:

"O.K., gentlemen, please 'get stuffed'... And line up against that wall. Excuse me, but a German soldier must always obey his orders. Heil Hitler... BANG! BANG!"

As we marched back along the road towards Kurstenfeld we managed to reverse the picture of a year before. Now, we were the smart ones, with two bedraggled-looking guards leading us. Some of the workers in the fields, even those from other villages, must have heard the news already, and were waving goodbye.

I could sense a new atmosphere as we approached the town fifteen kilometres away; cold and unsettling. In the main street were loudspeakers, posted at intervals, blaring out propaganda. As we passed the town hall we saw a company of soldiers marching towards us. When they saw who we were they struck up a marching song, ending each verse with a thunderous 'Sieg Heil' and clipping every line short, as if each one had suddenly tripped over a bump in the road. As an open staff car, carrying three smart-looking officers, glided past, their hands went up in an optimistically victorious Nazi salute. Now, prouder of our appearance, we felt the change in the way the people stared: the doubt in their minds. Were these different-looking prisoners really the beaten enemy? What sort of corrupt liar was this Doktor Goebbels? And, to add to our mood, a new sensation had come over us; the knowledge that here, by simply looking smart, we could at last get back into the war for the allies, and even help to win it.

Everything so far had seemed like a nightmare compared with life in Shaffendorf until, rounding a corner into a side road, Willis and the corporal at the front nearly collided with two cows pulling a load of manure. The smell of the manure brought me back to my senses; nothing, not even the whole nasty atmosphere of the 'Thousand Year Reich' that we had landed in, could beat that friendly diversion. The cows, not bothered by politics, the war or P.O.W.s, would have plodded on right through us if the old farmer walking beside them hadn't pulled them up with a "Yer-Harrr," to let us pass, greeting us with a genuine "Servus". Away from the cold indifference of the town we had, after all, landed back among friends.

Like new boys at school, we joined the fifteen men who had remained behind in Kurstenfeld a year before, in a camp very similar to the one we had just left: an old converted farm building separated from its neighbours, padlocked and barred. Saying goodbye to the corporal and the 'Pig' was, in its way, sad, as we had grown used to them like back sufferers do to a persistent lumbago. Between us and the 'Pig' had grown up a sort of love-hate relationship. He had learnt a lot, particularly that he couldn't easily browbeat us and at the back of his throat was always the pleasant taste of Player's tobacco: but, with his hand never far away from his rifle, he gave the impression that he still felt he was on the winning side. Within minutes of our arrival they had shaken hands all round and had gone off to join the active ranks of the Wehrmacht or, if their luck held out, to guard more prisoners and fill their stomachs with Cadbury's Dairy Milk chocolate.

On the first night it was impossible to get to sleep early with an Englishman and an Australian arguing until well after midnight. When I finally took my fingers out of my ears it came over loud, clear and pointless.

"Look, mate. We've got a horse on my farm, O.K.? It does everything: ploughing, manure spreading, the lot. So just keep yer mouth shut about yer bleedin' cows. They're about as much good as..."

"Cripes! Wait on. You can't milk a horse, Bruce. My cows can do anything your horse can do, and provide milk as well. What does your sodding horse contribute towards the strudel you eat and the coffee you drink? Ever heard of milking a horse?"

"Just a minute. Just a minute. What about the manure then? That's got you, hasn't it, Aussie, eh?"

"Come off it, Pommie. If we're going into details ... O.K. Yer cowshit ain't got the quality of yer horseshit but with two cows you've certainly got quantity even if you ain't got quality."

At this point there was a muffled shout from under one of

the blankets.

"Hey! When are you half-wits going to stop jabbering bullshit. Dry up, can't you, and let someone get some sleep."

Their voices faded away to nothing as I sank into a deep sleep, even more nerve-wracking. I was riding through billowing clouds of tobacco smoke in a chariot drawn by a huge four-legged owl, with the goddess Diana. We were both in the nude and I felt a bit cold.

"Keep your eyes on the road," she screamed as I stared at her.

"You're not a goddess," I shouted, "And anyway there's no road."

"Oh yes, I am. Remember that picture in your Latin book at school. Have another look."

As I happened to have the book with me I did, and there she was, just as I remembered her, scribbled all over; with a moustache, a hairy stomach and three extra nipples on each breast. I was thinking how beautiful she looked when she suddenly turned into Anna Wagner and, with a crash, the chariot springs broke. The crash, of course, had been the noise of the guard unbolting the doors. It was followed by the inevitable:

"Raus! Raus! Gehma! Gehma! Schnell! Schnell!"

What about the "Get stuffed"? I was gripped by nostalgia.

I had woken up confused, shivering, my blanket on the floor: now, with a shock, I realised where I was. Washed and shaved, we were taken to our new working places by the three guards. Wally, an Australian motor-cycle salesman, was left at the local vegetable gardens, Brummie at the cycle repair shop, Fred Bannister at a sawmill which had been confiscated from a Jew, who had subsequently disappeared, and the others on farms. At eight o'clock in the morning, with the sun already well up in a cloudless sky and promising to give Kurstenfed another hot early autumn day, I was marched through the gates of the biggest farm in the town; all part of Herr Schneider's gasthaus (hotel). Herr Schneider, a pale, greying, worried-looking plump man in his fifties, was waiting, nervously fingering a heavy gold watch chain supported on top of his pot belly, the top of his trousers and the bottom of his waistcoat looking as if they had last met many years before. As if there was a spring in his arm he greeted the guard with a smart salute which was returned and they both shouted "Heil Hitler" together. This ritual over, it was time for the handshakes but, as Herr Schneider had stretched out his hand, his wife had come in through the door behind him and the guard's hand shot up in another Nazi salute. Still not seeing his wife and obviously supposing that the guard had been caught up in a patriotic fervour Herr Schneider immediately answered with yet another salute but, by this time the guard's hand was outstretched to shake Herr Schneider's, which had just been there. Once more Herr Schneider tried to shake hands, but by this time the guard's was up in the air again. After they had sorted themselves out, Herr Schneider gave me a disinterested glance, said "Guten Tag (Good day)" to me and shot an abrupt order at the guard. A few more salutes and 'Heil Hitlers' and the guard led me away, through a high-walled, cobbled courtyard, festooned on all sides with healthy looking climbing grape vines, to the stables, where he introduced me to Jan, the farm manager.

Herr Schneider seemed to have left the handling of his newly acquired Englander to this six-foot-four-inch Polish farmer, who greeted me with a hearty handshake, a torrent of pigeon-German and a slap on the back. Squarely on top of his long narrow head he wore a dark blue beret, pulled forward over his big brown friendly eyes, set close on a face covered with an eighth of an inch of stubble which seemed to grow visibly as you looked at it. After the guard had gone, within minutes a grief-stricken Jan had told me that he had been taken by the Nazis from his farm somewhere near Cracow, leaving his two old parents and his sister to manage on their own and, with the tears still streaming down his face, had shown me how to get rid of the ten eggs be had stolen that morning from the hen-pen, by piercing them at each end and sucking out the contents of the whole lot within two minutes.

As I watched fascinated, not concentrating on what I was doing, I made it clear at the start that he was not to expect anything brilliant from me, by stepping back into an open channel full of horse's urine which came up to my knees. The sad tears became tears of laughter as he slapped me on the back again and called me an ignorant but amusing comrade, spluttering:

"Do a few more things like that and I'll die laughing, before Olga squeezes the life out of me with her fat legs."

"Who's Olga?" I asked.

Jan went to the door and shouted across the yard.

"Olga! Come here - you."

The next minute I was being introduced to his girl friend, a tractor driver from the Ukraine, clumsy, muscular, bandy-legged, bawdy and altogether as unfeminine a female as I had ever seen.

"She's a good bed-mate," he roared, as if he wanted the whole town to know. "Eh, Olga?"

She squealed as he pinched her behind, pointing with his spare hand over to a corner of the stable, where the straw had been flattened as if a battle had been fought on it.

"Do you sleep in here, then?" I asked him.

"Yes, comrade. I like to be near the horses, in case either of them gets ill in the night. Olga has a room in the gasthaus, with a lovely bed and a beautiful feather eiderdown, but she prefers a bunk-up with Jan in the straw. That's right, eh, Olga?" Once more his mutton-chop hand made a grab at her rear, but she was out through the door in no time, calling back coyly:

"Jan, don't be so naughty," and apologising to me: "Just see what raw eggs can do to a man."

Although Jan was fond of his girl friend, he loved his horses more and would never let them out of his sight, grooming and feeding them whenever he got the opportunity. With Jan and the two horses I started a new and more interesting life, going every-where; out in the fields, ploughing, turnip harvesting, spreading manure. The most he would ever let me do was to put on their harnesses, watching me carefully in case they suffered any discomfort, while I watched their hind legs, in case I did. While we ate our food, often salami, bierwurst or some other delicacy stolen from the gastaus larder, he recounted endless stories of his life in Poland, and how he had managed to get a six inch red gash drawn together by twelve ugly stitch marks, on his back. Within two days he had recited five different stories, ranging from a brawl in a Cracow tavern, when he had been directly responsible for the capture and conviction of an elusive ring of drug smugglers, to stopping a runaway horse and carriage in which the mayor was being driven to a meeting of the Warsaw city councillors.

I soon found that he was regularly trying to jump the queue and con his way back to Poland for a holiday. Most of the privileged Poles were allowed back home occasionally, but the queue was a long one, and they could not be easily spared. On three occasions he came back from the labour exchange cursing the girl in charge there, with the help of Poland's most popular swear word.

"Curvar! (At least, that's what it sounded like). Why couldn't she give me a pass? Curvar! ME... Jan. Curvar! She ought to be raped. That'd Curvar fix her."

I felt that a fellow like Jan, once let loose, could do quite a lot of...'fixing': a bad outlook for the women should he ever be on the winning side; especially this one, who was playing havoc with his ego.

Herr and Frau Schneider and their daughter, Gretel, well fed but as pasty as her father, quite tolerant of the fact that I had to live and breathe, gave me breakfast in the kitchen. When I was in there, hearing "Heil Hitlers" booming from the hall, I knew this indicated the arrival of yet another guest, whose importance in the 'Partei' I could judge by the quality of the stolen food arriving in the stables from the kitchen, soon learning to enjoy caviare mixed with chocolate mousse and asparagus tips garnished with brandy sauce, all laced with a fare sprinkling of horse manure. Unlike her husband, Frau Schneider wasn't always holding her breath when she came into the stables. A good-looking, blonde woman in her late forties, she would quite often bring us bits of left-over food, not realising that Jan already had his pockets full. Jan would laugh and joke with Herr Schneider and treat his wife with great respect.

"Now, there's a woman for you," he said to me one day."A real lady, I call her. She doesn't wipe her nose on her apron, fart and scratch her arse, like Olga."

"What will you do if the Russians ever get here and you've

got her at your mercy?" I asked.

His wide grin said more than words: but without warning, like the sudden darkness after an Indian sunset, his face changed.

"Do you know what I'll do with the 'Herr'?" he said.

Surprised at his sudden venom, I shook my head in expectation, knowing what he was for recounting the awful details. He licked his lips.

"I'll get a knife ... a blunt one. Then..." He was enjoying his carefully picked words. "I'll prepare him like a piece of pork. I'll make little cuts all over him and rub salt in until he squeals..." By this time he had specks of white saliva at the corners of his mouth. And now came the coup-de-grace. "I'll imagine he's a little pig and slowly cut ... off ... his...test..."

He stopped suddenly. The piece of pork, looking very alive and as healthy as it ever would, had just come through the stable door.

Jan jumped to his feet.

"Good day, Herr!" He was suddenly all smiles. "The horses are fed; the cows are groomed; I have cleaned the plough. I was very tired and was resting for two minutes. Now we are going out to the fields to spray them with your wonderful horses' piss."

"Good, Jan. Good," was all Herr Schneider could manage while holding his breath.

Life in the camp, a converted farmhouse with as unsociable an interior as the one at Shaffendorf, was exceptionally dull. Even the fleas were too lazy to multiply. The walls echoed petty arguments and boredom ate its silent way into our lives, like dry rot. To wangle a day off work became every man's aim and ambition; the need for some sort of inventive excitement was insatiable. After careful thought Arthur Griffiths, a small tough wizened Aussie from Wiluma, west of the Gibson Desert, with freckles on his shoulders and back the size of pennies, put the silver paper round his Red Cross chocolate to good use by screwing it into little balls, which he swallowed with water. Then he staggered into the guardroom and leant against the wall, hoping the chalk he had rubbed onto his face was making him look naturally pale.

"Mr. Corporal," he gasped. "I think my ulcer has come

back: the pain is awful."

"Your ulcer?"

The corporal looked surprised and slightly scared.

A kindly, insignificant Austrian from a Steiermark village, he wore thick glasses that had so far kept him away from the Russian front and on this occasion stopped him being suspicious. Arthur's eyelids were drooping: he was putting on a good act of just staying conscious as he went on:

"Yes. All my life, since I was a little boy ..."

He stopped — gasping. The corporal was taking no risks. Even the Nazis would not want too many dead Australians around. It didn't pay to be a negligent guard.

"Can you walk?" he asked, anxiously.

"I'll try. I'll try," gasped the Aussie. "But please help me, quickly. I think I'm going to die."

On the outskirts of the town was an up-to-date hospital, which served the whole district. Along a path across the fields, by a short cut, the corporal half dragged, half carried the groaning Aussie until, nearly exhausted, he hauled him into the casualty department. By this time Arthur's face was naturally white with the strain of the whole business and the flour had worn off.

"Nurse. Top priority!" called the Dutch house doctor, who had been brought in from Antwerp after Holland had capitulated. Arthur was rushed off to the x-ray room, trying not to look healthy as the flush of victory was beginning to colour his cheeks. Within half an hour, a serious-looking radiologist, holding a large piece of film up against the light, was convincing everybody:

"Yes," he was saying, as he pointed out the black spots. "This man is suffering from serious stomach ulcers. He must go back to the main camp for treatment immediately.

They rushed Arthur, triumphant and by now the picture of health, through the Austrian mountains, to the main camp near Wolfsberg. In the guard's briefcase were the x-rays. After a few days treatment, the Aussie was looking so well that they decided to x-ray him again, to be on the safe side before sending him back to work. But any black spots that remained had changed their position. In the camp hospital, on no account allowed to go to the latrine, he was given the privilege of his own personal Jeremiah, which was handed over to the now suspicious doctors after every performance until the first silver ball appeared. After this he was kicked unceremoniously into the Disciplinary Enclosure and quickly sent off to a coalmine in Poland, where he would be able to get real ulcers with no treatment, to his heart's content. The corporal got away with a severe reprimanding for his total lack of observance and, from that time onwards, spent a lot of time polishing his glasses. But this failure only had the effect of making us the more determined to succeed and before long the fixed idea of getting a couple of weeks off work became a disease, growing out of all sensible proportions.

During most of the days and nights I would be thinking, "How am I going to do it?" until, on a Sunday afternoon, as I stood keeping goal in the door of the latrine during a game of football and, noticing Alfie Owens' heavy studded boots, I suddenly got the inspiration that luckily only comes once in a lifetime. I was so excited about it that I let through the ball, which cannoned off the wall inside, hitting Fred Bannister, sitting on the long pole half asleep, on the side of the head and, plunging four foot down into the slimy seething trench, disappeared. When Fred, disgusted, at being woken up, had been pushed up to the end of the pole and the ball had been fished out and kicked about in the grass to clean it up nobody seemed anxious to go on playing, so signalling over to Alfie Owens I prepared him for his part in my wild scheme.

"I've got a job for you," I said. "One you'll enjoy, you bloodthirsty brute!"

"What's that, mate?" he said, quite unperturbed.

"I want you to kick me on the shin as hard as you can."

He didn't seem to mind a bit.

"How many fags do I get for that?" he asked, with a hint of boredom.

"A hundred," I said. "As long as you do the job properly."

"O.K. When?"

"No time like the present," I said.

We went behind the latrine, where I pulled up my trouser-leg and, gripping one of the thick struts, shut my eyes. It was too late to change my mind. All I could say, between clenched teeth, was:

"Well, what are you waiting for?"

He did the job well, opening up the skin nicely down to the bone. The hand grenade in Greece had only hurt half as much. I limped into the camp, with blood streaming down my leg, to get the cigarettes and something still more important and essential for the whole operation - a blue indelible pencil. The memory of my nanny, when she once caught me chewing one of these, was already beginning to chill me. But now it was certainly too late. I couldn't leave the plan half finished. Her wagging finger was clear in my mind, stuck into my face, looking as long as a broom handle. And the scolding, worried voice still rang in my ears.

"You dreadful boy. That's deadly poisonous. YOU WILL DIE."

"I DON'T WANT TO DIE," I screamed. "WHERE'S MY MUMMY? I DON'T WANT TO DIE?"

Probably my nanny thought she had overdone it:

"Oh! You won't die, my little cherub," she said "if you are good, and don't give your poor nanny any trouble for a week."

I was good — for half an hour: after which, I reckoned, the chance of dying had gone, because I had just heard my mother, who had been listening, giving my nanny the sack.

Kiwi, sitting on his bed as usual, keeping himself to himself, stopped singing one of his haunting Maori songs, to the accompaniment of a German guitar bought from a guard for ten tins of Red Cross bully beef, long enough to lend me his knife, which I used to scrape a fare pile of the powdered copying ink into a piece of paper. Then, with a masochistic satisfaction, I rubbed the lethal powder as deep as I could into the wound.

"Croiky!" said Brummie, staring wide-eyed. "I dunno about that ... yow'll sown be tellin' us yow've got blow blood in yer vines".

But it was too late. The battle between my red corpuscles and the attacking microbes had begun, as fierce as any yet fought at the front, and the only thing to do was to let them get on with it. For the next day or two I carried on with the usual routine, waiting to see what happened, the object of something between jealousy and horror, always looking for the first signs of poisoning, and secretly thankful when nothing happened. It seemed the microbes had given in, which said a lot for all the healthy delicacies I was getting from Jan. Being a natural work-lover he could not understand why I had gone to such lengths to avoid it.

"You look ugly enough with two curvar legs," he said with one of his hearty laughs. "God knows what you'd curvar look like with one."

After this abortive attempt, I gave up: but, to make up for it, the Heavenly Powers, realising I was a deserving case, saw to it that I caught a nasty chill a week later and, to the delight of the fleas, I was actually ordered to stay in my bunk.

The sudden silence, after the last man had left for work, was a better tonic than any medicine and within minutes I was asleep. Three hours later, when the brilliant sunlight was casting a threatening shadow of the bars across the window on the floor below my bunk, I was woken up by the sound of voices; this time German. Before the loudest voice had produced ten words I knew instinctively that it belonged to the biggest buffoon in the German army. With him was the corporal, who seemed to have forgotten I was there, and a girl. From my position I couldn't see them, but I could hear them well.

At the sight of the room the girl just exclaimed:

"Oh!"

She might have uttered it in disgust, amazement or sympathy, certainly not appreciation. But whatever it was, it floated over to me like a note on the flute in Debussy's 'L'apres-Midi d'un Faun'. But, like a verbal bulldozer, the Buffoon jumped straight in to hog the limelight. Though he was out of sight I had already taken an intense dislike to him.

"I understand you have thirty prisoners here, yes?" Behind each word there seemed to be a charge of gunpowder.

"Yes, Herr Uber-Feldwehbel (Mr. Sergeant-major)," said the corporal.

The Buffoon must have been testing the bars across the window.

"Not good. I shall put in for a double set. Can't have these men escaping, Ugh? You'll see that all boots and trousers are deposited in the loft every night after rollcall. You will keep your rifles clean and in good condition to shoot, if necessary, any man trying to escape. Under no circumstances will you accept any 'conserven' (tinned foods) from the prisoners. No man will be allowed more than one item out of his Red Cross parcel per day. You will immediately stop any patriotic or marching songs, such as, 'Pack up your kit in your old trouble bag!' (I hoped this would be his only attempt at English). Have the men ready and waiting here at eight o'clock this evening, when I shall make my methods clear to them."

"Yes, Herr Uber-Feldwhebbel."

I realised that this must be the new district comandant, in charge of P.O.W.s, everyone had been talking about. Chuckling to myself, I was still waiting for the girl's voice, while the uber-feldwehbel seemed to be looking round for things he could criticise. When he found Kiwi's guitar, he said suspiciously:

"Gott in Himmel! How did this get here?"

The corporal was quick-thinking; one of the reasons, together with his bad sight, which had kept him away from the Russian front. The other was that he walked with a slight limp, and so far Hitler hadn't enlisted the cripples. He seemed to be a naturally good liar.

"It belongs to Ulrich (one of the guards). He is very musical and, in order not to disturb me during the day when I am making out my reports, often comes in here to play. He seems to have left it behind by mistake."

At this point the girl broke in politely, but with a note of authority:

"Will this stove be enough to keep the two rooms warm in winter?"

"Fraulein Bayer, you think of everything."

As I listened to their voices I got the impression of a tonsilitic frog croaking besides a melodiously bubbling brook.

"I shall look into the matter," said the 'Buffoon'. If the prisoners are to work hard to win the war for Germany, they must not be cold - yes?" He gave a great guffaw at his own joke.

As they left, the girl seemed to be concerned about our latrine bucket, which nobody had remembered to cover, and the uber-feldwehbel was again promising his attention in this direction.

"Good," he said finally. "Corporal, you will please report to Fraulein Bayer at the Labour Exchange tomorrow to collect my written instructions. Come, Fraulein, we must go."

So this was the girl who had put Jan in his place. I wondered if her looks were like her voice and planned to ask Jan for further details.

"Heil Hitler," said the corporal.
"Heil Hitler," said the uber-feldwehbel.
"Auf wiedersehen," said Fraulein Bayer.

For some time, with nothing better to do, I lay thinking about the girl, trying to fit her into my mental picture. Probably tall, willowy even, and above all, contrary to common belief, she had made the German language sound unbelievably musical.

In the evening, I saw the uber-feldwehbel for the first time and, after half an hour, nothing had altered my opinion of him. His extra long arms, held slightly away from his sides, bow legs and habit of stooping forward, gave him the appearance of a gorilla dressed up in field grey. His head was as big as his voice was loud, his cheeks and abnormally protruding jaw, purple with stubble longing to be shaved, seemed to he trying to force the dark suspicious eyes back into his head. Immediately he came in, he spotted me still in bed.

"What's wrong with that man?" he asked the corporal.
"He is sick, Herr Uber-Feldwehbel."
"He doesn't look too sick to get up and listen to what I have to say." He beckoned to me impatiently. "Raus! Raus!" he shouted, and I began to move slowly.

"Bloody wog," I muttered.
"Schnell! Schnell! Mein Herr. Schnell! Schnell!"

I moved slightly faster, putting on my greatcoat over my pyjamas. When I had joined the others, his eyes rested on me for a moment, with cold reproach, as if it was a sin for an English prisoner to be ill, before he began his speech in German.

"Gentlemen, I am your new district commandant, yes?" he

said, each word clear and precise. "I want to make my methods quite plain to you, yes?" Those who couldn't understand tried to look intelligent. "You are to forget my predecessor and all his methods. I have my own, and they MUST BE OBEYED, yes?"

He waited for the words to sink in, then, like a verbal machine gun, he opened fire again.

"If you obey them without complaining, we shall get along like a big happy family. But..." again he paused for effect. "If you do not - if any one of you decides to protest — then I am afraid he will be treated like the naughty member of the family and will be punished. You understand, yes?"

"Yes, Herr Uber-Feldwehbel," answered Fred Bannister at once, in German, very solemnly and earnestly. "We understand perfectly."

"Good, good," said the 'Buffoon'.

Thinking he had found an almost intelligent Englishman at last, he made a half turn, clicking his heels, and began to address the rest of his speech to Fred. The drama he had created was gripping him.

"The punishments of war are drastic," he hinted, darkly. "Do you understand?"

"We understand, Herr Uber-Feldwehbel," answered Fred.

"Good! Good!"

So he went on, finishing each new veiled threat with a fresh, "Do you understand?" ... and staring all the time at Fred.

"We understand perfectly, Herr Uber-Feldwehbel," answered Fred each time, until Brummie was laughing so much that he had to find something to grip onto to stop himself from wetting his pants. Finally, the situation almost got out of hand, as Fred began to take tremendous risks.

The uber-feldwehbel had just said:

"Do you all understand you are now servants of the Third Reich and that you must forget your own country and work hard for our war effort?"

Fred turned to us and, as if asking our opinion of this and other points the uber-feldwehbel had made, said quietly in English, his face expressionless:

"Did you ever see such a stupid git? Stick his big head in

the piss bucket, someone! Yes?"

The 'Buffoon' seemed to appreciate more and more Fred's cooperation and enthusiasm, fixing him with his gimlet eyes, and too wrapped up in his own powers of oratory to notice the uncontrollable convulsions that had seized most of us. After half an hour of browbeating, he clicked his heels, raised his arm from the elbow in a Nazi salute, and left. A split second later, the whole lot of us exploded into fits of laughter, until the tears streamed down our faces and Brummie went and sheepishly changed his underpants.

After this, the guards, cursing the inconvenience, took it in turns to march up and down outside for a couple of nights, but soon things were ambling along as inefficiently as ever. The bars on the windows were not reinforced, but the thought that they might be prompted three inseparable pals in the camp to concoct an audacious plan to escape to Hungary, still a neutral, though pro-German, country and only thirty kilometres away. They would need time to get to the Hungarian border and cross it, wired, guarded and heavily mined as it was; then again to travel another thirty kilometres in order to pass an official demarcation line, beyond which, if caught, they would become prisoners of neutral Hungary. All this, if possible, before the alarm would be raised. If they were not caught, they would join the partisans in Yugoslavia, hoping eventually to be picked up by one of the British subs operating in the Mediterranean for this purpose. The 'Buffoon' had, as a result of his great zeal, given us an opportunity to use our brains for once, even if it was only to construct a concealed trap door into the loft, where the guards were still obediently locking up our boots and trousers every night. There were two problems to be solved: one, that of getting workmen's visas and train tickets to the border, and the other, of obtaining civilian workmen's clothes.

The trap door was easy: merely a matter of moving one of the panels separating our main room from the stairs which, in turn, separated us from the guard room and led up to the loft, performing a little skilful carpentry on it and returning it to its position, so that once more it would look a part of the whole structure. In order to do this, without raising the suspicion of the guards, we decided to form a choir of six men, who learnt some Austrian folk songs, and persuaded one of the guards, who had a piano accordion, to accompany them during an evening of 'entertainment' in the guard room. The sepulchral voice of Mike Burns, who had been a comedian in civvy street, singing and tap-dancing his way round England's flea pits, and who swore he had once emptied the theatre at the end of Brighton pier, did the trick, successfully obliterating the noise of the work going on only a few yards away. And so we opened the first stage of an escape route for anyone who cared to use it. Surprisingly, it would not be as easy to escape from here as from behind the barbed wire of one of the main camps. Every one of our faces would be clearly recognised in these parts. Many people knew us by name; also where we worked: and the police patrolled the area at night with Alsatian dogs. The disguise would have to be very good indeed.

CHAPTER SEVEN

I had been working on the gasthaus farm for about six months when one evening I was called into the guardroom. Expecting some query about my Red Cross parcels or a letter from home, I was surprised instead to see the 'Buffoon' sitting at the head of the table smoking a cigar, gripped between his teeth and sticking out at me like the barrel of a machine gun; with the corporal standing on one side and the two guards on the other, all three at attention. Taking his cigar out, his fat forefinger curled round it, he glowered at me over his spectacles like a belligerent bishop.

"Before you became part of this war, so senseless for your already beaten country," he said, " you were a commercial artist. That is correct?"

"That is correct," I said.

He shook his head, like a master trying to teach the dunce of the class.

"That is correct, Herr Uber-Feldwehbel..." He pronounced the last two words slowly and carefully, with a long-suffering smile.

"That is correct, Herr Uber-Feldwehbel," I said.

"Right, 5805," he growled at me, his bonhomie gone, reading from the file in front of him. "Because — possibly — you are good with your hands, you have been chosen out of all the prisoners to work for Herr Pfeffer, the town dentist."

I couldn't believe my ears.

"The dentist?" I said incredulously.

"Yes, my friend, the dentist. Not the butcher, nor the grocer, nor yet again the hairdresser but, (he paused for his sarcasm to take effect) the dentist. Herr Pfeffer is a leading member of the N.S.K.K., and surely even you don't honestly think a man of his influence should be lowering himself by making gold crowns for poor farmers who are not even active members of the 'Partei' and who, we know, would be chattering with them about the Fuhrer behind his back. Of course you don't. He needs a dental mechanic, but all our best men are at the front." (I chuckled to myself: a good reason why he wasn't there, I thought).

"But I don't know the first thing about making gold crowns, Herr Uber-Feldwehbel," I said.

With an imperious gesture he waved off my excuses.

"You can be taught, my friend." His nose was beginning to twitch, a sure sign that he was about to make a joke. The guards were getting ready to laugh. "If you make a gold crown for me, 5805," he said, winking at the corporal, "it will have to be more beautiful than the crown of the Great George the Sixth of England, or you will lose your privileged position — just as he will lose his, when the Fuhrer takes over Buckingham Palace." The guards laughed obediently.

"Now go! I have work to do. Yes?"

When I told the others, they were naturally envious. Who could blame them? But though, after a year of this confined life, 'bitchiness' was now a daily part of it, in this case it wasn't noticeable. Perhaps no one really wanted to work for such a prominent member of the 'Partei'.

"When you get fed up with doing back molars," said Fred Bannister, "give yourself some practice on the front ones, and knock the bastard's teeth in."

"Heil Hithler! Thieg Heil!" shouted Kiwi — his first joke for six months.

Jan seemed sorry to see me go. I had been a willing listener to all his stories and had made great friends with Olga, which pleased him. Slapping me on the back so hard that my tongue nearly shot out, he pushed a bag of stolen delicacies into the front of my jacket a moment before Herr Schneider came in to shake my hand and coldly wish me "Good luck".

On the following morning the corporal took me along the path through the fields and into the town, leading me like a V.I.P. to the dentist's house, a large three-storeyed building almost in the centre, approached under a high archway. Jutting out at an angle, a Swastika flag fluttered idly from its pole at the top of the arch, welcoming Herr Pfeffer's patients (or, at least his Nazi ones). I was taken into the surgery where a good-looking dark-haired girl in her early twenties was laying out the instruments ready for the day's activities. Giving the corporal a smile, and without looking at me, she went to call Herr Pfeffer. While we waited I had a chance to look round the room, with its modern dental chair, shooting out a frightening array of metal branches — drilling apparatus, x-ray camera, glass and spittoon — all the armaments guaranteed to cause a shudder, no matter how tough the nerves. On the wall, directly in front of the chair, hung a reproduction of a life-size portrait of Hitler in uniform, the fearless gleam in his hypnotic black eyes there either to give the patients courage in their sufferings or to make them tremble with fear, depending on how much or little faith they had in him. Though I hadn't as yet seen the dentist I could imagine him, from what I had heard, standing there, eyes fixed on his Fuhrer in fervent rapture, taking no notice of his patient's screams as he absentmindedly drilled a hole in his tongue instead of his tooth. I didn't have to wait long to confirm the image as the door from the hall outside into the private quarters had opened and my new boss was with us, complete with spotless white coat covering immaculate pin-striped blue suit, the neatly brushed grey hair of a man in his fifties, highly polished pointed black shoes on rather small feet and the slightest shadow of a sneer on a far too pale face. The rimless glasses balanced on a hawk-like nose finished off the picture of a man who could easily be imagined, transformed by a brown uniform with a black belt, into an officer of the N.S.K.K.

As I watched him exchanging "Heil Hitler's" with the guard, together with the usual salutes, I found myself getting annoyed by the sneer round his lips, even before he spoke. I must have sensed the sort of veiled indignity he was about to subject me to:

"Comment allez-vous, Monsieur le Prisonnier de Guerre?" he asked. Here was an Austrian speaking French to an Englishman: what the devil for? If he wanted to know how I was, he should have asked me in German. I looked as stupid as I could as I met the sardonic gaze and said in German:

"I am sorry, but I don't understand."

The shadow of a sneer became real as he shrugged me off as an ignoramus.

"They told me you understood French. They are inefficient. I was hoping to have someone intelligent to converse with instead of another dumb-cluck like, for instance, Fraulein Ida Schmidt." He was looking at the girl, who had blushed a deep red.

Without looking in my direction he beckoned to me to follow him into the room where I would work; a room so ordinary that, apart from a table with a bunsen burner and a few jars on it, a cabinet containing chemicals and, under another smaller picture of Hitler, a shelf with a row of plaster of Paris upper and lower grinning jaws, could have been a conventional sitting-room.

For the rest of the morning, while showing me what I was expected to do, he went on annoying me with his exaggerated patriotism and his remarks in French. Ida Schmidt seemed to enjoy being used as a doormat and in spite of her good looks, rapidly lost my respect. But, though he continued making remarks (now mostly to himself) in French and usually about the decadent British, a repetition of Hitler's frequent broadcasts, after two hours of flitting in and out of the room between patients, he had proved what a good teacher he was, and by the evening I had a reasonable idea of denture and crown making, even starting to produce an upper denture for some local underling in the Partei; carefully reinforcing it against the possibility of continually having to rattle out "Heil Hitlers". Making sure that the wireless was turned on each time the news came over, Herr Pfeffer did his best to pump me full of propaganda. In the late afternoon he joined me, proving again to be as patient with his technical instructions as he was intolerant and sarcastic about my German grammar and pronunciation. When he left me in the early evening with the job of cleaning up and rearranging the cabinet, told Ida sharply to go and disappeared into his private quarters, I was feeling like a human being for the first time in a year and a half, and almost looking forward to the next day's work.

Within a week I had become quite confident and was actually making dentures that fitted first time. Owing to the shortage of guards I was allowed to walk through the town to work on my own. When I arrived at seven-thirty each morning, my first duty was to clean out and light the two wood-burning stoves, one in my room and the other in the surgery. The wireless, which never seemed to close down, was always pouring out propaganda and by eight o'clock I already knew about all the latest German victories.

Soon, it was obvious that I had quite innocently landed in the middle of a volcanic domestic situation — a trio comprised of the dentist, his wife and his dark-haired assistant. Ida, always slightly gloomy, would bring me a cup of coffee every morning and afternoon and leave me without saying a word.

"Do you like your work here, Fraulein?" I asked her once, feeling that somebody had to say something. I was surprised that she answered at all. In fact, she sounded quite annoyed.

"It is not a question of liking my work. Whatever we Austrians are given to do, we must do it with all our might, the Fuhrer says, to help Germany win, however uninteresting it is. Besides, Herr Pfeffer needs all the help he can get."

It seemed that she had been indoctrinated.

"Ah, yes," I said. "Herr Pfeffer must have help. But do you think that, by pulling out teeth, he is contributing towards England's downfall?"

"And sending people back to work for the Fatherland with no distracting toothache: Yes."

A devout Austrian Nazi. Not many of these about, I thought.

"Herr Pfeffer is a good dentist, isn't he?" I was getting a kick out of this.

A very good dentist," she said. "A very great man."

She was blushing again, spilling some of my coffee as she put it on the table, and leaving the room in a hurry. The poor girl was obviously off her rocker: but that was the most human reaction I had managed to get out of her and I congratulated myself on the achievement.

Whenever the surgery door was open I could see Ida handing the dentist this and that or replenishing the patient's mouthwash; but she never smiled or looked in my direction. Often, when she was alone with the dentist she would be crying, but my natural reaction was: "Let the stupid Nazis get on with it". Frau Pfeffer never spoke to me or the girl. Like her husband, she was in her fifties but, in her case, still quite attractive in an angular sort of way, her face already showing the wrinkles of long forgotten laughter when, perhaps, she and her husband had been in love. Spending most of her time in the living quarters she occasionally glided past my open door like a shadowy spectral with an eye on the surgery and Ida.

In the mornings, after I had finished the two stoves, Herr Pfeffer would suddenly appear through the door of the living quarters and take up his position in the dark passage, watching me; on his head a black velvet skull-cap, his white shirt hanging loosely open at the neck, contrasting with his black well-creased trousers and his face deathly white. Given a pair of big gold earrings he could have been the ghost of a Spanish pirate, except that he would be wielding the 'Volkischer Beobachter' national newspaper of the Third Reich, instead of a cutlass. I could sense, without looking, the sneer twisting his thin grey lips as he would come over and put the newspaper on the table in front of me. At first it was depressing: day after day the same sort of black headline of inch-high type:

ANOTHER 100,000 TONS OF BRITISH SHIPPING SUNK

...Depressing until after a while I realised that the whole British merchant navy had been sent to the bottom at least three times, when it became comical. But there was no doubt about the fact that England was going through it: no question of feeling any security. Any optimism I showed was a difficult effort of play-acting.

I soon discovered that Herr Pfeffer, though an influential member of the N.S.K.K. with an example to set, was taking drugs. Quite often, he would stagger about the surgery until he would find his way through the door and sink down, head in hands and shaking, onto his usual seat in my room, an unopened barrel of plaster of Paris. At other times he would be highly elated and happy, once even making Ida laugh. When he was in a normal state he was a good dentist and certainly his patients seemed to suspect nothing, or were too afraid of the consequences to visit the dentist in any other town. Ida, with the looks of the Sphinx on a face which should have been open and pretty, watched him every minute of the day on these occasions, as if she expected him to fall over. These bouts of unnatural behaviour prepared me for anything and I was not surprised when, arriving one morning, I found him sitting on the barrel in his long white nightshirt, his twisted skull cap almost falling off his head, and his face sickly grey as hardened putty. As I came through the door his eyes rolled back, his mouth opened and with a dry gasp he toppled off the barrel onto the floor. For a second I stood and stared at him, wondering what to do. Then I rushed out into the passage and knocked hard on the rattling glass door of the living quarters. A minute passed and I knocked again, almost as the door was being opened by his wife, with a red dressing gown over her white nightdress and her hair in curlers. Showing no signs of the panic I had expected, she said, speaking to me for the first time:

"I'm not deaf, you know, young man. You needn't have bothered to knock twice. What's the.....?

"Your husband," I burbled, pointing towards the workroom. Something's happened. He's ill. I think he's unconscious."

"Of course he's unconscious," she said. "He's as unconscious as you would be if you had swallowed all his tablets: but he won't die. Oh no, he'll see to it that Herr Pfeffer doesn't die."

She shrugged her shoulders, went ahead of me into the room and, without showing any signs of surprise, bent down and pushed him onto his back.

"It's the same old business," she said. "I'll go and phone for an ambulance."

I was so hypnotised by her lack of concern that I couldn't speak. Though I hadn't got much use for her husband he was, after all, a human being of sorts. Coming back, looking slightly bored, she said:

"I'm sorry. Please excuse all the trouble, and don't be alarmed. This is all quite silly. He makes such a habit of this, he is driving me crazy."

"A habit of what?" I asked.

"Oh, you wouldn't know, of course. He just swallows all his tablets, lies down and goes to sleep. Never enough to kill him, you know: he makes sure of that. He just causes a lot of trouble."

In another two minutes we heard the shrill bell of the ambulance. Frau Pfeffer looked flustered for the first time.

"Oh, dear! Again, they've caught me in my nighty. He really is so inconsiderate."

I went to let the two ambulance men in. Obviously rather annoyed, they pushed Herr Pfeffer about, finally loading him onto a stretcher and into the ambulance like a sack of flour. As if nothing had happened, with Frau Pfeffer out of the way in the private quarters, I carried on with a very special gold crown I was making for a lieutenant colonel, until Ida arrived.

"Good morning. Excuse me, where is Herr Pfeffer?" There was a fluttering note of anxiety in her voice. Not wanting to rub it in, I said:

"Herr Pfeffer? Oh, he's had a bit of an accident, but he's all right."

Her eyes were staring, frightened.

"W-what happened?"

Her face had turned pale. There was nothing for it: I had to tell her and, as I explained the real facts, she sank into a chair, her head in her hands, sobbing. At that moment Frau Pfeffer, carrying a shopping bag, came into the room. She looked haughtily at Ida.

"I don't see what there is to cry about, Fraulein Schmidt. You know we've had all this before." She paused. "Unless, of course, you have a conscience. He is where he should be and it is no concern of yours. Would you mind stopping snivelling and ring up, cancelling all appointments until the day after tomorrow."

It was embarrassing. At first Ida kept her face covered, even after Frau Pfeffer had left, then drying her eyes she excused herself for being silly.

"I am sorry," she said quite normally, but looking at the floor. "You must think me stupid. You are English and none of this matters to you. In fact, you are probably secretly enjoying it all. Nobody cares about Herr Pfeffer, just because he has done it before." She covered her face again. "Sometimes I wish they would let him die, then I would kill myself and nobody would have to bother any more."

"How much misery can you cram into half a minute?" I muttered, in English.

She looked at me searchingly, as if I might come up with some magic answer to her problems, but as I didn't even know what they really were, other than that she was madly in love with a maniac, there was nothing much I could do.

During the next day or two, while Herr Pfeffer's patients wrapped poultices round their aching jaws, she sat in my room taking my attention off the dentures by chattering continuously about Herr Pfeffer, backed up with lurid details of how his horrible wife treated him; but always with one eye on the door in case she should come in.

"Why don't you go and see him in the hospital?" I asked.

She stared at the wall, her face a mask of misery.

"Because he would only curse me for going and say it was all my fault. It seem it's my fault even to be alive."

In spite of an instinct to say "Why do you love him? He's crazy", a narrow-mindedness which I should have had from the start was making it seem almost obscene to bother about the private lives of the enemy. So I said nothing, wondering how anyone could fall under the spell of such a man.

When he came back in two days, Herr Pfeffer made no drama of it; but walked through the door as if nothing had happened and without so much as a glance in our direction, went straight over to the appointment book.

"Colonel Gebhard has an appointment in half an hour, Fraulein. Get everything ready, please."

He turned to me.

"How are the Colonel's dentures, Stooart?"

"Finished," I said.

"Good. Let's hope you have made them well — and a good fit. He told me that when a shell landed near him at Volkhor his last ones vibrated for a week." His face cracked into a rigid smile. It was a relief to see him fairly normal again.

After a day or two life floated back onto an even keel, as if nothing had ever happened, until Herr Pfeffer had to roughen it up again, taking me completely by surprise after the last patient had gone, followed by Ida.

"I've got toothache," he said with no warning. "If you will hold the mirror, please, I've got to extract a back molar."

"You're going to take your own molar out?"

I wondered if I had heard correctly. Though he was admittedly a man who did unusual things he seemed, this time, to be really over-stepping the mark.

"Yes, why not? I shall be more careful with myself than any other dentist would be, especially Herr Gruber (the dentist in the next town). He got kicked out of the N.S.K.K. for interfering with a member's wife while he'd got her under gas and, as I took most of his patients, might want to get his own back on me....Who knows? Anyway, if it hurts too much, I shall scream and beg myself to stop. He gave one of his short dry laughs, grabbing his jaw and wincing with pain."

As I stood, holding the mirror while he sat in the dental chair, gathering all the necessary instruments round him, I knew I was about to have a unique experience and watched the whole operation, mesmerised. When I had the mirror in an upright position he made a noise, his mouth wide open, sounding like a mixture between a wailing siren and a barking fox, which I took to mean "Keep it there". Then, taking an ugly-looking syringe in one hand, while keeping his mouth open with the other, he plunged the needle deep into his gum and squeezed slowly. After he'd done this about four times, crying out "Aaah!" each time and scolding himself for his own incompetence, it looked as if his conceit was about to disappear together with his back molar. At this stage, he suddenly got up and headed for the door, saying he would be back in five minutes, when the cocaine had taken effect.

"Perhaps you would like to make yourself a coffee in the

meantime, Stooart."

He sounded quite concerned. If this was what toothache did to him I hoped he would get it more often.

Back again, his face grimly determined, he settled himself down comfortably in the dental chair, carefully picked out a large pair of pincers and, adjusting the mirror into the right position, got himself ready for the final coup de grace. By this time my hand was shaking so much that the mirror kept on shifting, which made him stare helplessly his mouth wide open, and make angry noises. With the pincers closed well and firmly over the tooth, he elbowed the mirror out of the way disgustedly, closed his eyes and began to fight a battle with the tooth as if he was trying to pull his head off. With a series of "Aaahs" and grunts, his eyes fixed reverently on the portrait of the "Fuhrer," he finally got both hands to it and pushed and pulled and twisted until, with tears streaming down his face and the light of the conqueror in his eyes, he pulled out his pincers gripping the decayed tooth, its four roots sticking out like primeval stalagmites.

"Sieg Heil!" he shouted like a delighted schoolboy.

The operation over, he wished me goodnight as if the whole business had been an everyday occurrence. After this, I respected him more and even began to give him a tin of Red Cross bully beef, jam or fruit every time I got a parcel.

As the news from the Russian front gradually grew worse, he was visibly losing confidence. Instead of continually asserting that Germany would win the war, he began to harp on what he would do if they lost. Like all senior N.S.K.K. officers he owned a Luger, which he kept locked in a drawer in the surgery. Frequently he would take it out and caress it lovingly speaking to it as he would to a pet animal or child,

"If Germany should lose the war, my shining beauty," he would say, "you will be my salvation!" With this he would point it at his head dramatically swivelling round in his chair to face the picture on the wall as if to gain the Fuhrer's approval. With your help I shall have a clean German death. So help me, my sweetheart, and never let me down ... Heil Hitler!"

As I watched him stroke this murderous-looking object,

sometimes for ten minutes at a time, unload it, polish the bullets and always put them carefully back into the chamber I was worried for his wife and Ida in case he should use it on them, never dreaming that I would be the chosen one myself.

When I arrived next morning at seven-thirty as usual I found him sitting at his desk in the surgery, not yet dressed, bent over and staring at one of his patient's files, his black skull cap on his head and, hanging loosely round him, an expensive-looking black silk dressing gown hiding his white night shirt. The look on his face showed that he was quietly slipping over the brink into lunacy. The tingling hairs at the back of my neck told me that I was facing a madman rather than a town dentist. It was a pity that the realisation had come too late. It looked as if al the trouble over his girlfriend had turned him within a few hours into a skeleton. His face seemed to be a yellow skull with eyes in it. For a moment he stared at me inscrutably: then, with a Napoleonic flourish, he pointed at a broom propped up against the wall, at the same time shooting out a staccato command in French:

"Sweep the room out!"

Taken aback by the side of his character which I had thought I would never see again, I made no move but just said:

"You know I don't understand French."

His face, suddenly losing its paler, reddened with anger.

"Sweep the room out! Schnell! Schnell!" he thundered in German.

A little voice inside me was trying to break through the noise. "Hey, you can't do it, just like that, without any protest,"

It didn't take much effort to fight against it. My common sense was warning: "He's got a gun in that drawer and, if I know anything about German Lugers, it could drill a hole right through me and halfway through the wall as well. And he's crazy." But, whether I had managed to rake up a bit of courage from somewhere or was completely mesmerised, (it didn't matter much at the time), I would not touch the broom. To crown everything, though I could have put my next remark in so many different ways, for some reason or other I chose the worst and most stupid:

"Say please." I managed to stammer, as if telling a pet spaniel to beg for its dinner. His eyes blazed with all the hatred of hell. From the depths of his lungs he let out a muffled, half whispered scream:

"SAY PLEASE! You say to ME — secretary of the Kurstenfeld branch of the EN-ESS-KAA-KAA? You damned cocky Englishman. You know you are a prisoner of war. You are here to do what we tell you and, by thunder, you will do it."

Probably a packet of drugs had given him back his confidence.

"Your country is doomed. All England will soon be our slaves. The Fuhrer has secret weapons, ready to use. He is enticing you all into his net and will wipe your miserable countries and armies off the map — send them sky-high through the clouds. Your damned Churchill will be tortured, beaten in public and led to his execution through the streets of London lined with jeering people shouting: 'Traitorous Rat!' Your ignorant people will work in our mines and on our roads and railways, begging us for enough bread to keep them alive to work harder... And you have the nerve to stand there and tell me to say PLEASE!"

He drew himself up in his leather-padded seat. His eyes seemed to have sunk an inch further into his head: there was white foam on his lips.

"Now!" he shouted hoarsely, "CLEAN THE ROOM OUT!"

By this time I was so petrified that I couldn't have moved if I'd tried. But my seized-up mind was working enough to remind me about what a missionary friend of my father had once said to me: "The best way to beat a man-eating tiger is to stand still and stare at it. While I was trying that little remedy, Herr Pfeffer was slowly sliding open the drawer with the gun in it. I was waiting to be killed, of all places, in a dentist's surgery. Luckily, the people at home would probably never find out. At that moment some senseless thought of bravado told me that I would see him in hell before I did what he ordered. Everything logical was screaming at me to turn and run, but how can you run when your legs are made of jelly? Surely he wouldn't shoot me in cold blood. BUT HE WAS MAD. OF COURSE HE WOULD! The hairs down the back of my neck were standing up trying to avoid each other.

"You will never get out of this room alive."

His voice sounded like an echo in a vast mortuary, filling my head as I managed to drag one foot after another towards the door. A silly thought struck me: that I should run, zigzagging, even though there were only two yards to do it in. But at the same moment, I saw him in the mirror and realised what a fool I had been. His head was resting on his arm on the table, near where the gun lay, his shoulders were heaving and he was sobbing like a little boy deprived of a ride on the 'dodgems'. At the sight of this I sprang like a hare through the hall and out onto the road, nearly knocking over the first patient of the day on his way to an uncertain fate.

With my heart trying to beat its way out of my chest I made for the camp. When I got there I reported to the corporal exactly what had happened. Now, completely gutless, given the order, I would then and there have gone back and swept out not only the surgery, but all the other rooms in the house: in fact, nothing less than a straight jacket would have stopped me doing the washing up as well. But, to my surprise, the corporal just said: "Ach, Ja. The dentist's mad. Everyone knows that. Perhaps we should have warned you."

With that, he picked up the telephone receiver and rang the 'Buffoon', who appeared to have been coming round anyway about some other matter. The corporal ordered me to wait in the camp, where I passed the time trying to persuade myself that I hadn't been a total idiot.

When the 'Buffoon' arrived he got straight down to business.

"You will report to Herr Gruber at the Gartnerei tomorrow," he said, looking at his file. "Phelps, the Australian, will show you the way."

As if my presence in the room had been a necessary evil, he told me I could go, waving me off with an imperious gesture of his stubby hand.

The situation had become ludicrous. Though the Hungarian border was only twenty kilometres to the east and the Swiss border two hundred to the west, the shortage of guards had made it impossible to control the prisoners who, gradually turning into V.I.P.s, had all the privileges any prisoner could wish for — except of course one very important one. It would not be much good shouting, "Please, don't!" if an order came through from Berlin to shoot the lot of us.

CHAPTER EIGHT

On the following day, I went off at seven in the morning with Wally Phelps following a path across the fields towards the far end of the town, walking for two hundred yards along the main road and finally through the gates of the Gartnerei, a curious array of various sheds, two very large greenhouses and about four acres of ground, planted with vegetables and flowers and flanked with rows of plant beds under glass. The possibility of an Allied bomb landing in the middle one day was interesting: even the Germans couldn't cover up their latest defeats in North Africa. Wally led me down to a shed that seemed to be reserved for us. This tall, dark, crop-haired motor-cycle dealer from Adelaide had decided to combat his problem of boredom by taking his work in the Gartnerei reasonably seriously and, laying down his own set of rules had, it seemed, become the 'Gaffer's' right hand man. We were the first arrivals.

"When does the 'Gaffer' arrive?" I asked.

"Wait on." Wally had his head through the door. "Which way's the wind blowing?"

"What's that got to do with it?"

"A flamin' lot, cobber. If the wind's blowin' down from his house up there, you know when he's coming. He eats garlic like monkeys eat cocoanuts — and for breakfast, too. Come on, we'll have a smoke."

He took out a tin of St Julian and some cigarette papers, managing to fill, roll, and light a cigarette with one hand. When the 'Gaffer' arrived unexpectedly (indicating that the wind was in the other direction), we were still smoking. Wally not bothering to get up, introduced me from where he sat. I had heard about Herr Gruber. He had started as an employee in the Gartnerei when the Nazis in Austria had been a hounded band of trouble makers, had become an active member of the Partei and, after the Anschluss (Hitler's annexation of his country), had rocketed to the top. Like a film star he had flounced into the shed, his hat at a jaunty angle, his lined features chiselled and healthy-brown above his open-necked shirt. He wore the usual blue apron and, as it was a bit chilly, a jacket — with a tiny swastika brooch on the lapel — over his shirt. Immediately, in spite of the brooch, I took a liking to a man who was obviously intelligent enough to treat his prisoners who could one day be his masters, as men and not animals.

"Volly," he said, "When you have finished your cigarette would you please water the cucumbers in the cases and get Stooart to help you."

I caught a weak whiff of garlic.

"Get it?" said Wally after Herr Gruber had left the shed. "He can only discuss his bleedin' politics with garlic eaters, thank God. He's a pain in the arse on that subject. The others soon clear off, except the creeps who don't mind a spot of torture to get a cheap turnip or two."

We had started watering the cucumbers when the first employee arrived, a smallish boy of sixteen with a fresh, open complexion and a friendly smile to go with it.

"Ah! Good morning, Crusoe" shouted Wally across from where he held the lid of a case open, while he hoisted a can of water up with the other hand.

"Crusoe?" I said, shaking hands with the boy. "That's not a German name."

He looked a bit sheepish and Wally saved him the trouble of answering.

"Robinson Crusoe: that's his name, or that's what I call the joker, anyway. Eh, Crusoe?" He slapped him on the back, nearly toppling him into the cucumber case. Seeing my puzzled expression, he said:

"Let me explain. Here, before your very eyes, is the biggest patriot in Austria and Germany together — and an inexplicable miracle of Austrian youth: a nice Nazi. Eh, Crusoe? But funnily enough he's more interested in desert islands than Brown Shirts.

And guess what, cobber: his hero is not the Fuhrer, like it should be, the naughty boy, but Robinson Crusoe. He knows more about Robinson Crusoe than the joker who wrote the story. He spends his life when he is not tearing around here for the 'Gaffer' like a blue-arsed fly, reading the book... hides it away like a family heirloom. I think it's on Hitler's 'forbidden' list. He's a nutter. Once, when I said 'Look out, or it'll be the Russian front for you,' he answered, quick as lightning:

'That's just where I want to go. The more Russians I can kill before I die, the better.' "

The 'Gaffer' had poked his head out of the glasshouse and Crusoe, obviously scared out of his wits, was busying himself with any chore he could find to do. By a quarter past eight, the three of us were well into the morning's work. I was hoeing near the border fence to the main road when I heard a loud "Psst!" Looking round, I saw two women waiting at the fence, ready to climb over.

"Where's Herr Gruber?" asked one of them a good-looking wiry blonde. She seemed scared.

"It's all right, he's in the potting shed. Come on," I said.

"Who are you?" asked the other, rather older, woman in her thirties, with 'nosy', dark eyes, set rather close in a face which reminded me of a sulky Pekingese. She sounded suspicious, as if the 'Gaffer' might have found some novel way of spying on his workers. As soon as they saw that the coast was clear they both clambered over the fence, were in and out of the tool shed within seconds and hoeing away as if they had been there for half an hour.

"We're supposed to arrive the same time as you and Volly," said the blonde one. "Oh! I'm sorry; I'm Frau Kempfer and this is Frau Tatt."

I was just introducing myself when Wally arrived with the 'Gaffer'.

"Good morning," shouted the Australian to the two women, winking at me as he made it obvious that they had only just arrived. The 'Gaffer' scowled at his two employees without replying to their rather sheepish "Good morning, Herr Grubers" and, uttering something directed at them about everybody's natural duty to work hard for the war effort, he asked me if I was getting on all right and walked off, followed by Wally, leaving me to find out more about the two women.

I soon realised that, in spite of the fact that Frau Kempfer's husband was at the Russian front and Frau Tatt's was a prisoner of war in Canada, they bore no resentment and considered me as an equal. The dark-haired one took me down the garden to the lettuce section where a woman of about fifty-five, with a grey head-scarf and apron over a neat black dress, was bending down weeding as if she had always had her head connected to the ground.

"Servus, Auntie. This is Stooart."

It seemed that she had arrived on her bicycle from a neighbouring village, even before Wally and me, ridden straight down the garden path, parked the bicycle on the ground and immediately got down to work, determined to stay in her bent-over position for the rest of the day. But when she realised the new 'Englander' had arrived she straightened up, smiling.

"Don't take any notice of me," she said. "I like work. Those two work because they are terrified of Herr Gruber. But you, young man, mustn't work too hard, because you're English. Why should you work for Hitler, the big turnip?"

At ten o'clock Frau Haunsel, Herr Gruber's daughter, came down from the house carrying a tray-full of cups of milk.

"Come on," Wally shouted to me, coming across from the glass-house where he had been watering the tomatoes. "This is what they call 'Yowzen', or at any rate it sounds like that. It's 'elevenses' an hour early."

Frau Haunsel took the tray of cups round to all the workers, finishing up with us. When Wally introduced me, she shook hands limply but didn't alter her expression. I felt that, though the dark features could have become reasonably attractive with a smile, they had not seen one for sometime. She said nothing, and hurried off, purposely unfriendly.

"Don't mind the 'Misery'," said Wally when she had gone. "She's a bigger Nazi than her old man. He only shouts 'Sieg Heil' round these parts to keep up his position as King of the Vegetables. But she's genuine 'Partei' and dangerous. Her husband's at the Russian front and, according to Frau Kempfer that's what annoys her. She thinks that if he'd played his cards right and 'Heil Hitler'd' a bit more, he might still be here where he'd be a bleedin' sight more useful. She hasn't heard from him for months, and reckons he's dead. The more the poor sod fights his knackers off the more she hates men. I reckon if he showed up unexpectedly she'd run away screaming and if he has the cheek to come back after the war she'll either jump in the river or zip her fanny."

We sat and drank our milk.

"Don't make a face," said Wally. "You'll have to put up with it. She's as tight as a duck's arse and you're lucky it's not water. She let's the milk stand, skims the cream off and is supposed to save it for the cooking. But Frau Tatt says she sells most of it under the counter."

Crusoe stood and drank his down in ten seconds, hoeing with the other hand. Auntie managed hers in the bent-over position, while the two younger women sat drinking theirs with one eye on the shed where they could see the 'Gaffer' using his to swig down the garlic he was munching. Within five minutes they were back at work, looking enviously at Wally and me, who had just started a quarter of an hour's smoke.

"Hey, Crusoe," shouted Wally. "Come over here."

Crusoe ran over like an obedient puppy, repeatedly glancing at the 'Gaffer's' shed. When he got to us, Wally said in a low voice:

"Show Rob your medal."

Crusoe looked sheepish and guilty.

"Come on, don't be bashful." He turned to me. "He's got an Iron Cross second class, dinkum."

Crusoe, looking round to see whether anyone was about, undid his shirtfront to show the medal dangling from a piece of string round his neck.

"Tell him how you got it," said Wally, and as the boy hesitated, "Never mind, I will". After making sure there was no one within earshot he went on: "He pinched the bloody thing from the barracks where the 'Gaffer' sent him with a load of seed potatoes. Cool nerve, eh? There was a hoo-hah that fizzled out:

there are plenty of spare Iron Crosses about. But, if he'd been caught, they might have shot him. Then you would have missed your chance of shooting a Russki, eh, Crusoe? Poor lad, he's very proud of it, aren't you?"

Crusoe retaliated, his face red but defiant.

"One day I shall wear it in the right place."

Wally chuckled.

"And never be able to sit down without screaming."

"How many Russians will you expect to kill first?" I asked.

"It doesn't matter," he answered after a pause. "The Russians are no better than pigs' offal. The only pity is that bullets cost money."

The 'Misery' gave Wally, myself and Crusoe our midday meal up at the house, which was rather like an English suburban semi-detached, except for the overhanging roof and triple-glazing, ready for the Austrian winter.

"We have set meals here," said Wally. "Today it's 'slaughterhouse sweepings', tomorrow it will be 'beans in putty' and 'opium pudding'."

The slaughterhouse sweepings certainly lived up to their name in looks but tasted reasonable and kept us going until we could get at our Red Cross parcels in the evening.

After a day or two I was finding the work hard, healthy, boring but just bearable, and feeling that, as a dental mechanic, I had been as near the top of the ladder as I ever would be. Friendly with everyone except the 'Misery', we still found the women a bit hesitant when it came to fraternising, with the main road only a few yards away and one or two Wehrmacht officers among the civilian customers. Away from the freedom of Shaffendorf we noticed a definite tension and automatically kept to ourselves most of the time. Crusoe the ardent patriot who would have died rather than shoot an Englishman or an Australian but could not wait to shoot a thousand communists, was our great companion. The 'Gaffer' was too busy keeping up his political image to come and breath his garlic fumes on us, except when giving us instructions.

Occasionally, especially if there was a glut of customers, Frau Gruber, the 'Gaffer's' wife, came down into the gardens to work, unlike the 'Misery' whose job it was to remain behind, do the cooking and think up new methods of making money or currying favour with her father-in-law by selling under-the-counter items to the right people. When Frau Gruber, a plump homely woman in her late forties would arrive, she would always be carrying something much too heavy for her, giving the impression that, like a worker bee, she would die if she was not busy.

"I bet she changed her own nappies when she was a baby," said Wally.

But there would always be a smile peeping from behind the endless bundles and baskets and a pleasant remark for Wally and me. Like Auntie, she was rarely to be seen upright when not carrying something and somehow managed to get her nose even nearer the ground. Wally had nicknamed her the 'Scratcher' after the hens which she loved; often crying when the 'Gaffer' would take one down the garden and chop off its head with an axe, leaving it to run around headless until it would topple over, twitching. When the 'Misery' wasn't busy concocting new ways of shrinking our stomachs and expanding her purse she was trying to get as near to any conversation as she could in order to be able to report the slightest anti-Nazi remark to the 'Gaffer', who had to pretend he was interested in order to keep up his image. Consequently, she was very unpopular with the three women workers, who called her 'Madame Gestapo'.

One morning, after I had been there for about a week, Wally got out a large flat hand-cart from the shed, loaded four six-foot potted palm trees, which he had first carefully dusted, onto it and said:

"O.K., cobber. let's go."

"Where?" I asked.

"Don't ask questions. Just move your arse!" He gave me a friendly kick. "If you want to know, we're going to make a beautiful friend of yours look even more desirable. Be careful going up the hills," he added. "If one of those bloody things falls over and breaks, you'll have to go to Istanbul to get another; though, come to think of it, even that might be better than this dump."

We trekked through the town, pulling the ludicrously wobbling plants. Every now and then Wally would say: "Steady! Eyes off the women!" as groups of civilians watched curiously. When we reached the kanzlei (town hall) we unloaded the palms and lugged them up a wide staircase to the conference hall where, in a moment, I saw the joke. Framed and well over life-size, the Fuhrer hung above the stage, painted in oils by an artist who must have found it difficult to stop his hand shaking, such were the stern lines he had created in the relentlessly obstinate face, under the almost life-like lock of carefully plastered hair. When I gazed at the array of swastika flags surrounding the picture I could well imagine the stirring notes of 'Deutschland uber Alles' ringing through the hall that evening as the Burgomeister, or somebody even more important, would rise to open the meeting. Underneath the great picture we arranged the palms, making sure that one large leaf covered the swastika on Hitler's armband and another the Iron Cross on his breast pocket. The job complete, Wally clicked his heels together, stretched out his arm in a Nazi salute and shouted, so loud that I thought I saw the famous Chaplin moustache twitch:

"Heil Shitler!"

Two days later we had the job of transporting these sad plants, which seemed to be drooping even more after so many hours under the Fuhrer's remorseless glare, to a large house, edging them through several narrow doorways and arranging them round the corpse of a prominent member of the 'Partei', who had died of a heart attack after eating too much at the town hall function and had, without so much as a murmur, been waiting for his Fuhrer to finish with them. Because the undertaker's barber was down with 'flu', this once proud leader, noted for his suave good looks, now had a growth of beard a quarter of an inch long and was still waiting for some unsqueamish person to shave him. Apart from that, he looked very peaceful and glad that his timely death would probably save some executioner a bit of trouble at the end of the war. When we finally got the plants back to the Gartnerei, they needed watering so badly, after all they had been through, that Garbi, the 'Gaffer's' dog, being very intelligent, cocked up his leg and piddled on them.

After carrying hundreds of cans of water, two at a time, from the stream at the bottom of the garden, and pouring them over various vegetables, or standing for hours with a hose-pipe and spraying the paprikas (green peppers), I decided that working in the garden was even more boring than building a road, and was usually relieved if somebody in the town died when I would sometimes be commissioned to make a wreath. The 'Gaffer' took on the costliest and those for the higher-ups in the 'Partei', Wally the second best and I the lower grade wreaths, mostly for the poor farmers. Crusoe, having to work twice as hard outside, hoped nobody would die, while we hoped as many as possible would. A not so interesting 'stint' imposed on us by the 'Gaffer', first making sure that we were in a position to be seen, was that of straightening out used nails, several hundred at a time; just another way of showing what a patriot he was, saving steel for armaments by using seconds. But usually it had to be raining before we were put onto this soul-killing job, while the 'Gaffer' would potter around, often in the rain, washing down garlic with pints of skimmed milk.

With the winter of 1943 approaching, in and out of the Gartnerei streamed a variety of people: young and old, male and female, fat and thin, Nazi and sensible. Sometimes, wandering about inside the greenhouses, they would try to avoid us, especially if the 'Gaffer' was around, scared to take the risk of appearing too friendly.

One in particular, unknown to me, was to shape my future. Her voice I had heard in the camp when I had been told to stay in bed with a mild dose of 'flu, the voice which had compared so melodiously with the bombastic bragging of the 'Buffoon'. Yet how different was this rather diminutive girl compared with the image I had formed of a tall, elegant business type. She was about five foot three, blonde and outstandingly pretty. She moved gracefully, dressed in a tight-fitting costume, and couldn't have been more than eighteen. Yet she had the unpretentiously confident look that went with her position. She it was who had probably got me into my present job — with the 'Buffoon' no doubt grabbing all the initiative for himself.

The 'Gaffer' had just said: "Guten Tag, Fraulein Bayer," accompanied by one of his blandest smiles, raising his hat and replacing it at an even jauntier angle. Carrying the flowers she had bought, she had left without looking in my direction.

As the winter tightened its grip the people began to rub their hands and wear thicker clothes, the weeks crawled by hitting us with ten-foot snowdrifts and temperatures so low that the farmers only lost the icicles hanging from their noses by sneezing. For the more patriotic, there was bad news from the Russian front.

On Christmas day 1942 we were locked in at seven o'clock with the few bottles of wine that the 'Buffoon' had allowed us officially to buy through the guards and a large pot of 'hooch', brewed, unknown to the 'Buffoon' or the guards, from Red Cross raisins and sugar — a deadly mixture that was to produce several semi-corpses. When they heard us apparently getting drunk on nothing, the guards crossed their fingers and kept their rifles at the ready in the guardroom, while we shouted toasts to "next Christmas" — which would be spent at home. Willis, the self-appointed leader and smoother-outer of 'incidents', stood sipping lemonade, his back to the false panel to stop the Aussies giving the whole show away by climbing up into the loft, letting themselves out through the window and dancing in the moonlight. The three 'inseparables', ever more determined to escape, at night, to Hungary, were to use this as their exit. Two setbacks had so far stopped them doing this; the lack of civilian clothes and workmen's passes for the railway. There seemed to be no way of beating this baffling problem until, by the middle of January, it unexpectedly began to work itself out. Discipline had been getting more lax; the 'Buffoon's' 'blitz' visits less frequent. Apart from being locked in at night we had become as free as the Poles and Ukrainians. In the mornings, Wally and I would leave in time to get to the Gartnerei by seven-thirty, spend most of the day in the greenhouses and sheds out of the snow and saunter back on our own at six-thirty in the evening following a route along the main road for a few hundred yards and then taking a short cut from the town to the camp, along a path passing between the fields, flanked by the few blacked-out houses and farms on the outskirts. The worst January on record had produced so much snow and ice that a narrow path had been shovelled out between two-foot solid white walls. Wally, after rubbing his nose with sandpaper, stuffing cotton wool up his nostrils and peeling an onion near his face, had managed to persuade the corporal that he had 'flu: consequently I was walking back alone on a dark evening, with solid black clouds scudding across the sky, occasionally letting through the light from the full moon and dazzling the countryside into detail for a few seconds at a time. When I reached the path I began to walk brusquely, hoping there would be no one to pose the problem of who should climb up the side first when, as one of the gaps in the clouds let through the moonlight, I saw a trim figure approaching. There was no mistaking who it belonged to. But why there... and at that time? It was dark when she reached me and stopped because, in that confined space, she had to.

"Good evening, Fraulein," I said breaking all the fraternization rules.

With the moon out again she was looking round to see if there was anyone about, but what I had half expected had not happened: she was in no way perturbed — merely cautious.

"Good evening," she answered.

Steeped in British tradition I forgot the main opening gambit of any conversation in a guaranteed cold climate is not always the weather.

"Very cold, isn't it?" I said, lamely.

Smiling, she waited for me to make way for her and knowing that the recognised way of dealing with women caught fraternizing, under such conditions, with P.O.W.s was to turn them over to the Gestapo who, among other more unpleasant things, would shave their heads down to the skin, I didn't blame her; but for some reason I knew I had to hang on.

"You have the right clothes for this sort of weather," I said, admiring the way she wore her fur coat and hat and Russian-style boots. "All you Austrians are wise and know how to keep yourselves warm. Do you often come out at night like this, Fraulein, in the cold? Wouldn't it be better to sit in some nice cosy room reading or listening to the wireless?"

The anti-British moon was shining persistently and again she was glancing round to see if there was anyone in sight; but the coast was clear. Looking at me, puzzled, she said:

"You are curious. Surely you know you ought not to be talking like this to an Austrian girl — alone and in the dark."

I went on to excuse myself:

"It's a bit dangerous for you, Fraulein, I know. My only excuse is that I haven't been able to thank you for getting me the job in the gardens. I'm sure you must have been responsible.

"Ah," she said, "you must be Stooart...Yes, I was. I really didn't know who you were, but I thought you might like a companion after being stuck with Herr Pfeffer. Anyway," she added. "above everything, let's hope you have forgotten you are working for the Nazis. At least three-quarters of the people here are non-Partei."

"I'm sorry," I said. "But we are fighting three countries — Germany, Austria and Italy. Three names, if you like. I never wanted to fight the people."

"Why don't you forget you are fighting anybody or anything?" she said. "Just work for yourself, to keep yourself healthy? Wouldn't that be better? Just keep watering Herr Gruber's tomatoes and, when they're big enough, I'll come and buy some."

Looking at the soft curve of her face in the moonlight I was finding it difficult to concentrate.

"And if they're not nice big tomatoes, you won't come back," I said absently.

"No, of course not, except to arrange for your transfer back to Herr Pfeffer!" she laughed. "Now, please, I must be going. I am on my way to see my aunt who lives over there."

She pointed out a little house, rather like a doll's house and just discernable, about a hundred yards way. "She is ill and my mother has given me some apples to take to her."

She took out a juicy looking red apple from the bag she was carrying and offered it to me: but I shook my head.

"No, that's very good of you but they're for your aunt. I couldn't accept it. But thank you."

"Do you ever get apples in the Gartnerei?"

"Apples?" I gasped. "Good heavens, no. I'm afraid they're definitely not on Frau Haunsel's menu."

"If I have to come past here again tomorrow evening I will bring some for you," she said. I was about to thank her but she went on: "There's just one thing. Please, be very careful not to tell anyone where you get them or let the guards see them. Now, you must be on your way back or they'll wonder what's happened to you. Goodnight," she said, and disappeared into the shadows.

As I watched her disappear into the darkness I felt that a new alliance had struck up between England and Austria, which could well be turning a few ears red in Berlin, and the sweet sense of danger had set my nerves tingling. If this bewitching lover of life wasn't one of us, the moon in the sky was a cake of soap.

I wasn't really expecting to see her the next evening. She would probably be embarrassed by the danger of keeping a rendezvous with an Englander, especially in her position, and had promised the apples in a rash moment. The moon in an absolutely clear sky was doing its best to warn her of the danger as well. Yet, of course, this meant the shadows were deeper and to my surprise, to prove I had been wrong, she was there, almost invisible and hidden in the recess of a high wooden fence.

"You thought I wouldn't come?" she greeted me, noticing how I started. "I would only have waited another minute or two. I think one of the Englishman's good points seems to be punctuality."

"At six-thirty sharp I down tools and I'm off."

I was looking down at her: she was really quite small, I thought, but her complexion in the moonlight was as smooth as the snow around her.

"Excuse me," I said, "but why should somebody like you bother about somebody like me? What of all the stories you hear about the Gestapo? You're taking a terrible risk, aren't you?"

"I don't think you get enough vitamin C," she said simply; but her answer didn't really convince me. "Here," she said, handing me the promised bag of apples.

Then she gave me a long searching look, as if summing me up. Would I keep my mouth shut? Then, she made up her mind quickly. With the next remark the curtain was lifted and I knew I had been right.

"Listen carefully," she said, "The Germans are being beaten back at Leningrad. We listen regularly to the news from London."

I needed no more convincing. From this Austrian girl's lips I had heard the best piece of news in the war so far. And she was obviously glad about it. She went on to give me more details. Three infantry divisions had been driven back over the river Luga and a division of heavy artillery withdrawn from Novgorod; a very distinguished general had been replaced and Goebbels was having a difficult time trying to persuade the Germans and Austrians that everything was all right. All this seemed to delight her, until she finally got to the part about the thousands of prisoners taken by the Russians.

"I'm sure half of them will die," she said sadly. "I'm terribly worried about ..." she hesitated. "But that's not your concern."

"No, but what is my concern," I said, "is why are you risking an important position, and perhaps torture and disgrace, for a British P.O.W.?"

"Of course, you must be wondering." She seemed apologetic, as if she had expected too much. "The real fact is I want to help you and your friends. And so does my mother. We began to think about it when we first saw you all arriving, scraggy and starved, nearly two years ago. My father is a Hungarian and hates the Nazis. He thinks Hitler is a usurper — a clever nonentity, and a madman. Without him there would never have been a war. He once worked in partnership with a Jew, a clever man and a great friend, until his partner disappeared and has not been seen since. To him, Austria is still the Austria of the Hapsburgs and the good old days of the Austro-Hungarian empire. We have always been pro-British and very, very anti-Bifki." She could see I was puzzled. "The 'Bifkis'? - Oh, they're the Germans — the arrogant, ignorant Prussians."

She went on to tell me about the rape of Austria - things that had never interested me. How little President Dolfuss had been murdered by the Nazis, and the next president, Schussnig, thrown into prison because he wanted a 'plebiscite' to see just how many Austrians would vote for Hitler.

"In my house are still the rips on the settee where the first 'liberating' Prussians flung their jackbooted feet, as if they owned us and our furniture."

"Yes, now I see", I said. "In England we had little knowledge of all these things. Too complacent, I suppose." The whole thing was becoming logical. "But you must hate the regime very much to be willing to risk so much for the British."

"Poor Austria," she said. "I'd take any risk for my once-free, once-great country."

"You are brave to do it," I said.

"Not all that brave. Perhaps a little too adventurous. And one other reason," she laughed. "We have so many apples we don't know what to do with them."

"You are the born optimist," I said. "Nothing will ever happen to you. You are sure of that, aren't you?"

"Of course! Now listen, I must go."

She gave me the apples and held out a gloved hand. When I held it, through the fingers seemed to come the message to throw care to the winds.

"May I see you again?" I asked. "Alone, I mean."

For a moment she hesitated.

"If I get some more news from the Russian front I will see you a week today at the same time. Don't forget, please, give them a surprise in the camp and tell them you got the apples from the Gartnerei. And, by the way, my name is Hildegard—Hilde for short."

I let go of her hand reluctantly. Thank you for the apples," I said, and she was gone.

CHAPTER NINE

Bringing Wally into my confidence — a 'must' — was a risk but, though his mouth was open most of the time, I was certain he could be trusted to keep it shut when I explained the circumstances. A week later he co-operated by going on ahead, leaving me to make my own way to the arranged rendezvous. In the shadows I stamped my feet and rubbed my hands together to keep warm, caressed by giant snow-flakes floating down like feathers from a dark grey ceiling of cloud. I waited until I had almost decided she wasn't coming and was about to go when I saw the dim outline of her figure coming quietly down the path. Obviously in a hurry, she said: "Now look. There's not much time. I can't tell you much, but I do know that you're going to learn something soon about a place in Russia called Stalingrad and it will be news you want to hear."

"However do you get this news?" I asked her. "I hear the German news sometimes and it's been quite optimistic lately — advances on the Russian front and so on."

"Simple," she said. "But a bit dangerous, that's all. We listen to London. It's a risk to get the truth, but it's the only way. Concentration camp, if you get found out." She sounded as matter-of-fact as ever.

"For God's sake be careful."

"All right." I knew she didn't really mean it. "You can tell the news to the others as long as you don't say where you get it."

Somebody was coming along the path and she went in a hurry, whispering:

"Quick! I will see you again."

As I strolled along, looking quite innocent, I said: "Gruss Gott" to the farmer's wife who passed. Though I had never seen her before, she knew me.

"Gruss Gott, Stooart," she answered to my surprise, and walked on quickly, showing how well known we were around these parts, surrounded by gossiping tongues.

Back at the camp I kept my news to myself, deciding to let it out when something definite happened in Russia. I knew now that I would see the extraordinary girl I had fallen madly in love with again and that she would keep me up-to-date, now that the war seemed to be turning our way. On the way to the Gartnerei the next day Wally said:

"Hey, cobber, what about this rendezvous of yours?. Can we go back together or have I got to keep out of your way?"

"As long as you keep your mouth shut we'll go back together," I said. "I don't think she'll mind. Anyway, I've no idea when she'll turn up."

After this we were back to normal, strolling back and keeping an eye on the track ahead, sometimes in the moonlight, sometimes in the pitch dark until, a few evenings later when the moon, down to the quarter, was softly discernable through the overhead mist, we met her. For a moment she hesitated and was about to go, when I stopped her.

"Wally's all right," I reassured her. "He may have a big mouth, like most Aussies, but he's discreet, like hardly any of them." I introduced him.

"I hadn't the faintest idea who you were when I chose you for the Gartnerei," she said. A motorcycle salesman wasn't necessarily going to be interested in plants but I took a chance. I'm very glad to meet you now. Perhaps I was right, because Herr Gruber is very pleased with you. Don't work any less hard because I told you," she laughed.

"Glad to hear it," said Wally. I only work for my health — not for the love of it, but if somebody's happy about it, that's all right with me. Nice to meet you. Now, I must be going ..."

"No, stop please," she interrupted. "You might as well hear the news. You will like it as much as Stooart will."

"Cripes! I don't know what we'd do without you, Fraulein. Dinkum!"

"All I can tell you at the moment is that a huge German

army has been surrounded at Stalingrad and that all attempts to get out have failed. The British news says a quarter of a million men are there and rapidly running out of supplies. It's terrible for the poor boys in those temperatures. So many of them are Austrians. But it's good for you."

"Praise the Herr Gott," Wally whispered reverently. "This is really something. O.K., I'm off; and thank you, Fraulein, but be careful."

As he disappeared she was already taking hold of my arm.

"After the last time, I made up my mind it was too dangerous here," she said. "Come on, we're going somewhere else."

She led me along the track and off at a tangent over untrodden snow.

"Won't they give the show away — the footprints, I mean."

"Not where we're going," she said. "Come on quickly."

After a while, more footprints joined ours from two other directions. As if reading my thoughts, she said:

"Don't worry, Bob. The nearest house is a quarter of a kilometre away, and anyway they're far too afraid of ghosts round these parts to come up here at night."

In a moment I knew why: she had opened the gate into the Protestant cemetery.

"There we are," she said, brushing the snow off one of the flat tombs. "What's wrong with this seat, apart from being a bit cold?"

"It'll make a change for the occupant," I said. "He must be dying of boredom."

Within minutes we were shivering uncontrollably while what was left of the moon was trying to light up probably the most decidedly unromantic scene in the whole of Europe at that moment. With my arm round her, I kissed the only part of her face not covered with furs, the tip of her nose, as she stroked the thick scarf wrapped round my head, whispering to it through chattering teeth. Though she was blue with cold, I still felt her warmth coming through to me.

"Hilde," I breathed. "I love you. You're so beautiful and so brave." And as she pulled me to her whispering "I love you too," a tiny part of the alliance between England and Austria, which a mad dictator had broken, was mended in this macabre enclosure where the sombre shadows of fifty headstones towered in their loneliness, silent friends that would never witness against us.

Three more times we met in the cemetery and, though Hilde seemed happy to go on like this, giving me the usual little bits of news and whispering into the scarf over my ear, I had had enough. At the end of the third meeting I said:

"Hilde, I could get to your house tonight."

Of course, she was totally astonished.

"That must be a joke, she said. "The uber-feldwehbel has always boasted how efficiently he has got you all locked up."

"That's what he says to you," I said. "But he's an idiot. There is a way out. Three of the fellows were going to use it for escaping but Wally and I have thought of a way of tricking the guards better than Ml5 could do it."

I told her about the concealed door onto the stairs and how we had thought of the idea of cutting through the bars on the lower floor, the obvious escape route, and still leaving a way out through the loft, which no one would ever suspect, for future escapees.

"But how are your men going to escape? They'll be recognised everywhere round here. They'll have to go as fast as they can to the border and get across somehow, and then thirty kilometres beyond, before they get out of the German clutches. Hungary is a pro-German satellite state, you know. And they must do all this before the morning's roll call."

We were both silent. While I was still thinking of the prospect of being with her in a warm room instead of a sub-zero cemetery, she had already hit on the most audacious plan so far.

"I can help," she said. Under all the fur I could see her eyes sparkling. "In fact, I WILL HELP. Leave it to me. Tomorrow I will meet you here for the last time. Perhaps it is getting a bit dangerous, anyway. I will bring a disguise for you and a plan of the route to my house, which you must memorize and burn. You must get everything into the camp without the guards seeing. On the first stormy night you must come to my house and meet my mother — not my father: he would be too worried — and listen to my plan. Then, if you agree with everything, you can tell your friends to be prepared to escape within a fortnight."

"You certainly seem to want to alter everybody's life for the better, Hilde," I said. "But you don't seem over-worried about your own. If they find out, you and your family will certainly be shot."

I might as well have sneezed, for all the notice she took.

The next night she brought a parcel with her.

"If you get caught with this we're for it." For the first time she seemed a little anxious.

"Trust me," I said, hoping my own anxiety didn't show.

It was fairly easy to smuggle the parcel into the camp and examine it without anyone noticing. The disguise was simple but effective — a leather jacket, blue beret, false moustache and a pair of spectacles with plain glass in them. In the blackout, it would be impossible to see that my trousers were khaki and with any luck I would look like the average nondescript worker — probably Polish.

I couldn't wait to put it to the test; but a week and a half went by before the weather was suitable: sub-zero temperature, windy with sleet blowing almost diagonally over the fields. Only an idiot (and I was one) was going to be out on a night like this.

Willis had had to be told; also the three escapees who were obviously going to keep their mouths shut in their own interest. Amongst our little group of six the excitement was intense. The three had waited so long that they were now prepared, without asking too many questions, to take any risk. Willis was happy about anything that would put one over the Germans, I was glad that something worthwhile was about to happen after nearly three years of non-achievement, and Wally was looking forward to doing his little bit; thankful not to be out of it. Gnawing at the back of my mind was the thought of the risk being taken by Hilde and her mother — even her father, who didn't know what was going on — but the intoxication of her vitality and enthusiasm to help us smothered any decision I might have made to finish the whole business and stop seeing her.

As the guards were in the habit of waking us at six-thirty lights in the camp, by everyone's agreement, were usually out by ten o'clock and by ten-thirty the majority were asleep. The resulting noise, like the approach of a tornado, made it easy to get to work in the other room, remove the false panel and, leaving Willis to replace it, disappear up the stairs into the loft at eleven-thirty, only six inches away from the corporal, whose bunk was the other side of the timber partition. The disguise outfit, which had taken the place of the straw in my pillow and which I had put on just before, had caused a laugh but at the same time a gasp of admiration, from the other two.

"A pig's arse looks more like a P.O.W. than you do," said Wally. "And better-looking."

"Mind what you say," I warned him, or I'll pull your bloody toe off when I get back!"

As his bunk was near the window he had agreed to have a piece of string tied to his big toe, with the other end hanging through the bars, to be pulled as a signal, so that he could get up and remove the panel again. In theory the whole thing was foolproof.

"Don't get back too late." he said. "I don't fancy doing all the bleedin' work myself tomorrow, while you trip over Crusoe with your eyes shut."

Up in the loft, alone and looking through the top window, I felt like the Prisoner of Zenda about to be thrown into the sea in a sack. The weather was so bad that I could hardly see the ground outside. But so far everything was going according to plan and with the rope Willis had stolen from his farm attached to a joist, and hanging through the window, at the other end of the building to the guardroom, it was quite simple to climb down and slip away, as far from the guards as possible, round by the hedge to the end of the field and over the fence, with the lashing sleet and the wind giving the feeling of comparative safety.

I had learnt the route to her house thoroughly before burning the plan ...Out along the path we usually took to the Gartnerei for two hundred yards; a sudden turn left along another path between ploughed fields; then a hundred yards along the main road (this would be the tricky part in good weather); between the high walls of farms each side of an eight foot wide lane; out into the open again; across a little footbridge over the stream which laughed its way to Shaffendorf; and around the edge of the town's football ground to her front gate. Though I had seen a few chinks of light shining through blacked-out windows, I hadn't seen a single person. Cold and wet but relieved that everything had gone so well, I walked quietly up the path to her front door, looked for the window of her room at the side and tapped gently on it three times. Within seconds the door opened two inches to show her face and the look of relief as she saw who it was. Quickly she pulled me through the door into the darkened passage.

"I just wouldn't dare let myself believe you would make it, in case something went wrong," she said excitedly. "But you have. It's wonderful. Mami and I have been sitting with our fingers crossed and couldn't even concentrate on the news from London."

Once the back door was closed, she put the light on in the hall and looked me up and down, laughing at my comical get-up and worrying about my wet clothes at the same time.

"Come and meet Mami."

She took me through the pleasantly decorated hall to the sitting room, opened the door and introduced me to the living image of herself, in another generation. Immediately, I liked her mother. There was nothing suspicious, no doubt or uncertainty in the look she gave me as she said:

"Gruss Gott, Stooart. Hilde has told me quite a lot about you. We wanted to give you the news but we were too anxious to take it in. But it is good, we know that. Hitler is being beaten on all fronts and we are glad. Austria will be free again unless..." Her face suddenly became grave. "The Russians, they will come here. The soldiers coming back say they are terrible - murderers and rapists."

"Perhaps the stories are exaggerated, Frau Bayer, like so many in wartime. I'm quite sure, for instance, the Germans never threw babies up and caught them on their bayonets in the first war, in Belgium. You mustn't believe too much: surely our allies can't be as bad as all that."

She looked relieved.

"Well, if you say so. Anyway, we must accept anything —

as long as it will bring an end to this pointless war. Now, you must be hungry." She gave me no chance to answer, slipping out into the kitchen and leaving the two of us together. Hilde wasted no time.

"I have got the escape all worked out," she said calmly. 'When you come here next I will give you the three disguises. They certainly won't look any funnier than yours. Please get that awful moustache off. Mami won't even know what you look like. She'll think I have terrible taste in Englishmen."

"What about Austrians?" I said, managing to tear off the black wad of hair in bits.

"Don't change the subject. And listen ... they must be ready to go tomorrow week. Do you think you can saw through the bars in that time? On that night there is going to be a small party at the barracks, a 'farewell' party for the C.O. who is retiring. You can imagine how old he is — even Hitler won't have him any more. Your 'stupid' uber-feldwehbel has asked me if he may take me and, of course, I have accepted. Sometime around midnight I shall get some of the officers there to drive me and one or two of the other girls to the border. It's always been a sort of tourist attraction. People go to see those big poles at the barrier being raised and lowered if they've got nothing better to do. In the meantime your friends will be hiding nearby. Everything will then depend on getting the guards talking to take their attention. I think I can do it. And while I'm doing it your friends will cut their way through the wire fifty yards further down, crawl through and go like mad."

She sensed what I was thinking.

"No, there are no dogs there yet. There are mines, so I have heard, but not laid too thickly, and your friends will have to take a chance. But mind, they must realise that the guards' rifles will be loaded and that they have been trained to shoot and never miss."

"God! What a risk you are taking. How can you do it? Suppose they get caught. You know what they'll do - torture them until they get the truth."

"If they obey instructions they won't get caught. Now listen, please don't tell Mami. It's going to worry her too much.

My father, I have told you, is very old. He is upstairs and doesn't know anything about you; but if he does see you, I can just say you are a Polish friend; and so will Mami."

Before I could raise any more objections Frau Bayer came in with a very large omelette, bread with a quarter of an inch of butter on it and a bottle of wine, and made me sit down and eat while she asked me questions about the camp and gave her opinion of Hitler and the way he had treated her country.

"Hilde is very cute," she said. "Cute enough to hold down a good job and yet hate the 'Partei' and everything to do with it. I remember so well the Duke of Windsor when he was the Prince of Wales, coming over here: how popular he was. Your Rudyard Kipling has stayed in a castle only fifteen kilometres away and I have seen Unity Mitford driving through the town in her little red sports car. But she's stupid: swept off her feet by a big talker who can charm women as easily as he can kill Jews. Why do some people worship Hitler? I can't understand it. Most of us are afraid of him, I suppose, but anyone with any sense knows he's led this country into war and is not to be worshipped for that. Herr Gruber, at the Gartnerei, is part of a circle of opportunists. I'm sure he is anti-Nazi at heart but he hasn't got the guts to do anything about it - not like Hilde."

"And you," I said. But she waved the remark aside.

"His vegetables are good: so who cares? Let him get on with it. I don't buy many from him because I grow my own. Last year my lettuce plants ..."

"Mami's a wonderful gardener," broke in Hilde. "And a big gas-bag, like Hitler."

By midnight I had finished my meal and between us we had drunk the bottle of wine. In my veins was the lingering challenge of danger. I could see Hilde felt the same: but amongst my secret thoughts was the ever-present warning of danger.

"You don't have to kill anyone to do something worthwhile in this war. But you don't have to take risks, either, you know," I said, making a last half-hearted effort to put a timely end to a mad adventure.

"You do if you believe in a principle and want to keep up your self-esteem," said Hilde, and her mother nodded approval.

It was one o'clock when her mother went to bed.

"Now, come and see my room," said Hilde. "But you must go soon."

She showed me into a small room: neat, tastefully furnished. A bed-settee, white dressing table of a French design, small armchair with embroidered cushions, flowered curtains: exactly the sort of room I would have expected; the predominant colour an eggshell blue, the lighting quietly soft.

"I bet you did this all yourself — thought it out and decorated it," I said.

"Yes, I did," she said. "Do you like it?"

"I love it. It is you — just beautiful you."

Looking around me, I felt dirty.

("Bloody fleas," I begged silently. "be good chaps and don't desert me now. We've been together so long. There's no place for you here. You're used to tough surroundings. For God's sake stick to the devil you know.")

She was looking at me as if she knew my thoughts.

"Don't bother about what you've become," she whispered. "Just be what you used to be — your real self."

Suddenly, the scent she was wearing was too much. The fleas were forgotten and had 'carte blanche' to hop where they liked — to bite anyone they liked after I had gone. For the first time they were no longer part of my life. The whole object of living had become the soft voice, like the ripple on a golden pond, the velvet of her skin, so eagerly accepting the touch of my blistered hands. The little room seemed to have become the Garden of Eden until the end of time.

But, lurking in the background was the serpent, in field-grey and jackboots, in the holster attached to his belt something even more deadly than a viper's tooth. The thought of the 'Buffoon's' stubble-covered face was trying to kill the romance as sure as sand kills a fire. And finally, as commonsense took over, we both knew that in the midst of this mad adventure was the speck of common sense we would have to hang onto if we were all to survive.

"You must go," she whispered, reluctantly pushing me away. "It's three o'clock. I'll keep my fingers crossed."

When she put the centre light on everything seemed different. The plan for the escape had suddenly become important again.

"You know all the instructions," she said. "You must come here exactly a week from today and take back the disguises, the passes to the border, the money for them to buy their railway tickets and a compass. Everything will be ready. I'll give you the final instructions then. In the meantime, you will have told the escapers everything — except who's behind it. That will be the great secret, which they must never know."

Outside the front door the night was pitch dark but the storm had died down and the wind had dropped. She brought my hat and jacket, which had been drying in the kitchen, and the few pieces of black hair, once a moustache, which I somehow stuck back on my face.

"If you see anyone just stand still — they'll think you're a scarecrow," she chuckled. "Now, whatever you do, be careful."

She put her arms around me. "I love you, mein liebling — I love you so much."

I went out into the black night, without the weather on my side, walking fast back the way I had come. Now was the danger. Anyone out at this time of night would look very suspicious. We knew about the policeman and his Alsatian: he might be anywhere, but neither of us dared speak about it. Silently, with the soft shoes that were part of the disguise making the going easier, I moved like a shadow as near the walls as possible along the main road and back between the fields, reaching the fence near the camp without seeing anyone. The silence of the dim white building gave me a curious feeling of security. Surely, if everything had been discovered, the guards would be out with their rifles: there would be voices, a light in the guardroom, a sensation of panic. I crept up to the window where the rope hung down from above it. The string was there at the corner of the frame — everything must be all right. I pulled it and waited, until I felt the slight tug as the faithful Wally answered back. Climbing the rope to the top window was simple: they hadn't left this out of our training. I crept through the loft and down the stairs, with the friendly, unsuspecting snores of the corporal only a foot away. Silently I greeted Wally, who had removed the panel. Nobody seemed to be awake in the other room and he was just managing to keep his eyes open.

"Everything's O.K., cobber" he yawned. "Get moving. I want to get back and finish off my dream."

"Thanks, Wally," I said. "I'll never say a nasty thing about you useless big-mouthed Aussies again!"

As I lay and drank the cup of tea I had brewed, I shuddered at the thought of what might have happened. But in the background was the little voice I had got so used to.

"Remember, you've got to be a fatalist. All the biggest idiots are fatalists, and think of the idiots who get away with it. Hitler, for instance... So far!" I added with slight misgivings.

A week later I and the uncomplaining Wally were all set for the next venture, this time in brilliant moonlight, after a day of more sleet. As I set off across the field I felt as if I was walking through a crowd, naked. All objects; trees, haystacks, fence posts stood out in detail, mocking me, asking me how I thought I would keep my luck. Desperately trying to escape from my shadow bobbing ahead along the path, I made for the shelter of the walls on the main road. And then, at eleven-thirty, when I hoped every farmer had gone to bed, and was rounding the corner near the little bridge, I came face to face with the last man on Earth I wanted to see. It was too late to hide. The time had come to put the disguise to the test and I walked on, head slightly lowered, cap pulled down over my eyes, waiting for the "Hallo, Stooart. What are you doing here?" But it didn't come. Though I had expected a farmer who might have recognised me, instead I was walking past an official-looking person wearing a 'Partei' badge.

"Heil Hitler!" It came across like a bullet.

There was nothing left but to bluff it out.

"Heil Hitler," I answered in the most matter of fact voice I could manage, showing unexpected respect for the Fuhrer who could have had me shot within the next five minutes. The official, dressed up in his light-coloured trench coat with wide lapels and trilby hat turned down at the back, seemed dissatisfied. The hairs at the nape of my neck told me he was looking back, hesitating. But, perhaps because he was in a hurry, he went on. As his footsteps died away I felt elated. If it was all going to be as easy as this, why worry? I got to her house feeling quite calm, even a bit blaze about it all, but it was not long before she had knocked this out of me. The instructions I was to give to the three escapees did that. But first they made me eat.

While Frau Bayer was still up she fussed and bothered around me, hurrying in and out of the kitchen with coffee followed by a liqueur. But soon, knowing how reluctant her daughter was to get her mixed up in the escape plans, she excused herself and went to bed. Hilde cleared the table and spread out a map.

"You've got to be really clever and remember a lot of things," she said, showing me the railway to the border marked from Kurstenfeld to Seltzen. "Your friends will get off here and walk down the road to here ..." and she pointed out the exact spot where they would cut through the wire. "I shall be here where the barriers are, but I might not be able to hold the guards for more than five minutes — so they must move."

She had put everything in a large box — workmen's' clothes, a duplicate map, compass, forged passes with the Polish names they would have to remember, wire-cutters; nothing had been forgotten.

"They've got to practise saying their names and also 'Seltzen'. 'Seltzen' will be important when they buy their tickets at the station. They must not get flustered but just remember that they are Polish workers going to Seltzen to work in the quarry for a day or two, if anyone asks them. Sometimes the Gestapo check everybody on the train — but usually only if they suspect that someone they are after is on it. So we must trust in our luck."

Time was getting short when I hurried back along the deserted route, and it was four o'clock before I was through the trap door. Wally, yawning, said he had been waiting for an hour, combating boredom by thinking out a completely do-it-yourself method for me to get away and back with no assistance; by fixing two nails on the inside of the panel and doing one or two modifications, which would make it possible to put it back in position from the inside.

"Now I'll be able to get some bleedin' sleep, so I can do your work for you at the gardens. I don't know how she puts up with it. She's far too nice to take up with a useless Pommie, like you. Come on, tell me what's on and when."

In spite of the way he spoke, I knew he was falling over himself to help three more useless 'Pommies' to escape.

By this time, everyone knew what was going to happen on Wednesday night. Without being aware of too many details they all knew how I was getting out and why and were waiting, but that was all. It had not been difficult to saw through two of the thick bars on the lower window, with the hacksaw Willis had managed to get, while the men collected their Red Cross 'konserven' from the guard room each night, as noisily as possible. A quarter of an inch of cutting every evening, carefully filling the gap made with boot black, would see the bars ready to be bent back by the Tuesday night; and though the guards, terrified of the 'Buffoon', conscientiously examined them before locking us in, they still didn't see the marks screaming at them, and trekked up to the loft carrying all our boots and trousers, which could all have been retrieved within five minutes.

On Wednesday, as the time approached nine-thirty, when normally the corporal and one of the guards would come in, count us and lock up, the tension grew. When there was still no sign of the guards at ten o'clock Willis sent Brummie in to ask for an aspirin for his imaginary toothache. When he came back he looked disgusted.

"The boogers are plyin' cards," he exclaimed. "Oi owp they'll shift their fat arses soon or oi'll gerra nervous broikdown."

The three escapees were getting jittery. While Jo kept looking at his watch and checking the equipment he had hidden under his bunk Roger chain-smoked and Arthur sat on his bunk muttering to himself: "Ich will ein Billet nach Seltzen kaufen." (I would like to buy a ticket to Seltzen.)

Hilde had decided that they would have to ask for their tickets in their own way, to allay suspicion, and not try to learn the correct German.

At two minutes past ten the corporal and a guard came in,

slightly drunk and luckily not in the mood to examine the bars too closely; counted us, took the boots and trousers from each man and started on their way out. Then, to everyone's disgust, at the door, the corporal turned and came back.

"Please," he said to Fred Bannister. "Can I beg a cigarette off you. We have smoked all ours — not one left."

Though Fred guessed the corporal had a few packets tucked away under his mattress, he couldn't refuse. Instead, he was forced to light the cigarette and carry on a conversation for another ten minutes, yawning all the time and hoping the hint would get home. When we eventually got rid of the corporal at ten forty, the clanging of the doors being shut was like sweet music. Big Tom, an Aussie fruit farmer from Swan Hill, Victoria, with arms as thick as young apple trees, was already bending back the two bars, his face purple with the effort, while Brummie watched fascinated, whispering "Fookinell!" His face was as white as a rabbit's underbelly. Every now and then he stared past the ceiling in the direction of heaven.

CHAPTER TEN

At eleven o'clock the lights were out and Arthur, the fattest of the three, was trying not to get stuck in the gap under the bent bars, with two men pushing him through and another holding a sock over his mouth to stifle his curses and moans, but once he was out the rest was simple — the equipment going through next, followed by Roger and Jo. Cautiously they tiptoed to the corner of the building and looked round it:

"Goodbye, lads, send you a postcard from Blighty," whispered Arthur, and they were creeping off towards the wall down the side of the field, as far away from the guardroom as possible. But through the window a dozen pairs of anxious eyes, staring at their dim receding figures, saw them suddenly stop dead in grotesque positions, a dark mass of shadows, frozen to the spot. Shattering the silence, the door of the guardroom had been thrown open, directing a brilliant shaft of light onto the wall only five yards in front of them. One of the guards, too lazy to go to the guards' latrine, had tottered away from the card game to say goodbye to a litre of good Burgenland wine in a long abandoned session against the wall. With a democratic freedom he let himself go both ends, frightening the nightlife with his thunder. His flies still open in his anxiety to get back to the card school, he hadn't noticed the unnatural quietness from our quarter or the three statuesque figures with their haversacks, poised like a tableau of the wise men carrying their gifts to Bethlehem. As he shut the door the light disappeared and so did the escapees and, with a general sigh of relief the rest of us got into our bunks hoping for sleep.

In the morning the fun was on. Naturally even the sleepy guards could not help seeing the gap, which we had done our best to make obvious, in the window. With a seismic crash they slammed and padlocked the doors again and, while one of them stood tensed and angry outside the window, the corporal rushed in mad anticipation and terror into the guardroom to telephone the 'Buffoon.' Taking advantage of the panic, some of the men went back to bed. Half an hour later no earthquake could have rocked the camp with more effect than the 'Buffoon's' furious bellow as he charged into the room like a bull full of pep tablets.

"'Raus!' Raus! Gehma! What do you think you're playing at? Get out of bloody bed. Line up outside. Schnell! Schnell!"

This was it then: I thought we were going to be shot. But not before they would find out the truth.

From nowhere appeared three majors and a colonel, all with hangovers from the party at the barracks the night before. While we waited on parade, stony-faced, Willis was ordered into the guardroom where he was questioned for half an hour. But he had prepared for this and, acting dumb, created an even more convincing impression of the decadent enemy than the officers already had, giving nothing away. In fact, he asserted, he had not had the faintest idea that anyone was going to escape or had escaped until that morning when the guards had woken him up; adding convincingly:

"I'm a little disappointed that my comrades don't trust me, and am considering resigning my position."

Once out on parade we were told we would be shot if we lied, but all managed to appear as surprised as he was. The 'Buffoon' had lost his arrogance and slunk here and there like a spaniel which had messed in a corner. In his eyes was the mad stare of most malingerers threatened with the dreaded 'Russian front'. The colonel made angry remarks to the 'Buffoon' who passed them on to us, trying to cut down his voice from an agonised scream to an unemotional statement of fact.

"The Herr Oberst (Colonel) says that you will all be sent to the coal mines in Poland unless you open your bloody mouths and tell us more."

So they had decided not to shoot us.

It was an empty threat and we knew it: we were far too useful here in Burgenland. And, guessing that the colonel needed to get back to the barracks and drink black coffee, we stood our ground.

"This whole unfortunate business will be dealt with later," the colonel shouted and, turning to the 'Buffoon', whose face was still as grey as his creased and sad-looking uniform: "Uber-Feldwehbel, you will report to me at twelve o'clock sharp. In the meantime send the men to work...(It was no good saying, 'with the guards': there were not enough of them and he knew it but he had to make his parting thrust.)Your friends will be caught. They have not got a chance. And when they are caught they will talk. The Gestapo have many 'refined' ways of making people talk. Yes...It will be sad for them to be in the Gestapo's hands and not in ours."

We could detect the slight scorn. The hatred of the Wehrmacht for the Gestapo was common knowledge.

For the next three weeks, when the frozen snow squealed under the weight of the guards' jackboots at night, as they yawned their way backwards and forwards outside our window, I lay low: there was no possibility of leaving the camp. The 'Buffoon' had gone, as we knew he would, replaced by a more intelligent feldwehbel, whose valour at the front had lost him an arm, who knew he could not be sent back to Russia and who showed his appreciation by allowing the guards to have a good rest at night. As long as our work was satisfactory he didn't worry; no more questions were asked and everyday life was back to normal. As the colonel didn't come back to say "I told you so" we guessed that Roger, Jo and Arthur had made it. When we heard snatches of news, now slightly pessimistic, coming over the guardroom wireless, it was difficult not to give the guards the true details, which I was again bringing back from Hilde and her mother. Some of the farmers and civilians must have known the facts but the threats of the Gestapo kept their mouths sealed. Then, at last, Berlin had to announce that at Stalingrad the German armies had suffered a very grave setback.

For us, hearing this actually coming over the German network was like crawling out from under a cold dark stone into the sunlight.

When a group of officers escaped from an oflag in

Germany, we didn't know they had nearly all been caught and executed. There were certain atrocities, like the extermination of the Jews, which nobody ever heard about; but in a day or two we understood that the Fuhrer had decided to let us know exactly where we stood, by means of a four foot poster, pinned to the camp wall and leaving absolutely nothing to the imagination. Under the six inch swastika the heavy red and black type screamed the message, specially for us, from the Fuhrer himself ... All guards throughout the Reich or any country in Europe under German occupation, together with all members of the civilian police and Volksturm (Home Guard) had been ordered to shoot any prisoner or suspected person — seen outside a prisoner of war compound between the hours of dusk and dawn — who did not immediately answer their challenge, raise his hands and give himself up.

The situation now was not merely dangerous, but suicidal. How could I possibly go to the house again? It was out of the question. But the threatening poster had not been in Frau Bayer's sitting room, and, true to form Hilde visited the Gartnerei a fortnight later, managing to leave a note in a geranium pot at the end of the row I was watering.

THE RUSSIANS ARE GETTING NEARER, BUT YOU SEEM TO BE GETTING FURTHER AWAY. COME AND SEE ME.

With Hitler's reminder shouting at me from the wall in the camp I still hung on, until one night when the moon was well behind a solid bank of cloud I gave in. I had to see her again, and I knew she wanted to see me too.

Wally already knew about the note.

"You crazy Pommie bastard," he said. "If you're dead the next time I see you don't say I didn't warn you!"

As it happened, of all the nights this was the wrong one. I had pushed a great coat and one or two bulky objects under my blanket, working the whole lot into the shape of a sleeping person, and had spent a tense five minutes carefully removing the false panel two feet from the corporal's ear, replacing it from the other side and blessing his vibrating snores. Then I had lowered myself down from the window where I had left the rope dangling against the wall and, with the usual plain glass spectacles, slouchy jacket and soft-brimmed hat pulled well down over my eyes, was gliding quietly along the path between the fields. It was too late to turn back when the moon left the cloudbank and I recognised the two dark shapes ahead on the path, one with two legs the other with four. With no warning the great black hulk of the playfully murderous Alsatian leapt at me. Though it had been taught not to tear a man's gizzard out until it had been given permission, the look in its hungry black and yellow eyes showed how loath it was to stick to its training. As it stood as tall as me, propping itself with its hard-as-leather paws against my chest, its red tongue hung out and its fishy breath blew smack in my face.

My brain had stopped working and the rest of me had turned to jelly. But the fact that the policeman was reeling from too much schnapps gave me just enough time to pull myself together and, with idiotic nonchalance, I patted the dog and smiled like a good dog-lover at its dripping jaws. The curious noise which came from the throat of the policeman, floating its way to the dog on a blanket of alcoholic fumes, could have been, as far as I was concerned, either "tear out his jugular" or "get down". Luckily the dog seemed to know and contented itself by running round me in circles, sniffing at my legs and licking my boots in anticipation of what might be a fleshier meal later on. The policeman stared with beery eyes, looking at me fixedly as if not sure whether I was there at all.

"What are you doing out so late at night?" he asked, when he had decided what sort of an object I was. Because I had persuaded myself that it would never happen, I had not bothered to rehearse an answer — probably a good thing: If I had learnt something off by heart it might have sounded too obvious. As it was, I mumbled the first thing that came into my head. The dog had stopped its antics and was studying my leg. If it were not allowed to bite it, it would at least use it as a lamp post. I was quite prepared for anything it might do: better a living urinal than a dead hero.

"I am on my way to Neubauer's." All I could think of was the name on the tomb Hilde and I had sat on in the cemetery.

Who he was, where he had lived or what he had done I didn't know.

"Ach, so!" said the policeman. "On your way to your farmer, eh? (Luckily for me he had thought I had said to 'mein Bauer'— which meant —'my farmer!'). "You know it is very late. Where have you been?"

Though semi-mesmerised by the dog that was lying down with its wet nose on my toe, now waiting for permission to eat it, I had managed an amateurish lie.

The policeman swayed deep in thought his hand on his forehead debating whether to go to the trouble of locking me up or to tell the dog to drag him back to the police station without me. But, however conscientious he might have been normally, this time his lazy nature got the better of him.

"Gehma! Gehma! Schnell !" he croaked. "Get back to your farm and don't let me ever catch you out at night again. You Polish workers get treated like bloody lords."

Without another word he lurched off down the path, pulled along by the dog, intent on sinking its teeth into someone's throat before the night was out, and leaving me staring up at the stars and wondering how long my extraordinary luck could last. But Satan had one card left up his sleeve to complete the night's entertainment.

Hilde managed to get the blood flowing back to my cheeks with two bowls of soup and I was just sitting down to listen to the news from London when her mother came in from the hall.

"Quick!" she said. "It's snowing. You must go."

Our worst enemy — the snow. Within two minutes I was out through the back door and hurrying back towards the camp whispering, "Keep snowing. Keep snowing." Within ten minutes, I was back through the window, with the snow still floating down, obliterating the footprints, and reading the note pinned to the shape under the blanket.

WELCOME HOME. BE CAREFUL HOW YOU TREAT
THE FELLOW IN THIS BUNK. HE'S NOT AS
HEALTHY AS HE LOOKS!

How did they expect me to work out a cryptic message like this at that time in the morning? I watched the snow from my bunk near the window, finally going to sleep with the effort. Four hours later, I was woken by a loud whisper six inches from my head.

"Are you feeling better?"

I was looking straight into the anxious eyes of the corporal. Behind him as a hazy vision I could see Willis signalling frantically for me to say "No".

"Not very much," I said.

"Then you had better stay in bed today," said the corporal.

"What was all that about?" I said to Willis when the corporal had gone.

"Christ! The stars are shining for you," he said. "They must have told the hauptmann to be more efficient because he ordered a 'blitz' inspection last night for two o'clock. Luckily he didn't turn up himself or he would certainly have commanded all that load of crap under your blanket to jump out and line up with the rest. The corporal asked me what was wrong with you; so I told him you'd got a severe chill from standing in the piss bucket to cure your chilblains.

'Leave him alone', I said, 'and the blighter might be better in the morning'. I had a hell of a job to stop him feeling your pulse; especially when he said he couldn't hear you breathing."

"What do I do now?" I asked after recovering from the shock.

"Stay in bed 'til the evening, sport; then make a miraculous recovery."

And so I did. In fact, I was so well again by the next morning that I couldn't even use the 'sick' excuse to delay what fate had in store. When I was just about to leave the camp with Wally, one of the guards stopped me.

"You! The corporal wants to see you."

In spite of the friendly, unflustered atmosphere in those days you never quite got rid of the feeling that you might only have a short time to live. Death seemed to be like a rheumatism that might crop up at any time, given the right circumstances: and on this occasion there was nothing to reassure me.

"Get your things ready. You are going to the main camp." My heart sank.

"Why? For how long? Am I coming back?"

"I don't know."

I believed his innocent expression, and shuddered at the thought of what might be the real truth. In that bleak moment of uncertainty I knew the Gestapo had found out and were onto us. Hilde and her parents were probably already in custody. In the pit of my stomach there was a corkscrew — twisting.

Even if I had felt like enjoying the magically beautiful mountain scenery around Wolfsberg it would have been difficult, without continually staring past the grim profile of the silent guard I had been landed with — an unsympathetically aloof stranger. At various points along the route we picked up other unfortunates: Allied, French, Poles — soon all sitting separately with their guards; forbidden to talk and looking either dazed, resigned or scared. At least, I had something definite to be scared about.

If I had done a stretch in the glasshouse military prison at Aldershot, I might have been prepared for the 'Disciplinaire' section of stalag XVIIIA. As it was, in total ignorance I was plunged into the midst of a crowd of deliberate or accidental criminals; arguing, cursing, fighting, queuing up around one small stove; lousy, noisy, blustering, shy and introvert — all mixed together in a separate thickly barb-wired open area. There was one consolation: I got no food whatsoever, which showed that I was a short-term visitor. After a sleepless night surrounded by snores and gastronomic thunder, I was ordered to sit on a long bench in a passage opposite the door into the office of a major in the German Intelligence Corps— together with three or four others, all as ignorant of the reason why they were there as I was, apart from one French P.O.W. who had been caught with an Austrian fraulein while trying to escape to Switzerland.

"What do you reckon is going to happen to you?" I asked him in German.

"Nothing much," he said with an air of innocent satisfaction.

"What about the girl?"

"Trudi?" Putting his finger against his throat he drew it slowly across. "It's the end of her, I'm afraid. The Gestapo don't mince matters. Never mind, it was good while it lasted." His grin did nothing towards improving my impression of the French.

"Cretin!" I muttered, remembering the word was French.

At that moment the door opened and he was beckoned in.

When he came out half an hour later he looked crestfallen and avoided looking at me as he was led away to whatever the Germans had in store for him.

I hardly noticed the others going in and coming out and not particularly concerned about their troubles I sat making up my mind to keep my mouth shut at all costs: trying to get rid of unpleasant memories of films and books about the primitive tortures used by the Gestapo. Towards the end of the morning my turn came. The expression on the face of the major opposite me, behind the desk, as I stood rigidly to attention, was ambiguous. He might have been going to tell me, with regret, that my execution had been fixed for the next morning or he might have been about to say that I was being sent home on a prisoner-exchange scheme. Though he was tall and smart there seemed to be something lacking until I realised that he was the first German officer I had seen without an Iron Cross. On the almost bare table in front of him was a thin file. In that file, I thought, desperately, was the key to possibly several lives and, looking at it from a distance I wondered for a moment whether I should ever have been born. The major fixed a monocle in position and stared at me with his one natural eyeball, but, just as he was about to say something, there was a knock at the door.

"Herein!" he called briskly to the orderly outside, who came in and saluted.

"The colonel would like to have a word with you in his office straightaway, Herr Maior (Mr. Major)."

The heaven-sent opportunity.

The room was empty - the file there to be looked at. To move round the table was too risky. The only thing to do was to lean over, open it and read it upside down. Seconds later there were footsteps in the passage, the door, left half ajar, had been pushed open, the major was halfway across the room and I was standing where he had left me, at obedient attention — but wiser by two words, 'PFEFFER' and 'KONSERVEN' — two little words which, in a flash, had been laughing at me, soothing my ruffled nerves. I knew now why I was there. Herr Pfeffer and the Red Cross parcels. A prominent member of the N.S.K.K. accepting konserven from a British P.O.W.: by German standards — unforgivable. I could imagine him ... Privaat Pfeffer at the Russian front, trudging through the snow, a frozen dew drop on the end of his nose, muttering:

"To hell with the Fatherland, bloody sauerkraut and gnodls! DAMN HITLER, AND ALL HIS WORKS!"

Silly devil, I thought. Surely he should have known better. He must have been storing the stuff in his pantry, and what more likely than an act of revenge from the banished girlfriend. I hardly heard what the major was saying when he asked for my excuses.

"Yes, Herr Major," I said. "I gave Herr Pfeffer a few tins of konserven. He had been a reasonable enough boss before he went a bit peculiar. I didn't see much harm in the whole thing."

I thought it better not to ask why they had gone to the trouble of bringing me all the way from Kurstenfeld to answer a couple of questions. As far as I was concerned I had had two days off work and an experience of relief, which I should never forget. As I had proved that even a 'sehreiber' could have his uses, I was fairly sure nothing would happen to me.

The next day, I was taken back by a much more talkative guard, who seemed proud to act as guide to the Austrian countryside; the only P.O.W. in a train full of civilians, mostly curious to find out who I was, where I had been and where I was going; and trying to get the answers out of the guard, not me, without much success. Back at the camp the other P.O.W.s, soon tired of listening to my stories, reverting to playing cards and arguing like old women, until the whole episode was forgotten.

With the fishy smell of the Alsatian's breath still in my nostrils, I waited for the next stormy night before venturing out. When I saw Hilde and told her what had happened, at first she showed no sign of worrying about herself.

"But if the Gestapo gets you," I said. "What then?"

To my surprise at last she showed that, underneath the optimistic exterior, she knew the danger.

"All right. It would be very unpleasant indeed," she said. "But we have got away with it so far, so why turn back now?"

"The war is nearly over," I said. "All the more reason why we've got to be careful. This last little episode has woken me up a bit. The Russians are already at the Platten See in Hungary. According to the news from London, Hitler has decided to defend the area with Rumanians, and you can't tell me the Rumanians are tumbling over themselves to die for the Fatherland. The Russians are coming through soon. The British and Americans are advancing from the west..."

"One thing is certain," she said. "Berlin won't consider leaving the P.O.W.s in Austria."

"Then somehow I shall have to lie low and wait for the Russians to come in."

"But why not try to escape to the British lines, when they are nearer?" she said. "Why the Russians always? Why do you think the damned Russians are so marvellous?"

"The Russians are our allies. I don't know whether they are marvellous, but they certainly can't be such a bad crowd. They've got guts. And anyway, any nation which produces a Tchaikovsky and a Borodin can't be bad."

"Tchaikovsky and Borodin didn't have their houses burnt down. The Russians are doing what was done to them."

"Propaganda."

"So you think it's propaganda. I thought the English were more intelligent. You don't believe the stories of the soldiers coming back from the front — the stories of how the Russians behave every time they move into another town or village. Why should our boys lie to us?"

"I think they exaggerate. I absolutely promise you will be perfectly safe if there's an Englishman around."

"An Englishman around? You're determined to escape into the arms of your red comrades, then?"

"Only to be near you," I said.

There was no way of telling what she thought. Her roots were in Austria. But in that moment I knew that as long as she wanted me I could never leave her. As for the Russians, for some reason I was convinced that any nation fighting beside the allies must be a pretty good one. At the time, as the Russians were my friends, I didn't want to know much about their seamy side.

I decided to play safe and leave it for a while before the next visit. We knew how much could happen in that time, and promising to let me know if there were any developments, she told me to look out for her in the Gartnerei.

"Whatever is going to happen, I shall probably know before-hand because of the necessity of distributing the remaining labour round here. Somehow I will give you the details but, in the meantime, lie low for a week."

As I left, the vibrations of danger lingered in the kiss she gave me. With the Germans losing, apprehension and insecurity hung over us like a menacing shadow. The snow had gone, leaving the ground wet and slushy as the spring of 1945 drew nearer. With its approach came the relentless air raids on Graz and Vienna, rattling the glass in the greenhouse from a distance of sixty kilometres and scaring the workers. Over Kurdstenfeld, flew the formations of American bombers from Italy, filling Wally and me with a sense of triumph as we stopped work to watch, first them and then the faces of the 'Gaffer' and Crusoe, grim and at last resigned to ultimate defeat. Day after day the massive planes roared their encouragement, flying ever lower as Germany ran out of fighters and fuel. When one bomber was shot down we sadly watched the nine white parachutes, and waited for the other two which never appeared, as the plane with its crew of eleven, slowly dropped lower, black smoke pouring from its tail. Seconds later the air was split by the fury of two fighters tearing low just above the town — the Hungarian Messerschmidt which had shot down the bomber chased by an American Marauder ripping it to pieces with thousands of rounds of ammunition. Cowering under the rain of empty cartridge cases that cracked the glass where they fell, the women looked across helplessly at us, as if it was our fault.

`"A pity it isn't Russian!" was all that Crusoe could say, while the 'Gaffer's' jaws worked harder, chewing an extra ration of garlic to steady his nerves and prepare him for the explosion as the Messerschmidt hit a field outside the town.

In the middle of this new and final development of the war Hilde arrived, and I knew instinctively something was wrong. But I wasn't prepared for what I read in the note she left, in a pre-arranged spot, tucked away behind one of the plants in the greenhouse:

KEEP AWAY. THE HOUSE IS BEING WATCHED.

No message could have been more final. There was only one consolation: they might not arrest her without proof. Somehow she had been able to find out in time — perhaps just in time. I had paid my last visit to the house and yet felt instinctively that this was not the end. The Russian guns would soon be heard in the distance: the war must be drawing to its close and we all knew that, at any minute of any day, we would be told to pack our things and be ready to go... unless, of course they had decided to shoot us.

"They won't know it's you," said Wally. "But don't worry, cobber. They'll be keeping tabs on her."

Yet, within a week she was back again, carefully concealing another note where only I would see it. Five minutes later I was behind the shed, reading it...

"The camp is being closed down next Thursday. At 1 p.m. you will be taken away in the direction of Dreisdorf. You will spend the night somewhere in that vicinity. PLEASE try to get away. We have room for you, and one other, at my grandmother's farm in Mattesdorf. No 38. It will not be far from where you are. Follow the little stream called the Vaalt that runs through the village. At 3a.m. on Saturday I will meet you in the orchard above the farm. Take great care and LOOK OUT FOR THE VOLKSTURM. I know it will be difficult to find your way, but you will. We will hide you until the Russians arrive. Then...Who knows!"

CHAPTER ELEVEN

After I had memorised her instructions, I burnt the letter and dropped the ashes in the latrine bucket. Then I climbed into my bunk and spent the next hour reciting the names and times over and over again until, unable to sleep, I lay on my back staring at the ceiling and began the long wait for Thursday.

As I had decided to tell nobody except Wally about the 'close down' I had to look as surprised as the rest when Brummie ran in from the guardroom shouting:

'Ey, fellers! Gerroff yer arses. We're gowin."

We had the morning to get our belongings into bags and haversacks, together with as many konserven as we could manage. At one o'clock by the agitated corporal's watch we set out, sandwiched between loaded rifles at the ready with bayonets glistening in the sunlight, turning off the main road through the woods with the eyes of the jittery guards darting everywhere as if the squirrels might be Russian spies. As we left the town the farmers showed complete surprise but were fobbed off with shrugs when they tried to get information from the guards. The slow awakening of fear showed itself on some of their faces as the only friendly link between them and the dreaded Russians headed away up the road and off along one of the paths through the fields. We soon found out why Fleisinger, a new guard who had only joined us a week before, was looking so cheerful when he told us that he actually came from the village that would be our first stop.

"I have only been away from my dear wife for a few days," he said. "And now I can see her again. She has been running the farm on her own. She will have something good to eat for me: you will see."

True to his promise, when we arrived at the village his wife came out to meet him carrying a large dish of gnodls, which he swallowed together with most of the stones, standing up hugging and kissing the fat woman between mouthfuls, his hands straying up her leg and under her skirt while she giggled and talked to one of the neighbours about the turnip harvest. While we sat and ate konserven he caressed his wife amicably, flinging coarse remarks every now and then to us as we cheered him on. When it was time to go, he proved to be a very good comedian as well; bursting into tears, smothering his wife with kisses and wailing so loudly that he set the dogs off barking at the other end of the village, while the corporal tried to drag him away. For a hundred yards he walked backwards up the hill, tripping over his heels, keeping up the wailing and drying his eyes and nose on his jacket sleeve until, once over the top and out of sight he changed like a chameleon, whistling and singing as if he had never seen the strings of a woman's apron. We travelled by short cuts through the woods away from the roads for another twenty kilometres, arriving in the evening at the village of Dreisdorf, as Hilde had promised in her letter. Somewhere near here would be, hopefully, the chance to escape. As we passed through the village, we were gazed at by friendly people who had never seen an Allied prisoner but were waiting secretly for the allied victory. Soon we reached the main road, where we were ordered to get into single file, keeping to the side while the retreating Wehrmacht thundered past in an endless procession of tanks, guns, infantry trucks, carriers, armoured cars — all the disorganised debris of an army in full retreat. Then, after an hour, the guards swung us suddenly off the road into a large farmyard, dominated by a towering red brick barn with a tiled roof. It was still too light to think of escaping and, at the sight of a contingent of Wehrmacht infantry gathered near the farm building, my heart sank. How was I going to get out when the nearness of the Russian armies was putting every German soldier on his guard and keeping him ever more vigilant? How could a man, unless he was invisible, get past the machine gun emplacement that they were already beginning to set up for the night?

When it became clear that we had landed in the middle of a line of defence, the whole project of escape seemed doomed to failure. But it had not been Hilde's fault: how could she have known, when all she'd been able to find out had been the time and place? Where they were going to put us was obvious: the great barn with its powerful oak doors seemed built for the job and as sound as Fort Knox. Surrounded by German soldiers, we were allowed to wash under the same tap with them and, before long, were finding out how pathetically confident they still were in ultimate victory. Speaking with no particular malice, they repeated the optimistic jargon we had grown used to. The Fuhrer had secret weapons: his enemies, including the Russians, were walking into a trap — a web he had spun to catch them. Why hadn't the British joined with the Germans against the Russians?

Whether they believed what they said was difficult to guess at but, not really worried about this, I was still trying to assess the possibilities of escape. When a shroud of misty darkness began to spread itself over the turbulent scene outside, I was foolish enough to think that escape might be easy and still quite optimistic, after the guards had taken us inside the barn and carefully counted us. The corporal seemed confident that the barn was secure, as he slammed and bolted the big oak doors, but the moon had been behind a cloudbank and the chink between the two loose tiles high up above the rafters hadn't shown. It didn't take long to climb up and discover that the tiles could be pushed apart enough for a man to get through. When I climbed down again, I looked hopefully at the hole I had made.

"I'll be through there later," I said to no one in particular. "Who's coming with me?"

"You must be daft, cocker," said Fred Bannister. "With bloody war nigh over, who wants to stick 'ead through 'ole and get t' bloody ting blown off?"

"Bob does," said Wally, pretending to know nothing about the plan. "With what he's got in it, it's no good to him anyway."

Some of the others laughed their approval, glad that they were about to get rid of a potential troublemaker. So for the present, as no one seemed keen to go with me, there was nothing to do but lie on a pile of straw and stare out at the sky through the hole in the roof, fighting against a creeping doubt as the moon gradually rose above the mist and cloud.

Though it was some consolation to realise that the hole was at the opposite end of the building to the machine-gun emplacement, I knew our guards would be outside and to be contended with, even if the retreating Wehrmacht, rolling past nose to tail, might prove helpful; preventing the possibility of being heard and commanding the attention of the machine gunners. As, one by one, the men stopped talking and went off to sleep, most of them convinced that decision to escape had been 'big talk', I was getting used to the idea of 'going it alone' when Jerry Hayle joined me.

"I'm coming with you," he said. "It's a piece of cake: all we've got to do is wait a couple of hours, get out of that bloody hole, and run like mad."

"I hope it's as easy as that," I said. "O.K., I'm glad you're coming."

I had always liked Jerry and was quite happy to have him with me. After a few whispered words we decided to take absolutely nothing with us except a lot of hope and a full stomach and, with this in mind, began to eat all the Red Cross food we could manage. After this we lay still, waiting for zero hour, which we had decided would be 3 a.m.

Exactly on the dot Jerry said, "O.K. Let's go!" and within seconds hoisted himself up over the rafters and was crawling above the snoring men and sticking his head, three parts covered by a balaclava, very slowly out into the moonlight. I climbed after him, onto the steeply sloping roof. The moon, now a brilliant white shape casting eerie shadows, was looking down at us amazed, as we sat absolutely still and stupidly conspicuous, searching furtively for the guards.

"If you want to hide your money, stick it on the ceiling," Jerry said, encouragingly.

He was right. Twice the two guards (without the corporal, whose snores were probably competing somewhere with the noise of the traffic) passed underneath us without looking up; Fleisinger moaning about his nagging wife, the other yawning with boredom. After the second time, as they disappeared round the corner of the building, I looked at my watch: a minute and a half went by before they appeared again. So we had a minute and a half to slide down the roof and get away. I waited for them to get out of sight once more before pulling Jerry's sleeve and shouting, "NOW!"...above the noise of the traffic. Then, taking a few more tiles with me, I clattered down, followed by Jerry tumbling sideways like a crab. Quickly we crept along the wall to the far corner and peered round at the backs of the two machine-gunners, only eight yards away, covering the road. The moon showed the second-hand on my watch clearly: ten more seconds to get out of sight.

"Come on!" I shouted, and we ran out towards the road, five yards in front of the machine-gun, with the traffic lumbering past just ahead of us, stopping the men from shooting.

Well-shielded, we raced between the back of one blacked-out truck and the front of another. Just able to hear the excited shouts of the Germans, we were halfway across a field and heading for the outline of the woods before they had time to get through the traffic, aim and fire.

"Look out, there's a ditch here," shouted Jerry over his shoulder, unable to stop himself falling in and sinking up to his waist in the slimy water.

With the energy that comes from stark terror I leapt over the gap where the water lay, grabbing hold of the root of a tree on the other bank and hauling myself out. By now the flashes from the rifle barrels were only a few yards away and, catching hold of Jerry's arm, I pulled him up the bank and ran ahead of him into the trees and out of sight.

"Christ! Those goons are rotten shots. If they're all like that no wonder the Ruskis are winning," he gasped with a great show of bravado when the firing had stopped and we could just see the two dim figures running back over the field. "I think they got scared without Mother Corporal to tell them what to do."

"Don't talk too soon," I said, quaking. "They might have gone back to collect the whole bloody contingent."

The scene outside the trees was flooded in moonlight and it was possible to see all the details of the traffic still only three hundred yards away.

"Let's get moving," I gasped. "It'll be safer in amongst the trees.

In the woods the feeling of comparative safety was preventing us from keeping as alert as we should have been and within minutes we nearly walked into the middle of a group of men from a Panzer regiment lolling around one of their tanks in a clearing, eating from dixies full of some concoction from their field kitchen and apparently more interested in their stomachs than the approaching Russians. Thoroughly scared, we crouched down behind the bushes about fifty yards away and waited. After a few minutes, we crawled back slowly and stopped at a safe distance, holding our breath and listening for Germans following. Everywhere was silence except for the gentle rustle of the leaves and we settled down to review the situation. Suddenly we realised that the night had grown quite dark and that we were being slowly saturated by a tormenting, soaking drizzle.

We're bloody fools," said Jerry, handing me one of his five Goldflakes. "Think of those bastards asleep in the straw."

"Better not to think about them," I said. "They may not be so lucky later. Keep the butt ends: we might need them."

After we had been searching for the stream, which would hopefully lead us to Mattesdorf, for half an hour, the woods suddenly ended abruptly. Out in the open we could see the dim shape of silent buildings, only yards away, clustered together in a disorganised jigsaw of timber and corrugated iron rooves.

We moved slowly, ready to make a dash for it if challenged and edged towards what appeared to be a saw mill, with the welcome sound of water churning its way past the stationery mill-wheel and proving that the stream must be near. We had done enough, gone far enough, and were wet enough to decide to spend the rest of the night, if possible, out of the rain and, as we crept round the deserted buildings and sheds, locked up for the night, we found the best spot under cover at the bottom half of the twelve foot mill wheel — antiquated enough to be a relic of the Hapsburg empire. Under its shelter, we took it in turns to keep awake, so that we could get away and hide somewhere before the whole surroundings would be astir, managing well enough until the butt ends ran out. Minutes after this we were both fast asleep.

We had been like this for some hours when somebody somewhere pressed a button and the wheel started to move. With a startled shout, Jerry pushed me out of the way, rolling over just in time to prevent himself getting his problems sorted out for good, as the great wheel clanged and groaned its way into a terrifying rhythm. With the turning of the mill wheel the situation had become dangerous. There would be workers around: some of them still hopeful of getting their devotion to the Fuhrer recognised — men who wouldn't hesitate to turn us over to the authorities if they knew who we were. We only had time for a rapid conference. At any moment one of them might arrive in the wheel shed and, even if his sympathies were with us, would probably turn us over unless we could overpower him first. Hilde had arranged to meet us that night. If this was not going to turn into a fiasco, we should have to be there. There was only one method open to us — bluff! We would have to brazen our way out: neither run nor walk, but just get out as quickly as possible without causing suspicion. Taking a tremendous risk, we walked out into the open — praying. As they downed tools and stared, somebody called out:

"Hey. Look! Englanders." But when we passed him, smiling, the fellow next to him exclaimed:

"There's one born every minute, Herman, and you're one of them. Don't you know a Hungarian uniform when you see one?"

One of them called after us in Hungarian some word that neither of us had ever heard.

"Shout something back quickly," hissed Jerry.

I made a noise, which I hoped was a fair imitation of Hungarian, reasonable enough for a man with his heart stuck in his throat. We didn't wait to see whether it had worked, but disappeared into the woods, running until we found the stream. After ten minutes we were out in the open again, on the path and following the running water. The sun was up and the path lay ahead in a long straight line, terminating in a little wooden bridge. A hundred yards further on we were just able to jump out of sight into a dip, well down below the road, before a cartload of soldiers rounded the corner. From a distance they looked

British or French but, through a peephole at the top of the dip, I recognised the khaki uniform of six Hungarian privates and an officer with red epaulettes. Quickly, I pulled myself down out of sight to let them pass but after five minutes realised that there was something very wrong. The cart, drawn by a horse so thin and bony that even Herr Tagmeier would have had a conscience about putting it in harness, had got one of its wheels firmly stuck between the planks of the bridge.

The suspense, after five minutes of curses and groans from the men and snorts from the horse, was becoming unbearable and, taking a chance, I crawled up to peep over the top — as luck would have it, right into the eyes of the officer in charge. Taken by surprise, he shouted a warning, reaching for his pistol, and within ten seconds six rifles were pointing at my head. But this one was easier; we were getting into practice. I pushed Jerry, who was crawling up behind me, back into the hole with my boot; then I got out, grinning sheepishly as if I had just finished pulling up my trousers. But the officer, suspiciously nervous, shot several questions running at me in Hungarian. When he saw that I didn't understand, he shouted in German:

"Who are you, and what are you doing here?"

God, who was I? What was I doing here? What was the name of some village in the vicinity? My brain was clogged with treacle: I could think of nothing. But Jerry saved the situation.

"You're a Pole from Roderturm", he whispered harshly. (I had heard of the nearby village.)

The officer was tired of waiting.

'Well?" he shouted, his finger twitching nervously on the trigger.

"I'm a Polander from Roderturm," I faltered.

Surely this was the lamest excuse anyone had ever made. But the officer looked relieved.

"It's all right,' be called to the others. "He's only a Hollander (Dutchman) from Rotterdam."

Once more, I thanked God for my bad pronunciation, which had saved a nasty situation.

"You're a Dutchman. You have been working for the Germans. Good! Good! Now you can work for us. Come and help these lads."

Never had there been a more willing helper. It seemed as if I almost lifted the cart out of the rut on my own. The horse co-operated well, pulling at the same time after a sharp jab from a rifle barrel. With the Russians so close it was obvious that the soldiers were as keen to get on with their journey west, as we were to go east.

After three minutes they had disappeared and after another five we had nearly managed to stop laughing.

"No more of this. Come on, you bloody Dutchman," said Jerry, between splutters. "It's getting too late to be safe. We've got to take cover for the day. What about those bushes?"

About twenty yards ahead and slightly back from the path was a thick clump of brushwood and brambles, which would probably give us good cover.

"We don't want to get too far from the path and lose it this evening."

Under cover, we soon went to sleep — but not for long. The distant drone of the U S bombers, getting louder, was as good as any alarm clock. When at least fifty of them flew over at less than ten thousand feet, we had a job to keep from jumping out, waving and shouting.

"Ruskis one side — Yankees the other," Jerry called out above the noise. "God! This is marvellous. The war's nearly over."

For ten minutes there was silence and then, seconds after we felt the earth tremble, we could just hear the shattering noise of the bombs falling on Graz — mercilessly flattening a city already in ruins. After this we managed another half hour's sleep before the bombers came back, flying south to Italy.

"Not a Messerschmidt anywhere," Jerry's shouted above the noise, delightedly.

Through the day we slept fitfully, keeping an eye open for strangers until, late in the evening, the moon rose above the trees and, crawling out, we headed east towards Mattesdorf which I calculated was about fifteen kilometres away, always keeping as near the stream as possible. We had been walking on silently for some time when Jerry suddenly grabbed me by the arm.

"Hey, listen," he exclaimed.

As we stood still, just above the hooting of the owls and the night noises we could hear a low rumble — like distant waves breaking on a beach.

"Ivan the Terrible!" breathed Jerry, his eyes shining. Already more than half way through Hungary, the Russian steamroller was rolling flat out towards the Austrian border. Not even the distance could muffle the boom of the heavy artillery. We smiled and, full of fresh hope, travelled on into the night.

At one o'clock in the morning, as the moon was slowly disappearing again behind the mists of a rainy sky, we could just see the shape of the village at the end of a steady downward slope: like Shaffendorf, a large group of farms dominated by a slender church steeple. Any one of those farms could have been the one we were looking for: in the dark it was impossible to guess. Probably, half of them had orchards somewhere near them, and this fact alone would make it very difficult to find our meeting place. As we tried to solve the problem we both started with surprise when we saw a man staggering towards us only yards away, as if he was bouncing off an invisible wall. Jerry made for the field at the side of the path, but stopped suddenly.

"What's the use?" he called out. "Never mind, he's old and he's pissed." We kept on walking. "With any luck he might even help us." The alcoholic fumes had already reached us.

"By the looks of things, he won't know who we are in this light."

He was wrong. The old man had made up his mind exactly who we were. Leaning on Jerry's shoulder, staring up into his face with the wrinkled smile of an ancient toothless angel, he said with conviction:

"Good (hiccough) evening. It gives me great pleasure to welcome you Russian gent.... (Hiccough) gentlemen to Osh-Oshtria."

Jerry's shoulder was stopping him from falling over.

"Listen, old fellow," he said, "one of your prisoners of war told me in Moscow where we could find a nice farm when we got to Austria with good comfortable straw to lie on. It belongs to Herr Shandos (Hilde's grandfather). Can you tell us where it is?"

Safe enough, I thought. He would never remember a thing when he came to. The old man's face lit up.

"Shandos," he said. "Good old Shandos. (Hiccough) He'll be a good friend to you Rush - Rush - Russian gentlemen."

He did what he could to send us in the right direction, before sinking on his hands and knees and crawling off.

With a vague idea of the direction and position of the orchard, we moved on cautiously, remembering Hilde's warning about the Volksturm who by now could well be on the lookout: across a field of young barley, round the back of two farms and down a slope leading to the orchard, above another: though it was nearer and easier to find than I had thought, recalling Hilde's letter, I felt sure I was right. There was only one thing to do — settle down and wait. But when we were, as we thought, safely hidden amongst the apple trees, we were oblivious of one important fact. Only a hundred yards away was a member of the Volksturm doing exactly the same thing, and trained to shoot anything suspicious-looking on sight. In the stillness of the night our low voices had carried across to him and he was already moving, just discernable, a dim shape among the trees.

"Look like an apple tree for God's sake," Jerry whispered.

As we stood stock-still, we had the advantage. Luckily for us, the man's sight was as short as his world war one rifle was long. He was not sure where the voices had come from and, with his rifle at the ready, held against his shoulder, had turned uncertainly away with his back to us. In all the best war films the fellow in my position would have jumped out, grabbed him round the neck and throttled him. But in the cold light of reason, things were different. Supposing, for instance, it didn't work. Supposing he had a friend near. If we got caught how would we react to torture and what would this mean for Hilde, under suspicion already but in the heat of the Russian advance and German lightening retreat, temporarily forgotten? Jerry, with a more practical and less heroic idea, had quietly bent down picked up a stone and thrown it over to the side of the orchard where it crackled amongst the branches like somebody running.

As we watched the man move off in the direction of the

noise, I began to wonder just how much use the Volksturm really were. Jerry had thrown another stone further out beyond the orchard and it soon seemed that we had got rid of him altogether as he disappeared in the darkness, hot on the trail of whoever was running away from him. When, after ten minutes, he hadn't returned, we settled down to wait, breathing more freely. It was so quiet that we could have heard a mouse move in the grass.

"Are you positive this is the right place?" whispered Jerry.

I looked at my watch: it was three-fifteen, and I was worried. But luckily I hadn't shown it by the time I saw the familiar figure coming from the direction of the farm. At first, looking here and there, she didn't see us. Only when I whispered "Hilde" did she jump, startled, and come running over.

"Come quickly," she said. "It is very dangerous. Have you seen any Volksturm?"

I pointed over to the side of the orchard where the man had disappeared, and she dragged us both in the other direction. So far I hadn't seen her move with such urgency, and knew that the danger must be very real. We followed her down between the trees towards the dark silhouette of the farm, watching for more Volksturm.

As I looked at the dim figures ahead the whole unreality of the situation suddenly struck me. Was this all really happening? Were we in a net with a spider waiting in a corner somewhere to pounce? Was that really the rumble of guns, violating the stillness of a night fraught with danger, in a countryside where danger should have been a dirty word? A girl, whose life hung in the balance, supported precariously by the thread of her unwavering optimism. Two democratic Englishmen, who could by now have been comparatively safe in the big camp at Wolfsberg, waiting for their own countrymen to liberate them; at the mercy of fate and ready to throw themselves into the arms of the communists. Was it all really going on?

Even inside the darkened house there was still no real feeling of safety. Had the prying eye of some gossiping villager seen anything? I introduced Hilde to Jerry, cheerfully delighted to meet her.

"I am really glad you could manage to bring Jerry with you," she said. "I would have loved to hide more men but, when the two of you see where I'm going to put you, you'll understand why I couldn't."

She took us out through the back door, looking out first to see if the coast was clear, and across a yard to the bottom of the ladder into the hayloft, climbing up first and beckoning us to follow.

"I have tried to make it comfortable," she said; and certainly she had lived up to her intentions. In the light of the misty moon we could just see the straw, tidy, clean and neatly laid out to make two beds.

"You'll have company, I'm afraid," she added, "but never mind. Perhaps all the rats are Nazi and will keep away from Englishmen. By the way, there is another one of my family who knows nothing about this: my grandfather. It would only worry him stiff. He doesn't like the Nazis any more than we do, but he's a bit too old to be adventurous, so we've left him out of it. You can smoke: I have some of your cigarettes still: but be careful — not too much — your English tobacco smells so different. Now, if you can wait a bit longer without fainting from hunger, I will bring you something to eat. Mami is in bed, of course, but she has cooked some goulash and all I have to do is heat it up."

When she had gone, Jerry and I sat looking at each other, until his friendly, angular face broke into a beaming smile.

"Well, we made it,"

He sounded as if he didn't believe it and wanted confirmation from me. Yet it was true. We had done what we had set out to do: the lucky stars were still shining, and we were at last waiting for our great, warm-hearted Russian liberators. Almost as he said it, the first ten-inch shell roared overhead from the gun camouflaged in the woods outside the village, on its way to wish the Russians good morning, before blowing as many of them as it could manage to bits.

"Christ!" said Jerry. "They've only got to find where that lot's coming from and we've had it."

Rats seemed to fit in well with the general mad scheme of things, and anyway were preferable to the Greek bugs. Also, though the shattering noises of one shell screaming over regularly about every half hour, on its way to kill more Russians, was doing its best to lower our morale, we knew that when the final whine had come and gone either the Germans would have run out of ammunition or the Russians would be very near. By about five o'clock the last shell of the night had gone over and we were asleep, so soundly that neither of us woke up until dusk was once more descending over the little village.

Hilde didn't disturb us and when she came up with our food we were refreshed and ready for anything. During the next few days and nights she was our constant companion. The first thing I wanted to know was how she had found out that she was in danger.

"I'm not going to mention names," she said. "It wouldn't help anyone, but I have mixed with many who are 'in the know'. The man who warned me, being an important Nazi, should not have done so. He was the head of the firm I had worked for when I finished my national service — selling electric ironing machines, believe it or not — and he was fond of me. He just stopped me one day in the street and said:

"Hilde, be careful. You are under suspicion. They believe you are in some way connected with one of the prisoners of war, and they are watching your house at night.' He had no need to say more: I knew it was true. I am very lucky to have such a real friend."

The business of how it had all got out was unanswered. As it couldn't possibly be Wally, the only one of us who knew who she was, the suspicion must lie with some farmer who might have seen me on my way at night and followed, probably then passing his knowledge on through supposedly harmless gossip.

At night, in spite of the never-ending scratching of the rats, sometimes a foot away from our heads, and the occasional scream of the shells overhead, somehow Jerry and I managed to sleep. In the daytime, when Hilde was with us, if we mentioned the Russians she kept quiet or changed the subject. Food throughout the country was running short, a lot of it requisitioned for the troops and the bombed-out civilians. Perhaps, so far, it had been too plentiful. For the first time we noticed the pinch, as Frau Bayer began to produce truly economical meals, such as one made deliciously from young stinging nettles. But we always had enough and were never short of a bottle of wine. Limiting our smoking to after meals, we spun out the supply of Player's. If we climbed down the ladder to visit the outside toilet, we watched carefully for any signs of the grandfather or any visitors.

After about a week, Hilde couldn't contain herself any longer. Sitting with her knees drawn up under her chin, staring out over the parapet, she began to talk slowly and earnestly.

"Please", she said, "I want you to listen carefully. Your Russian friends are not what you think they are. When they get here, they will be cruel and relentless."

"We've told you they won't be as bad as you think. Why don't you believe us?" I said.

"Because, well - I haven't let you know before. What was the point? You have so much faith in them. But I will now. The day after you arrived, an Austrian soldier turned up in the village. He had been a prisoner and had escaped with two others from the Russians, hiding in the woods across the Hungarian border behind the Russian front lines and finally making a dash for freedom, leaving the other two shot dead. During the night, while they were hiding among the trees, a company of Cossacks had raided a nearby village and had ridden away with fifteen girls tied to their saddles, setting up camp only fifty yards away. After swallowing gallons of 'fire water', made from local stolen potatoes, they made the girls strip naked and dance round the campfire like the Bolshoi Ballet. Then they had raped the girls one after another, cheering each other on and queuing up for the muscular ones: but none of them, not even the ugliest, got away with it. Our Austrian boy didn't wait for an encore, though he had no doubt that there would be one, but got away while most of the Russians were asleep. Ever since he got here, he has been begging the village girls to leave before the Russians arrive. Some of them have already gone."

"Maybe he was exaggerating," said Jerry. "There must be some discipline in the Russian forces? Otherwise, how have they managed to drive your armies back so far?"

But Hilde wouldn't listen.

"It's true," she asserted. "I know it's true. Our own soldiers wouldn't lie to us. Why should they? Germans, yes perhaps, but not our Austrian soldiers.

"All right," I assured her. "We'll protect you against these terrible red monsters. But the Gestapo ... we can't protect you against them. What about them? They're the chaps you should be worrying about."

"It's just too late to think about them," was all she said.

The Russian artillery, ever nearer, was rattling the farmhouse windows and filling Jerry and me with a mixture of fear and hope. Every minute we waited for the first shell to land in, or somewhere near the village. It seemed impossible that they hadn't yet detected the gun in the woods. It had been getting rid of its ammunition at such regular intervals that we could tell the time by it; until it would stop occasionally for an hour or two, as if trying to give us the chance to lose some of the knots in our nerves. During one of these breaks, when Hilde had disappeared down the ladder with our dirty plates, we had just settled down to the usual after-meal smoke when, within seconds, she was up again.

"Put those cigarettes out quickly," she said and was gone.

We obeyed immediately, but the atmosphere was thick with Virginia tobacco smoke and our luck was once more in the balance as we desperately looked for somewhere to hide. Even if there had been any cover we couldn't have found it before we heard her again, talking quite normally this time to a man we couldn't see.

"Fraulein," he was saying. "I have my orders. What are we going to do with a division of Dutch S.S troops for the next four days? We must house them somewhere while they are waiting to join the reinforcements. We must search out every available corner in every house and farm. Your lives here depend on us — or would you rather have the Russians? Come now, let me see what sort of accommodation we can muster up here."

His foot was on the first creaking rung of the ladder. At any moment he would smell the tobacco smoke, even see the ghost of Jerry's last smoke ring lingering under the rafters.

"It will be a lot more comfortable than some of the places the men have slept in, and I will keep the numbers down to a minimum. If you don't mind, I will go up and look for myself."

Hilde, without a trace of the panic that had seized us both, was answering quickly.

"I don't think you could possibly take the risk, Herr Hauptmann (Captain). The floor is very weak. Only one at a time ever goes up there."

"I appreciate your interest in warning us, Fraulein, but nevertheless I must confirm all this for myself. As I said, I must obey my orders."

As the ladder groaned in protest, he began to climb up to discover us. In a moment we were shuddering, staring at the hands gripping the parapet. Fascinated and mesmerised, we watched the skull with its grisly crossbones, Todenkopf emblem of the S.S., grinning at us from the front of his helmet. Vividly, in that moment, it seemed that the whole adventure was over, and I saw the terrifying picture of Hilde blindfolded, standing, alone and very small, in front of a firing-squad. Again I cursed the day I had been born — for surely this was all my fault. The distance from the skull and crossbones to the centre of his eye pupils would be about two inches; two inches between the protecting edge of the parapet and death — unless we killed him.

I looked at Jerry: his penknife was open in his hand, the big blade short and rather harmless-looking, but lethal if it could be stuck into the officer's throat. In the dim light his face was deathly white. In one second, all the dreaded questions had run through my mind. What should we do with the body? Did anyone else know the man was here? Would they shoot the villagers in true S.S. style?

"But, Herr Hauptmann, I'm worried." Still no panic — not even a tremor. How did she do it? Perhaps she had a premonition of a charmed life. "Last week my grandfather was up there, putting poison down to kill the rats, when he got bitten by one. Now he is in hospital with septicaemia and a broken leg: poor old man, we don't think he'll last."

We stared stupidly at the skull and crossbones, mocking us, almost shouting with laughter through the grinning teeth:

"What am I going to do next?"

"A rat, you say, Fraulein? And your grandfather has a broken leg?"

"Yes," she said, "To start with, one of the rotting boards gave way and he broke his leg. Then, when he fell, he put his hand right on top of one in the straw and it bit him badly. I'm afraid we're infested with rats up there. These old people can't keep the farm all that tidy."

The skull, still grinning, seemed to be wavering. A few seconds seemed like an hour. The captain was weighing up the situation. Russians he could face: why not rats?

We waited, sweating with fear. Luckily a friendly draught was blowing away the smell of tobacco smoke. And then the hideous skull slowly began to disappear, followed by the hands. He wasn't going to make a fool of himself in front of one of these Austrian girls. The voices receded. Jerry's face still toned in nicely with the sack of flour he used as a pillow. My mouth was open: for a fleeting instant I remembered my mother telling me how God had given us all a guardian angel.

But the Russians weren't going to let our nerves get back to normal. In the evening the village of St Stefan, eight kilometres away across the fields, was completely gutted by fire from their incendiaries: fired from 'Stalin Orgls' (Stalin Organs), as the terrified Germans had nicknamed them, which pumped out shells, enveloping everything they were aimed at in a sea of flames. Wailing like the banshee — louder, softer, louder, softer - they had almost destroyed the village, with its wooden fences and gates and thatched roofs in five minutes, while we watched through the little window in the roof, waiting for our turn.

"Perhaps the shells won't reach here." I said, without much conviction.

Within ten minutes the 'Stalin Orgls' were quiet, leaving the village they had destroyed white hot and lighting up the countryside for miles around. After another hour we had made up our minds that they were not going to do the same to us; and some of the villagers, who had run out into the woods, had come back with the news that 'Big Bertha', with no more ammunition, had been dismantled and was on her way to join the rest of the sad retreating Nazi war machine. But the volunteer S.S. troops from Holland, feared by everyone and reputed to he more cruel and relentless than the German S S., were still in and around the village in their hundreds.

"That last little episode was enough for me," said Hilde when we'd settled down after the excitement. "You two have got a new home where nobody will ever find you."

Near the farm, but very much out of the way below the orchard, well camouflaged and let into the side of a steep bank, was the cellar where they kept the wine and cider together with the smoked pork, cheese and sauerkraut, which needed a cool temperature in the summer. At night when everyone was in bed Hilde took us over and gave us carte blanche to eat and drink as much as we wanted.

"Only don't make yourselves ill," she warned. "There's no question of getting a doctor for bilious attacks or hangovers."

Under the circumstances, with the three-inch oak doors muffling our voices, we slowly emptied the cider barrel and our unmelodious singing by candlelight was heard only by a small audience of cockroaches, who got their own back by crawling over us when we were asleep.

Hilde would often come in with proper meals, fruit and other delicacies, but for the rest of the time would leave us on our own...until, one morning the earth shuddered, torn apart as the first Russian bomb landed in the orchard. The doors were so thick that we hadn't even heard the planes. Hilde, who had only been with us for a few minutes, leapt for the door and was racing across to the house before we could stop her. With the door open, we heard the full thunder of them overhead, like giant coffee-grinders — a monotonous, terrifying rhythm. As the bulky shapes flew over at five hundred feet dropping their bombs a few seconds later on the woods west of the village, we suddenly realised that we were in 'no man's land', with the line of defence reinforced by the Dutch S.S. only a few hundred yards away, and that at any moment we might get blasted to bits. The bomb, which had landed in the orchard, had fallen short of the mark and might easily be followed by another. The Russian troops could not be far away and might shell the village at any moment.

Only seconds after Hilde had rushed out to get the others and bring them to the shelter we could see she had failed, at least with the grandparents. The only proof that the curious-looking object following her was her mother was Hilde's desperate shout:

"Come on, Mami. Quick, more planes coming."

We could just see Frau Bayer's feet sticking out from under a huge pile of eiderdowns and from the depths of all the feathers could hear a muffled:

"Where am I? I can't see where I'm going."

"Here!" shouted Hilde again from the steps as the next wave of coffee-grinders screamed overhead. "Oh, God! HERE!"

Frau Bayer somehow reached the steps under her bundle, then staggered off back towards the house.

"BRING THEM DOWN INTO THE CELLAR!" shouted Hilde.

"NO! I WON'T LET MY BEAUTIFUL THINGS GET DIRTY," came the voice from under the bundle. Now the planes were overhead and another bomb was on its way with an ear-splitting whistle.

This time we all thought we were going to get it. As the explosion ripped the air and the shrapnel cut the branches off the trees scattering them in all directions, Hilde was flung back through the entrance.

"MAMI!" she screamed.

The bundle of eiderdowns was wallowing about under the trees, its feet tripping over the severed branches. We could still here the muffled voice.

"Oh dear! My beautiful eiderdowns: they're going to be full of holes." But when the next bomb was half way down, the bundle had disappeared into the house again and we were holding Hilde down to stop her running back indoors.

"There's nothing you can do," shouted Jerry. "If she's determined to go somewhere, not even a bomb will send her in the other direction. What's so magic about those eiderdowns?"

"Nothing! Her great grandmother made them, that's all. But she's so stupid. She's going to get killed for the sake of the damned things. Now, let me go!"

But we wouldn't let her go — not until the last bomber was out of sight and we could venture out to see the damage. Even then, we had to be careful in case we were seen by anyone and were soon back under cover. The silence that followed the bombing was far more terrifying than the noise. While most of the villagers cowered under their roofs, waiting, even the geese and hens lad lost their busy voices.

When, in the afternoon, Hilde came back from the house her face looked drawn.

"I can't stand this deathly quiet," she said. "It's Sunday and not even a church bell ringing. The priest is either too frightened to open the church up or worried about the crowds who'll want to get a last confession in before the Reds come and eat them. Listen!" She paused. "You can hear the silence."

We held our breath. The usual dull thunder of the guns had gone. She went out for a few minutes and came back.

"One of the farmers went to the woods and the Germans had gone," she said. "What's wrong with the Russians? They don't seem to want to come here either. Grandpa and Grandma say they're going to jump under the table again if the 'planes come back. Mami's found three holes in her eiderdown and is crying over it, as if it was a pet animal. It doesn't seem to sink in — I mean the fact that they might have been in her instead. She's going to..."

"Wait a minute," Jerry broke in, holding his finger to his mouth. "Listen."

At last we could hear a noise, like a distant drum roll getting louder: unlike anything we had heard so far. Within seconds we realised that it was the pounding of horse's hooves on hard ground and were looking through the gap made by the slightly open door. When we saw the rider we knew that our friends, the Russians, were with us at last. Galloping at breakneck speed, as if chased by a regiment of goblins, he tore past the bottom of the farm, churning up a field of young barley. In spite of his speed, we could see that he was wearing field grey trousers and tunic, not so blue as the German counterparts, over a white shirt. Down the side of his leg was a red stripe, contrasting brightly with the dull dried blood on the bandage wrapped round his head. He was leaning forward, digging his spurs into the steaming flanks of the black horse, the white flecks of foam from its mouth floating away behind it. In one hand he held his machine pistol while he clung onto the rein with the other. In an instant he was gone.

"He's been sent in to attract any fire," Jerry said. "To see if there are any snipers: one of the Russian methods. Some get away with it; others die like brave Soviet martyrs. We're lucky, I think; it means they won't turn the 'Stalin Orgls' on us."

We didn't rush out. Somehow the atmosphere didn't invite this. Besides, there would be a certain embarrassment as the villagers would see us for the first time. Some of them would welcome the security they thought we would bring, others might think of us as allies of the Russians, and not to be trusted. It would be a question of getting away from the darkness of the cellar first and then getting indoors and remaining there. For the first time we met the grandfather and grandmother, dumbfounded and rather touchy about the whole business: also Hilde's cousin, Mina, who had joined the family three days before. Unlike Hilde, she was straggly-haired and ungainly, apparently doing nothing about looks she felt were not worth trying to improve: also, very reserved and, though not antagonistic, still unsociable towards Jerry and me, her smiles of greeting dulled by the worry of uncertainty.

Quickly, the word had got round the villagers that now that the fighting was over they could expect the Russians any minute.

For an hour we waited until with no warning a large black staff car full of K.G.B. officials, drove up, parking right outside the farm. Five men and two women got out. They wore immaculate, dark blue uniforms and brilliantly shining high leather boots, their only decorations small silver stars on red circles of cloth and red stripes down the side of skirts and trouser legs. Obviously giving us no time to doubt their good intentions one of the women, with short-black hair brushed back close to her head, and speaking flawless German, introduced herself and her comrade 'liberators'.

"Your war is over," she said, with a friendly smile on her

dark, good-looking rather square face. "You can go about your business as you used to — work and grow your food. Forget the bombs and shells." Though I saw the look she gave as she glanced across at her comrades and heard what might have been a touch of sarcasm, I suspected nothing but, seeing how she looked curiously at Jerry and me, hastened to introduce Hilde and to relate in a few words why two Englishmen were in the village and what she and her family had done for us. When they heard this the Russians, especially the women, were soon clasping Hilde by the hand.

"What a wonderfully romantic finish to your war," said the woman who spoke German. "I am happy for you."

She turned to me smiling in her dark slightly mocking way.

"In a week you will be in England with your 'Zheria'." (wife)

She squeezed Hilde's arm. At this point one of the officers broke in as if reprimanding her for talking too much.

"Now we must go," she said.

By this time a group of villagers were looking on, as surprised to see Jerry and me as the officials had been, but when the nosier ones tried to find out more, Hilde was very short with them. She seemed nervous and not her usual optimistic self.

"So," I said as the staff car with its five occupants drove off. "What did we tell you? The Russians are a nice bunch. How can you possibly be afraid of them now?"

"I think you two had better go back into the hay loft," was the only comment she made.

Though we felt on top at last and relieved at our sound judgement, we still did what we were told, trusting in her initiative. Frau Bayer put her arm round us, kissing us and looking a little crestfallen. Mina had gone, as silently as she had appeared, leaving the two grandparents still looking rather edgy but less annoyed, now that they were getting used to their granddaughter's unpredictable ways.

Back in the straw, long after the K.G.B. had gone, I was lying staring at the rafters and repeating to myself "I mustn't feel too cocky over all this. After all, if I had been Austrian I would probably have thought the same about the Russians."

I was dozing off when the first scream stopped the birds twittering back in their old haunts. A moment later Mina, dark eyes staring in terror, ran gasping for breath back from the village and threw herself into the toilet, slamming the door and shooting home the bolt. Hilde ran out from the house.

"What's the matter, Mina? What's happening in the village?"

The terrified burbling from the toilet was drowned by a second chilling scream. Quickly we clambered down the ladder and followed Hilde, who had set off along the road to find out for herself but was already out of sight. At the sound of more screams coming from further down the village our hearts sank as we stared at each other stupidly.

"God, I've got to get Hilde out of this'" I was shouting when she appeared round a corner, walking slowly back, her face relaxed with a sad satisfaction. When we came up to her she hardly looked at us, but just murmured softly:

"I knew it. I knew it. Our boys wouldn't lie: that's why he wanted me to go. He knew what was going to happen."

"What is happening?" We both asked at once.

She had straightened up now, alert and alive again.

"You poor devils," she said. "So easily falling for your exaggerated propaganda. Why didn't you listen to me? Those people were just the icing on a cake full of poison. The poison's here in the village — seeping through the whole of Eastern Austria by now, I imagine. If you can visualize Ali Baba and his forty thieves, you'll recognise your Russian comrades when you see them." She turned on me sadly. "They've already raped all the women in the last three farms in the village, loaded up all their belongings and smashed the windows before driving away; and they're mad drunk. If you don't believe me go and ..." The sentence was cut short by another terrified scream.

"Come with us quickly," I said, holding her by the arm and turning back towards the farm.

"The bastards," muttered Jerry. "The lecherous bastards."

CHAPTER TWELVE

Within a few minutes we were back in the hayloft, which had become a sort of conference room. If our Russian so-called comrades were going to let us down like this we would have to work out how to cope with them; at least the drunk ones. The sober ones might be an easier matter.

"Please, you've got to stick to us," I said to Hilde. "They're bound to be here any minute but when they see we're British they won't do anything to you or your family. We'll stay up here for the present; but what about Mina and your Mami?"

Hilde climbed down the ladder and was gone for five minutes. When she came back she looked frustrated, shrugging her shoulders.

"Mami says she thinks she knows how to get round the Russians. She's already cooking and vowing she'll get to the soft side of their hearts through their stomachs. Mina's in the toilet, knitting a scarf. I think she really expects to have to spend next winter in Russia. She's quite sure one of them is going to come and take her away. I've asked her to join us, but she just sits and knits and shakes her head as if she's glued to the seat. Grandpa and Grandma say whatever happens to them doesn't matter anyway: they've lived long enough.

"So what are we going to do?" said Jerry. "Get out there and meet them or hang around and let them find us?"

We had no choice. At that moment we heard the harsh jarring tones of their strange language outside in the yard, the words seeming to come in jerks, as if the soldiers were on edge. There was something about the urgency in their voices and the clinking metallic noise of their machine pistols that brought back the sense of danger we had felt when the fighting had been still on. When they rattled the toilet door and no answer came out, we heard Frau Bayer trying to explain that someone was in there; and as we heard them shouting with suspicion, we had to hold Hilde, who was getting ready to go to Mina's assistance.

"Wait until they find her," Jerry said. We'll stop them then."

Suddenly he grabbed my arm and whispered: "Quiet."

The top of the ladder was moving slowly. Somebody was pushing it up slowly against a part of the loft which jutted out, full of bales of straw from the July threshing. Behind the partition, which divided our big loft from the small space at the back, we could hear someone scraping around on hands and knees and the noise of his gun banging against the beams.

"This is ridiculous", I whispered. "We've got to show ourselves before they think we're spies and shoot us." I began to move.

"Christ! Be careful!" Jerry warned as I slowly stood up.

For some reason, though the Russians were supposed to be friends, I had my hands up. With a stifled cry of fear, the young Russian soldier, seeing me in the dim light swung round from where he knelt, his machine pistol pointing straight at my stomach.

"Angleeski!" I shouted, the only Russian word I knew. Jabbering his disbelief, he climbed over the parapet, his gun pointing at all three of us in turn. As his gaze rested on Hilde for a second, looking her up and down he licked his lips, which were still trembling. By this time we were all standing and he was shouting to his comrades, who was about to kick down the toilet door, to bring the ladder round. When he began to climb down first, his hands fumbling round Hilde who was following, it was obvious he had got over his shock.

"Angleeski Angleeski," Jerry and I called repeatedly, but he seemed to be totally unaffected, making it clear that we should keep our hands up and jabbing us out into the sunlight with his gun barrel.

"What sort of a bleedin' mate are you?" said Jerry in English disgustedly, after an extra jab.

The soldier, a boy of about seventeen with high cheek bones and a cropped head, called out to his comrade who went into the house, coming back followed by the grandparents.

"Nix Frau!" He had attempted something vaguely like German, rubbing his stomach and trying to explain with signs that Frau Bayer had not been brought out, because she was cooking.

"Dobra! Dobra! (Good! Good!)" he said, sniffing the smell coming from the kitchen. "Frau, dobra."

After lining us up like prisoners in the yard covered by the other's gun, he ran over to the toilet and banged hard on the door, shouting abuse. As far as he was concerned whoever was in there had been long enough. Not a sound came from the terrified Mina.

"She must have fainted," cried Hilde and was starting to run across when the Russian grabbed her, pushing her back into line.

"Come on out, Mina," she called. "It's all right. Don't be frightened. They're not going to hurt you ...Stop him banging at that door," she commanded the one pointing his gun at us, who just grinned stupidly. Jerry and I beckoned to the Russian, indicating that he should get away from the door.

"Angleeski!" shouted Jerry again, pointing to himself. Then, in English: "Get your thick head screwed on. Leave her alone and she'll come out."

At last the soldier seemed to understand, moving back from the door and waiting, his revolver pointing at it. Nobody made a move until, very slowly after a tiny click of the bolt, the door began to open. Mina's black sunken eyes, in a deathly white face, were peering through the crack as if she expected to be shot on the spot.

"Come on out, 'mein schertzel'", called the old grandmother encouragingly and Mina, holding her knitting needles with the beginnings of a white scarf dangling from them, ready to jab them into the nearest Russian, crept out and ran over while the Russians looked on, roaring with laughter. The fact that we had insisted we were English had obviously done something to damp down what otherwise might have been a dangerous exuberance, but whatever it was all about, whoever we were, these two weren't going to go away empty-handed. They would leave the women alone, yes, but they would pinch whatever they could.

The Russian with the revolver, jabbing it into our stomachs one after the other and making grunting noises like a hungry animal, started with the grandfather, pathetically unshaven and bent over as if the weight of his shoulders was too much for him. Greedily, he began to take everything in sight. First to go into his pocket was the old man's gold watch and chain, worth a fortune; then Hilde's turquoise brooch, handed down through three generations. At this stage the two soldiers had both started to swig schnapps from a bottle found in the house and were beginning to reel about, looking more dangerous and less capable of using their brains than ever.

The next to go was a tortoiseshell comb from the back of the little grandmother's head: they both laughed, as her thinning white hair fell in unruly strands down over her shoulders, transforming her from her usual image of a neat little woman into someone who could well have been sitting beside Madame Lefarge at the guillotine. One of them caught hold of her frail wrists, laughing at her tears, while the other held his gun ready to shoot anyone who made a move. Jerry and I had given up trying to persuade them that we were English: what was the use? As they dragged Jerry's wedding ring off his finger and my watch off my wrist, our obvious hatred of them had no effect. Finally, when they had loaded themselves up with our belongings and stuffed a few small liqueur glasses and ornaments from the house into their pockets, they seemed to remember what they had been sent for. One of them shouted to the grandfather, pointing to the loft and making the motions of turning knobs on a wireless: then, putting his hands to his ears, tried to look as if he was listening to something through headphones. Wirelesses — he had been sent to look for wirelesses. The old man understood.

"No, nothing up there."

They nodded as if his word was enough, too drunk to climb the ladder and look for themselves. Finally, in their search, they found the deserted cellar.

"Thank God we're a couple of greedy alcoholics," said Jerry when they came out again. "There's nothing left for those bastards. Luckily for them they were so quick. I would have locked them in and let them starve to death."

They went as quickly as they had come; leaving the two of us feeling and looking ashamed of ourselves and our previous opinions. I glanced at the sad group of harmless people.

"I'm dreadfully sorry," I said, and really meant it.

Nobody bothered to answer and very soon Jerry and I were back in the hayloft, discussing how we were going to combat this new danger — our Red so-called allies. The problem of whether to leave Hilde and the others on their own while we reconnoitred in the village was a difficult one but, taking everything into consideration, we decided it was the only thing we could do; and safe, as long as we were not too long about it. When we suggested it, they all agreed. Our plan was to look for officers who, with that little bit more intelligence, surely would realise who we were. Also, they might encourage a bit more discipline. Hoping for the best, we set out to find one.

This proved to be easy. He was walking through the front door of the third farm down the road, carrying two large beautifully embroidered eiderdowns that he threw on top of some greasy guns and ammunition in a 12 cwt truck. A moment later a private, probably his batman, came out with two sacks full of crockery. We went straight up to the officer, who gave us rather a pre-occupied look and asked us a question in Russian. Jerry looked as puzzled as I did.

"Sounds like a gramophone played backwards," he said, disgustedly.

"Good day," I said in English to the officer. Then I pointed to my uniform and said hopefully and very slowly, pronouncing every syllable:

"ENG-LISH PRIS-ON-ER OF WAR."

The officer turned to his batman and made some comment. His expression was suspicious and unfriendly. How could we get these fellows to understand who we were? Had we tried everything in the book? Were we going to be treated as enemies until we could get away from them? I felt hopeless... until suddenly everything seemed clear. It was so obvious and yet neither of us had thought of it.

"Please — look," I said in English.

I opened my shirt and showed him my P.O.W. disc hanging round my neck with my number 5805 engraved on it. Then I took out a letter from home, which I was luckily still carrying, and pointed to the head of George VI on the stamp.

"We are English prisoners," I said, showing him the number against my name on the letter. "I am prisoner No 5805. We have escaped from the Germans." Luckily the numbers in Russian and English were the same. He looked at us long and earnestly, his fingers stroking the pistol hanging from his belt and then, like a dark landscape gladdened by sudden sunshine, his face lit up.

Again, he turned to his batman who, shifting his weight from one foot to the other impatiently, was obviously interested in sorting out the loot as soon as possible. At the same time he held out his hand delightedly.

"Angleeski!" he cried. "Angleeski"

O.K., I thought, as he gripped my hand with the strength of an ox, the penny has dropped.

From now on, if anyone showed any doubt, I would be an 'Angleeski'. Generously he pointed to the loot. What he was shouting was debatable but we decided it meant roughly: "Comrade, half is yours. Our two great countries must share alike." When I refused, he turned away hopelessly, though apparently quite relieved and, getting into his staff car followed by his batman, squashed in amongst the eiderdowns and bedspreads, smiled happily and set off down the road, waving goodbye. After this, we decided that looking for incorruptible officers was not going to get results and went back quickly to the house, in case anything nasty was happening there.

Hilde was sitting, talking earnestly with her mother and grandmother, Mina was in the toilet feverishly knitting and keeping a constant look out for Russians through a knot hole she had poked out in the timber wall, and the grandfather had followed the soldier, who had taken his watch, down the road. Hilde wasn't at all surprised to hear our story and had already arranged with her mother about getting back somehow to the house in Kurstenfeld before too much damage was done there.

"It was very difficult to know what to do," she said. "Mami says she wants to stay here: you can't drag her away from her valuables. Grandma is not worried and neither is Mina as long as there's a lock on the toilet door. But I am. Anything could have happened in Kurstenfeld."

And we agreed with her that we must go and see: then salvage whatever we could.

"Perhaps the troops will calm down after today," I said without much conviction, and got a pitying look from Hilde.

To get to Kurstenfeld, we would have to go through the woods where we might be able to avoid the Russians: the main road would be too risky.

"I shall be ready in half an hour," said Hilde, "I'm going to make myself look ugly.

"That's one of the things you won't succeed in doing easily," laughed Jerry.

As we talked to Frau Bayer while her daughter was out of the room, we discovered how confident she was about handling the Russians; and I believed she could do it.

"They won't do any harm to anyone who cooks them nice meals," she asserted. "If they're going to steal flour and butter and you make it clear you can cook something good with them instead, they'll leave you alone: they're wise enough for that. Anyway, probably some officer will want billets and that should solve the problem. Poor Mina's already dreaming about living in a villa on the River Don married to a handsome Cossack. She's expecting him to come along at any minute and rescue her from the ugly monsters she's seen through her peep-hole."

Hilde came back looking unusual but not the slightest bit ugly, as she had hoped. Though she had tried to hide her face as much as possible with a grey speckled headscarf and had put on her grandmother's calf-length grey skirt, black woollen cardigan and a pair of high lace-up skating boots, I still couldn't imagine her putting off a Russian. But I hadn't the heart to stop her convincing herself she was unattractive.

"I've got four pairs of Grandma's bloomers under this skirt," she said.

"But whatever for?" asked her mother, astonished.

"By the time they get to number three, they'll either have got put off or I shall have thought of a way to trick them." she laughed.

Within a few minutes we had said goodbye to her mother and grandmother and had shouted to Mina that this was her last chance to come with us.

"For heaven's sake, leave me alone!" she called back through the locked door.

"She'll knit enough scarves for the whole Russian army before she ever comes out of that den of hers," said Hilde. "It's no good worrying about her."

With a bag full of bread, smoked pork and salami, several cakes of soap, two towels and our last four packets of cigarettes, the three of us set off towards the woods through the village, where the one or two villagers who dared show their faces looked at us curiously, doubtfully greeting us as if afraid that we might in some way be dangerous. To the few Russian soldiers wandering aimlessly, with their deadly little guns slung over their shoulders, staring or stopping in their tracks, discussing us with each other and addressing us in Russian, we nodded; getting away from them as quickly as possible. At the end of the village we found Hilde's grandfather, apparently trying to explain to two young Russians about his watch, gesticulating and almost crying while they laughed in his face, prodding him with their fingers as if trying to burst a balloon. Before we could stop her, Hilde had run up to the old man and had her arms around him, telling the soldiers in German to leave him alone. To our surprise, they made no attempt to touch her. The grandfather, greeting Jerry and me half-heartedly, still seemed relieved to see us.

"No wonder they're behaving themselves a bit better," he said. "I've been told that there's a commissar visiting here tomorrow. He's the only man they seem to be scared of. As soon as he arrives I shall go and tell him about my watch and make sure I get it back."

Not wishing to shake his optimism we said nothing, but just waved him goodbye and good luck. Further down the road we stopped outside a farm.

"Come on inside," Hilde said. "The Haunsels are friends of the grandparents, we'll find out what's been happening."

In a small dark room we found the family huddled together — the farmer, his wife and two daughters, about seventeen and eighteen. When they saw us with Hilde they looked suspicious until she introduced us.

"It's all right," she said. "They're friends — Englanders." Frau Haunsel's eyes brightened up in her sallow frightened face.

"The English are here?" she cried exultantly.

When Hilde explained that we were escaped prisoners she looked disappointed.

"For one moment," she said, "I thought ..."

In the dim light Herr Haunsel's face looked badly bruised. A muscular, confident man in his mid-fifties he was obviously frightened and shattered. But now, slightly more at ease and nodding to us without trying to get any explanation, he launched straight into his tragic story, describing how four drunk Russians had kicked the door in, taken all the food in the house and then taken it in turns to rape his wife and two daughters in front of him while one of them had pinned him in a corner at the end of his gun.

"The foul swines," he blurted out, sobbing. "I'll find them and kill them. I don't care what happens to me, but one thing I swear......I shall KILL THEM. I must find them somehow. They all look alike but somehow I'll find the evil bastards." He was totally distraught.

Putting her arm around his heaving shoulders, his wife tried to console him, while Hilde soothed the terrified girls. Halfway through the afternoon, after giving them some of our food, we said goodbye and made for the woods. Outside the last house in the village stood an old farmer.

"Have you heard anything about Kurstenfeld?" asked Hilde. For a moment the man, who looked as if nothing would ever upset him, appeared scared.

"Kurstenfeld," he said. "Poor, innocent Kurstenfeld. My brother has just arrived from there. There's not a house that hasn't been plundered and hardly a woman who hasn't been raped. My brother says that even the assistant priest, young pretty-looking Father Bendel, was raped by a 'queer' colonel and that he's been in the church praying for forgiveness ever since:

poor fellow, as if it was his fault."

"Come on," said Hilde, pulling us away. "We've got to get to that house. What sort of mess will our dear friends have made of that, I wonder?"

We set off by the short cut through the woods. The fir trees were towering high above us, blocking out the sky in eerie silence. Only the intermittent firing of machine guns, perhaps a mile away, with the occasional louder explosion, showed that the fighting was not far off. We moved on carefully, trying not to make any noise. In the very stillness of the air immediately surrounding us was the smell of danger, the sensing of some presence we couldn't see. As we watched the ground to make sure we wouldn't snap any noisy twigs, we didn't notice the horseman until he was only fifty yards away among the trees, looking around him with a nervous alertness, nursing his machine pistol lightly, ready to squeeze the trigger. Down the side of his trouser leg was the familiar red stripe. His head was cropped: the lower part of his face deeply pockmarked.

"My God! Look!" whispered Hilde.

"Keep dead still," We could hardly hear Jerry's warning.

"Faces down. If he sees the slightest movement he'll shoot."

Still staring at the ground, unable to see what the Russian was doing, we held our breath, hoping that we had merged in with the surrounding bushes and trees. The crackling of the undergrowth under the weight of the horse's hooves began to get nearer — then silence. At least two minutes went by before we dared even begin to look up: and now we could see him, only twenty yards away, but facing the other way. Would he look round? But luck was with us again. Standing motionless and rigid, we saw the spurs press lightly, almost reluctantly, into the horse's flanks and watched his form slowly disappearing among the trees.

Cautiously we moved on, following the quickest route to Kurstenfeld and, within half an hour, were right in the front line; tricked into thinking the way was clear by the lull in the fighting. Suddenly we were in the middle of them, the Russian front-line troops; well-fed, well-equipped and well-satisfied by the looks of things — lying around behind their machine-guns and field telephones triumphantly on their priceless stolen eiderdowns, hand-made rugs and bed-covers.

The first group we came across were gathered around a huge lump of smoked pork, tearing it apart with their grimy fingers and swilling it down with stolen cider. As they were obviously in a good mood, this seemed the time to put the magic words to the test. One of them had already swivelled his machine-gun and was pointing it straight at us.

"Angleeski," I called out in a friendly tone, holding Jerry's arm. Then I remembered the K.G.B. woman and putting mine round Hilde exclaimed:

"Zhena." (Wife)

I was gratified to hear most of the soldiers repeating the three words and, relieved to see them smiling, I pointed through the trees and said:

"Kurstenfeld?"

The bearded machine-gunner turned to the others, grinning at Hilde and murmuring their approval: "Zhena! Zhena! Dobra!"

"Kurstenfeld," I repeated.

One of them seemed to understand, pointing south and trying to explain that it would be dangerous to follow our present route.

"Boom! Boom!" he cried, shaking his cropped head and warning us "Nix. Nix. Kaput," meaning that if we went that way we should be 'kaput' — finished. At that moment a serious-looking officer arrived, and the soldiers' explanation of who we were and where we were going did nothing to change his look of suspicion.

"Go!" he said to us in German. "Get out and think yourselves lucky we haven't got the time to arrest you for sneaking around here. Anyway, how do I know you are English prisoners?"

A few seconds later he was scrutinising our P.O.W. discs and my letter from home.

"O.K.," he said. "Perhaps you are telling the truth."

Then he pointed to Hilde. "But not the girl: she stays with us."

Behind the responsible look of the officer I could detect the crafty streak of the primitive peasant. A girl for his troops — this would make him more popular. They would obey his orders more willingly. Jerry came to the rescue.

"She is English too," he said in German. "An escaped internee from Vienna."

"You speak German," said the officer, for a moment suspicious again, and then quickly changing his mind. "But yes, as a P.O.W. you must of course have learnt some of the language. You have proof of what you say?"

"No proof," said Jerry. "All the proof she had has been stolen by you Russians," The officer hesitated. "You can't hold an Englishwoman, one of your own allies, prisoner," Jerry added.

The officer seemed uncertain, until the noise of a shell exploding a quarter of a mile away made up his mind for him.

"O.K.," he said. "But get back east, away from the front. Get out, and be quick about it."

He took a last lingering look at Hilde. What a chance to miss.

We needed no persuasion, but hurried off in the direction he'd indicated, leaving the machine-gunners alert and concentrating on the woods to the west, fingers ready on the triggers. For a further few minutes we kept going, finally turning south onto a cart track.

"This will take us there. I know the way: it will take almost an hour," said Hilde. "Jerry, you're a genius; I really thought I was for it then. All these hideous clothes don't seem to have made a scrap of difference after all, and grandma's bloomers — phew! They're so hot. How long can I stand it?"

We soon found that we couldn't avoid the Russian troops, scattered everywhere in the woods, nearly all of them decked out in some unusual garment, perhaps a coloured silk scarf round their necks or a pair of knickers pulled down comically over their helmets; their pockets stuffed with watches, cutlery and jewellery. As Jerry and I shouted continuously 'Angleeski prisoner' they would drop their menacing attitude, lowering their machine pistols, which had been at the ready and, approach us, their suspicion changing to friendliness and their bold attitude towards Hilde simmering down as they realised she was with Englishmen. But the time inevitably came when we were stopped by a higher-ranking officer and questioned. From the start he showed a cautious disregard for our assurances and within minutes had turned us over to a private who led us off, walking behind with his gun pointed at our backs, in the direction from which we had come.

"If only we could understand their impossible language," I said.

"What the hell are they going to do with us?" There was a slight tremor in Jerry's usually calm voice. Hilde looked tense.

After a few minutes walking through the undergrowth, the Russian stopped us outside a Nissan hut, obviously recently erected amongst the trees.

"Commissar!" He was obliging enough to tell us where we were, with probably the only word we all understood.

He banged at the door, then opened it and put his head through. From inside came the resounding chords of Tchaikovsky's 1812 Overture, with a scratchy background not a bit fair to the composer; but which showed us that at least somebody round these parts was musical as well as military. When the Russian private beckoned us to follow him, we found the 'somebody' sitting at a table winding up a gramophone as the music ran flat. Surrounding him were other stolen goods besides the gramophone and a few records — walking sticks, umbrellas, a two handled saw, saucepans, torches, beautifully carved pipes; on the floor an exquisitely hand-woven Persian carpet and on that various pieces of walnut, oak and mahogany furniture, all crammed together as if someone had pushed them through the door and left them. On the commissar's fat, ruddy, bespectacled face, as he looked up from behind a half empty bottle of vodka, was a friendly smile, directed mainly at Hilde — a smile disconcertingly opposite to the looks we had been used to. But behind it the small dark eyes showed just the slightest hint of sarcasm. Though he seemed to be drunker than he looked, he managed to take in the fact, explained by the private, that Jerry and I were British and that the 'Zhena' was an Austrian travelling with us. (We had thought it too risky to keep up the lie that she was also British.) There could be no doubt that he was inclined to believe our story when we showed him the usual proof; but the Austrian girl ... she presented a problem. Not only that but, to a man of his authority, who had been moving up behind the front line for months, she was more than a tasty morsel. The watery eyes trying to pick out the curves hidden by the voluminous skirt, showed it as he searched for an excuse to keep her for himself. Seconds later he had found it.

"Show me your hands, my dear."

His German was broken and comical, but understandable. Hilde reluctantly drew out her hands from the folds of the skirt. Reaching for them and holding them in a podgy grasp he turned them palms upwards, looking at her and pretending to be angry.

"These are not the hands of a worker. We only try to help workers, my dear, not members of the bourgeoisie." Hilde began to explain quite calmly that she had been working in an office in Kurstenfeld.

"She helped us to escape," I broke in. "She and her family have taken great risks for the allies."

"I understand this, comrade. But some of the soldiers you will meet will not believe you are British and consequently the fraulein may be in danger. Such a great champion of our cause must be protected from our,"...he gave a dry chuckle..."happy soldiers, exuberant in their victory: and must be protected by men with authority, like me."(What more were we going to hear from this overfed peacock?)

"But to make sure she deserves my protection, I must question her just a little more — a mere routine which must be followed, you understand. In the meantime, my two English comrades, you have my permission to go on ahead. Later, I myself will accompany the fraulein to Kurstenfeld."

"But..." I began.

"Enough." The smile had left his face. "We want no trouble. You are allies, I know, but we want no trouble. You are in the Russian lines and you must do what I, as commissar, tell you." He indicated to the private that he should accompany us back to the main track and set us on the right route to Kurstenfeld.

"We will not go without Fraulein Bayer," I said, hating the

little fellow and forgetting the risk I was taking.

The commissar staggered to his feet, his face red with a mixture of vodka and anger. His stubby finger was wagging near my face. "Englishman, you will do as I..."

But the impossible had happened. Hilde had covered her face with her hands and was sobbing bitterly. This was no act. The girl I had thought was so sure of herself was showing another emotion at last. I put my arm round her and looked at the little commissar defiantly, though I knew and he knew that I had no chance.

"I have the power to lock you up until I have satisfied myself entirely about your identity" he threatened.

Of course I knew that and, flattened and useless, I knew I could do absolutely nothing. Then, for the first time I was to find out that at least one Russian, drunk and nasty though he might appear had, tucked away somewhere, a soft streak.

"O.K.! O.K.!" he exclaimed, "I have had enough of this."Get out, the lot of you. Get away so far from the front line that an exploding shell sounds like an acorn falling. Now, Go!"

Though I still disliked him, I had to be grateful. If he ever found his way to the London Zoo, and I would be around, I would see to it that he would be given a first-class cage. We hurried off quickly, intent on getting as great a distance as possible between us and the commissar before he changed his mind. Hilde, laughing with relief, was embarrassed at her own weakness.

"Some Russians I've seen are not all that bad, but that greasy little monster made me feel sick. I'd rather die..."

"A kindly monster, thank God," I broke in.

"Hallo, You, there!"

The monster was at the door shouting. Everything inside me shrivelled up. Hardly daring to turn, I still had to. Come on, I thought, you're no medal earner but you're not going to let that swine have her back.

"Over my dead ..." I was shouting back, but he didn't let me finish.

"Don't worry," he called, "Just get to hell out of here and don't stop for thirty kilometres. The next commissar you meet might not be so lenient."

He was pointing towards the east — Hungary, Rumania, the Black Sea, Moscow — giving the impression that, as far as he was concerned, if we landed up there everybody would be better off.

"And look after your delightful bourgeoise 'zhena'."

He was swigging from the bottle, drowning his frustration and probably cursing himself for having been born with a touch of humanity.

CHAPTER THIRTEEN

Again, we set off through the woods, tired and hungry, but still managing to raise the energy to call "Angleeski" to the Russians scattered about like ugly sores on the quiet face of Mother Nature: some skin-headed and clean-shaven, some with dark unhygienic stubble and others with matted unwashed hair and thick beards. Within half an hour we were again being interrogated, this time by the most unlikely person in a Russian uniform we had met so far — an intelligent, sober colonel. Prodded at the end of a rifle into an empty woodcutting shed by a conscientious private, we were again explaining our circumstances, which he quickly understood.

"Open your bag, please," he said in German.

Without wasting time he was following the rules. A thoroughly business-like individual, I thought, and a pleasure to meet for a change, as I watched him carefully moving and searching under things in the bag. Looking up, he smiled but seemed to be hesitating.

"I am inclined to let you go on your way; but I wonder if I should." He paused. "Ah! Soap — and what a nice towel," he cried, as if he'd only just seen them.

Such subtlety we had not come across. He was rubbing his chin and pursing his lips.

"I wonder whether I should keep you here for the night." Continuing his special form of persuasion he had rubbed in the blackmail, and there was nothing for it but to play along.

"You like the soap and the towel," Hilde said. "Here, take these."

She handed him a cake of soap and the worst of the towels. Luckily he had missed the cigarettes.

"I like the flowered pattern."

He wasn't going to be put off the scent so easily. The best towel had the embroidered corners. Hilde gave it to him.

"Thank you. Thank you." His entire attention was on Hilde. "Yes, I love flowers, and these will always remind me of you." He kissed Hilde's hand with a flourish and within minutes we were on our way.

"Clever bastard!" Jerry looked disgusted.

"I don't see why we should have to go dirty just to oblige him," I said.

I was annoyed that he had tricked me into thinking he was genuine.

"Now," said Hilde. "Let's forget him and get down to business. We've got to find somewhere to spend the night."

She was looking anxiously at the darkening sky.

"What about Frau Fleisinger at Dreisdorf?" She said. "I know my way from here. We're never going to make it to Kurstenfeld tonight, unless we travel through the woods in the dark. Frau Fleisinger, with her husband away, will be glad of a couple of men to protect her."

When, after no more incidents, we arrived in the village, we found it almost void of Russians. A group of women, recognising us, followed down the street, firing questions at Hilde with the undertone of envy which she got from most of her own sex. By the time we arrived at Frau Fleisinger's farm several seemed to have made up their minds to get in there for the night.

"Where are all the Russians?" Hilde asked one of them.

"In hell, where they ought to be, I hope, choked to death by their filthy 'fire water'. Last night the village was full of them. It was horrible: they were so drunk."

With a flurry of her thick skirt and speckled apron and a saucepan in her hand, Frau Fleisinger came out to greet us.

"Ah! Two Englishmen. You are welcome, my friends. So welcome. Last night it was awful. We barricaded all the doors and windows and the devils were too drunk to break in, though they tried. One of them smashed the window opposite and cut himself and when Frau Fischer had finished bandaging his hand the two who were with him dragged her into the woods and raped her. I shall never forget her screams."

One of the women with us, a small rosy-faced farmer's wife in her fifties, was crying bitterly.

"I've been raped three times. Please, please let me come in with you tonight. I'd rather kill myself than go through last night again."

Pulling up the front of her skirt to wipe her eyes she showed the bruises on her muscular, blotchy legs.

"One of those Ruskis smelt worse than our pig. I feel sick when I think of him. Please let me come in."

"She's lucky to get raped once with legs like that," muttered one of the other women.

"We got here first. Wait your turns," cried two of the younger girls at once. "Anyway, what about the children?" One of them was pointing to a little boy and girl, neither of them older than six.

"The children?" I glanced at Jerry. "Oh, hell."

"Yes," said Frau Fleisinger. "The children are not safe either. It makes no difference, when the Russians are full of 'fire water'." Frau Meier took her little girl to the doctor in Putzdorf this morning. One of them had injured her terribly. The doctor sent her to the hospital in Kurstenfeld for an operation. Just think of it: she's only three."

"My God! I feel sick." Hilde looked pale and disgusted. Frau Fleisinger pushed the two girls away.

"I'm going to have ten people in my house, that's all." she said. "And selfish ones like you will be the last."

She stuck to her word. By the time we were ready to lock ourselves in, besides the three of us and Frau Fleisinger there were six others: the farmer's wife, still crying, the two children, an old half-blind man, another middle-aged woman and one of the girls. We had soon barricaded the big door with all the furniture not already up against the windows which had no boards nailed against the inside of the frames. Once prisoners inside the house, we waited for the night.

At the back of a cupboard Frau Fleisinger had managed to conceal the last of her stock of food, which she brought out, together with a jug of cider.

"We might as well drink this before the Reds get it."

She was pouring it into all the glasses. "You'll feel more like facing up to those pigs with full stomachs, especially if you're a bit tipsy yourselves," she said with a wry smile.

"My advice is to pour what we don't drink down the sink," said Jerry. He had seen what a belly-full of cider could do towards blinding a drunk Russian to our identity.

Though the old man and two farmer's wives were grateful for Frau Fleisinger's hospitality, they could only eat and drink a little, but the jug was soon half empty and a lot of the food had gone before Frau Fleisinger, Hilde and the girl who had been let in with us had cleared the table.

"Listen, I think I can hear them coming." The girl kept on repeating, her face distorted with fear.

"There, there, my pet. Don't worry: we have the Englanders with us to protect us."

The woman who had been crying earlier was comforting her.

Our responsibility was beginning to weigh on our shoulders. On the way through the village we had passed a group of soldiers sitting round a fire they had made in the street singing Russian songs and filling their bellies with 'fire water', made from stolen potatoes; and knew that they would be on the rampage later. Round the table sat the women, like frightened hens, while the old man stared at the wall he could not see clearly, muttering silent prayers to heaven to protect them all from the Red devils. Hilde and Frau Fleisinger sat talking in whispers, adding a sinister touch to the dimly-lit surroundings.

When the first thundering crashes came from down the road, as the drunken soldiers tried to break down the barricades, we waited silently for our turn, with the women staring wide-eyed at us, as if by waving magic wands we could stop the whole thing; and the two terrified children trying to lose themselves amongst the folds of Frau Fleisinger's long apron. At the table sat Hilde, holding each of the other women by the hand to try to calm them down, as the one who had been raped the night before trembled and sobbed. In a few minutes the screams from down the road were drowned by the noise of bellowing voices, half singing, half shouting outside our farmhouse. The barricades shook dangerously as the first boot tried to kick the door in. Now was the time to act: there was just a chance the plan might work. Jerry was the first to get his mouth near the door.

"Get lost, you lecherous bastards," he roared at the top of his voice."

A sudden silence...then a low, grunting discussion and we could hear their boots shuffling off over the hard dry ground. Thrown off balance at the sound of a young male voice, they were no doubt looking for places where there were women only — and there were plenty of them.

"That's fixed them. They won't come back here," I assured the women. "Now we must relax. If they drink themselves to sleep, we'll get some rest."

In the room at the back of the house was the only other piece of furniture, apart from the table with its two benches, not being used to barricade doors and windows; a beautifully carved, solid mahogany four poster, at least six feet wide.

"Come in all of you," Jerry called. "We'll get you in this room; then you can push the bed up against the door and Bob and I will keep guard out here."

"You've got to come in here with us." Frau Fleisinger seemed to like giving the orders, as it was her house. "The women and children will feel safer with you in here. If the Russians try to get in, you can shout at them again."

"Come on," said Hilde. "I think it would be best."

"Yes." The old man had clutched one of Jerry's hands, holding it in both of his. "You have a good strong voice, like Churchill. The Russian swines were scared."

"I'm not taking any clothes off — that's certain," said the woman who had been raped. "I'm sitting out here, with Anna and Hans, at the table."

"You're doing nothing of the sort," I said. We pulled the two benches into the bedroom, placing them against the wall. "Now, you can sit there if you like."

It took four of us to drag the heavy bed over and push the end against the door. When this had been done, everything seemed set for the night.

"It won't be heavy enough to stop them if they put their shoulders against the door." Said Frau Fleisinger. "We'd better weigh it down with a few of you. Hilde, you take the children, one each side. Anna, there's plenty of room for you too: and you, Gretl; you're a skimpy creature if ever there was one."

One by one they climbed fully clothed into the welcoming bed — not even taking off their shoes, until they were all lying beside each other, flat on their backs. The children were loving the fun, as Hilde laughed and played with them, with one ear listening for noises outside.

"Come on, Uncle Jerry." The little girl was laughing so much that the tears were streaming down her face. "There's plenty of room for a big elephant."

There was no question of getting the old man or the woman they called Lisl to leave their uncomfortable bench.

"I'm going to pull the bench away and jump through the window if they start knocking down the door," the woman said.

"I haven't been to bed for six years," the old man assured us. "I just sit in a chair, smoke my pipe and snooze. Saves washing pyjamas."

"That's it then, Stoo. Jump in the other side and make up my lucky number — seven, said Jerry"

Jerry had put the final touches to the picture - seven people in one bed, all of them ready to jump out at a moment's notice, yet so tired that their eyes were already closing as they were being slowly lulled to sleep by the quiet monotony of Frau Fleisinger's snores from where she had decided to sit on the bench; her head, still hidden by her blue head scarf, resting trustingly on the old man's shoulder.

From the stale tobacco in his worn old pipe came enough billowing smoke to suffocate us all before the Russians could get a look in.

Luckily, there were no more incidents and, when the first glimmer of light was showing through the curtains, Frau Fleisinger was up making coffee for everyone — with sour milk, if they wanted it, and the remains of her bread and wurst.

Though we would have liked to take the children with us

we had to give them back to their grandparents, living on a farm down the road, and leave them to their fate. As there were no Russians about, we did not wait to listen to the stories from some of the terrified villagers but set off through the unnatural silence, conscious of the lingering threat of more atrocities to come, leaving Frau Fleisinger examining the lock on the front door, broken by the Russian's boot, and cursing her husband for not putting a new and stronger one on, before leaving to guard P.O.W.s, instead of bemoaning the fact that he would not be there to protect her when the dreadful Russians arrived.

"The silly beggar. All he ever thinks of is jumping into bed with me — never doing anything useful."

By nine o'clock we were following the cart track which would take us through St. Stefan, the village which, only a night or two before, we had seen set alight by 'Stalin Orgls'. Occasionally, we spoke to the few Russians we passed in the woods, friendly enough to us when they heard our "Angleeskis Plenis" and enthusiastic about our "Zhena." In the village of St. Stefan the pathetic survivors, huddled together in clusters in the few farms left intact, told of the horrifying deaths and injuries from burning, of the Kurstenfeld hospital full to overflowing with casualties and of three escaped allied P.O.W.s being herded, at bayonet point, with German P.O.W.s into a pig-sty where they had been locked up — the Swastika and Union Jack side by side at last. Of the twenty village girls taken away to a spot outside the village, to 'peel potatoes' for the troops, only twelve had been seen since. Even with the Germans in full retreat old men were being made to dig trenches for the Russian second and third lines of defence. As we left the village we passed two machine gun emplacements, made comfortable with feather-filled eiderdowns as a protection against the cool earth at night, their crews alert and ready for the counter-attack that would almost certainly never come...a curious army, part highly disciplined, part uncouth and free to do as it pleased. Slowly it was dawning on us that these crawling masses of occupying troops, raping and plundering through the villages and towns, were there systematically to break down morale. Like gangs of escaped thugs promised immunity from the law, they were all round us, their mini machine pistols seemingly attached to them with glue, pursuing their one-sided war against non-belligerent civilians. Towards the end of the afternoon, when we were nearing Kurstenfeld, we met a group of soldiers who offered us some of their freshly brewed firewater. Jerry was the first to take a swig from the bottle and immediately began to hiccough, his eyes streaming.

"Good God! They must have guts of iron," he groaned.

"Uh! Uh!"

There was no escaping. One of them was almost pouring it down my throat.

"I'd rather have a pint of caustic soda," I gasped, as the Russians laughed at me in amazement.

"Zhena! Zhena!" They were toasting Hilde, too uncertain of themselves to touch her; understanding that we were English prisoners of war but still obviously puzzled about how we had got there.

"Dobra! Dobra!" One of them showed his appreciation as we shook hands and left. Hilde had moved to a few feet distance and was waiting.

"Auf wie... Auf wiedershi... Auf..." The Russian was doubled up with laughter, trying hard to stand up straight and say 'Auf wiedersehen'. At last he gave up and, blowing a kiss to Hilde, lay on the ground with his head back, the neck of his nearly empty bottle vertical in his mouth. After ten minutes, we at last found a lieutenant who spoke German. On the strength of the immediate respect he showed us, we came straight to the point.

"What's going on?" asked Jerry bluntly. "Don't your chaps know when to stop? We've heard that Kurstenfeld is in an awful mess."

The lieutenant smiled forbearingly.

"The Russian army is run on different lines to yours," he explained. "And for another thing, it's getting its own back. As far as knowing when to stop is concerned, well, Kurstenfeld, being on the fork of two main roads, is unfortunately a sort of temporary H.Q. for troops moving on. They don't all stop there — at least, not at the moment. So, comrades, Kurstenfeld is going to be occupied by fresh troops at least once every four or five days."

"Don't the men ever get disciplined? Can people make complaints?" I asked.

"They can make as many complaints as they like, but our soldiers have carte blanche to do whatever they fancy for at least twenty-four hours after occupying a village or town. This is part of the liberation process, if you like."

"Liberation?"

"Come now, anything's better than oppression under the Nazis. You ought to have seen the way the Nazis 'liberated' Russia; corpses hanging from the lamp posts everywhere. We don't like killing for the sake of it, like they did — but just having a good time." He sniggered, looking at Hilde "So you see, all I can do is guarantee a lot of sleepless nights in Kurstenfeld for a week or two. Anyway, what are you comrades worrying about — you are British? Aren't these people supposed to be your enemies? Haven't they been bombing your cities; perhaps killing your wives and families?"

Here was a difficult question to answer.

"There are some," I said, "who deserve whatever you care to dish out, I agree. But most of them are harmless, even secretly anti-Nazi and often pro-British."

"But not pro-Russian, eh? Pro-Churchill but not pro-Stalin."

"Perhaps not. But you know what it's all about. Every capitalist is anti-communist at heart; every Communist anti-capitalist; but the Russians have been fighting alongside the British and if they injure someone who is pro-British they injure someone who is supposed to be a friend."

"Try explaining that to these fellows." He swept his arm around embracing the whole landscape, where his men were crawling like ants on the roads and tracks and in the fields.

"They are incapable of thinking things out in such fine detail. To them an enemy is an enemy. Their families have been murdered wholesale by the Nazis and they are not going to forgive. Besides," he gave a short dry laugh, "they are looking for a reward after four hot summers of dust and human stench and four freezing winters of blood-soaked mud and snow, and to them that reward is anything with a soft skin."

I could see that he was not going to penalise any of his subordinates for following their instincts. It was no good arguing: time was running short. The 'blue room' with its dainty furniture was only five kilometres away and, like an old friend with happy memories, I wondered just how much the Russians had tortured it. The lieutenant had put the reason for it all so plainly. The Russian army, trotting across Europe like a donkey, every now and then getting a bite of the succulent carrot dangled in front of its nose. After a time when the carrot grows old, smelly, inedible, the Russian soldier, now used to it, eats it like he eats his breakfast. No longer novel, it has become a habit.

Along the route lay the litter of their particular war: hundreds of gramophone records smashed and scattered around like black slag from a coal pit, horses' harnesses, clothes, saucepans, farm tools, paper, notebooks, cutlery, valuable pictures, priceless broken ornaments, smashed-up telephones — all thrown callously over the road and into the ditches. Lying across an unexploded shell, face down, was a forlorn golliwog, which would never get back to the little boy or girl still crying for it. The road surface had been churned up by tank tracks five foot wide. Though the human bodies had been removed, the horses, killed while playing their part in helping them to murder each other, had been pulled off the road into shell holes, as if being punished, and left to rot and breed bluebottles and typhoid germs.

As the Russian soldiers gathered round us trying to get into conversation we suddenly realised we had lost Jerry. At the same time people were running past and along the track behind us, civilians, shouting incoherently. There had been some sort of an accident... "Children... Hand grenades"...we could pick the words out of a jumble of hysterical shouting. Momentarily the Russians had been forgotten. A woman, palefaced, ran past screaming: "Klausi ! Klausi! My little Klausi!"

When we saw a group of men, including one or two Russian soldiers, approaching, some of them carrying a blanket full of bulky softlooking objects by its corners, we began to realise what had happened. Jerry, his face ashen-white, was holding one corner, shuffling past the civilians who stared fascinated at the blood dripping from the centre onto the road. Answering our unasked questions he was finding it difficult to hold back the tears:

"Dead kids. Not even whole ones. Bits and pieces."

One Russian was helping a woman who was almost fainting, another trying to stop the woman who had passed us, screaming, from tearing the blanket open to find what was left of her child.

"But how?" Hilde tried to ask Jerry. I had never seen her looking so upset.

But Jerry just shuffled on, holding his corner, muttering:

"This bloody war. This bloody war."

That was the last we saw of the good-natured Jerry, who had helped to keep everybody's spirits up for a fortnight. Hilde called after him:

"We'll see you at..."But there was no time to explain where. The little procession had turned off down the road on its way to the mortuary.

"Don't worry," I said. "Jerry's not going to stop here any longer than he has to. He'll get himself sent back to England as soon as he can. There's no reason for him to stay."

"He was such a marvellous man. So nice...so kind," Hilde exclaimed sadly.

The civilians, coming back from the place where the children had been found, told us the grim story about a hand-grenade left lying in the wood, unexploded, the pin still intact. To the children who should never have been there in the first place, examining the funny-looking thing was natural and great fun until one of them had pulled the pin out. Only seconds before the explosion they had been heard shrieking with laughter. Who could blame the Russians this time? Which side the grenade had belonged to would never be known.

The road, busying as we arrived at the outskirts of the town, ran between the fields where the grain shoots, sewn by the farmers to provide them with next year's harvest, were being slowly eaten by the horses, stolen, brought in from Hungary and let loose to graze where they wished. But, used to all this wastage and sadism, the two of us were thinking only of one thing — of one place — as we hurried through the side roads to the house, which had sheltered the people, not so long ago, watched by the Gestapo. At the same time we hoped for what we secretly knew could not be true. Quickly we rounded a corner, almost ran round the side of the sports ground and threw ourselves through the space where the gate had once been. As we approached the house our feet crunched through the piles of broken glass from the windows. A thoughtful person had leant the door, smashed off its hinges, up against the side of the house, showing the wall behind the broken panel, kicked in by a Russian boot.

Hilde, resigned and silent, drew me into the hall and through to her small room, now a pile of rubble. On top of the bed, which had been stripped of its bedclothes, lay what was left of the blue wardrobe; beside it the axe that had smashed it to bits. On the floor was one of her early schoolbooks, 'The Life of Richard Wagner': but the great composer had not been allowed to grace the frontispiece of a book with a forward by Adolf Hitler. Instead, glaring up at us from the floor, defiant and all powerful even in that position, was one of the composer's most devoted fans, the Fuhrer himself.

"Oh, God!" gasped Hilde. "No wonder they smashed everything up. Of all the bad luck. They just saw the picture: that was enough."

But she had not gone to pieces; was not trembling with rage and frustration, as I was. Instead, looking almost apathetic, she was going round methodically looking in those drawers and cupboards not pulled out and broken to bits.

"Nearly everything's gone," she said quietly. "All my clothes — all my jewellery."

From the bedroom we went to the dining room. Here, the Russians had managed to control themselves from breaking up the table and chairs so that they would not have to eat off the floor; spreading out all the valuable china from the walnut dresser, normally there for show, for what must have been a giant feast. With little room to move without treading the broken crockery and odorous vomit into the carpet, we picked our way through the debris.

"They've been dancing on the table."

Hilde had found the lumps of horse manure, shaken off amongst the bits of left over food and plates smashed by their exuberant boots. What could I say? I felt miserably ill equipped to deal with the situation. Before we'd had time to fill in all the details, one of Hilde's friends, a woman who lived a few houses away, called from the entrance where the front door had once been.

"Anna," cried Hilde. "How nice to see you. Are you all right?"

"Oh, I'm all right. I hide in a trunk at night; but, my poor child, what have they done to your house? How can you ever clear up this mess?"

"If we do, they'll probably do it all over again. You can't win against them. If only we could speak their damned language."

The woman, attractive, dark and rather muscular, a type some of the Russians seemed to go for, looked desperate:

"When's this rotten war going to be over?" she gasped.

When Hilde had introduced me and explained our situation, we sat for a while outside on the patio, while Anna related some of the dreadful things that had been happening in Kurstenfeld. Three people had been killed; one of them a man, shot in the stomach while trying to protect his thirteen-year-old daughter. Two French escaped P.O.W.s, wearing civilian clothes, had been taken into the woods and shot, as spies — with no trial.

"But why?" I tried not to let the tingling in the back of my neck affect my voice.

"Why?... They're even suspicious of the rabbits, and that's it. It was the civilian clothes they were wearing that did it. So look out. Keep your battledress jacket on."

She went on to tell us that all the shops had been ransacked, including the electrical shop, owned by the man who had tipped off Hilde about the Gestapo.

"Where is he now?" asked Hilde.

"Gone, I'm afraid. Like all the others on the 'important' list.

Nobody knows where. Herr Brenner, for instance, disappeared after they found his Volksturm uniform in a wardrobe. You don't stand much chance, unless you're very lucky."

"What about Herr Pfeffer, the dentist, Herr Gruber of the Gartnerei and Herr Schneider of the gasthaus?" I asked.

"Oh, they'll all have something to tell you — except Herr Pfeffer, of course. He shot himself before they got him — right under that picture of Hitler in his surgery." She smiled mischievously. "The Burgomeister was very annoyed about it because Herr Pfeffer was in the middle of making him a new set of dentures: he had been very sick after drinking too much wine and had lost his others down the outside loo. Of course, none of his family would look in the bucket for them in spite of his orders. At his first meeting with the new commissar he had to keep his mouth shut for once in his life, which probably saved him from being locked up."

"Exit Herr Pfeffer; one more misguided Nazi," I muttered. "So he did what he always promised he would do — and I never believed him."

"We must go along to the Gartnerei tomorrow after we've cleared the house out." Said Hilde.

"Good idea," I said. "I'd love to know what's happened to the 'Gaffer' and the 'Misery'. And perhaps we could call in and give big Jan a surprise on the way."

When Frau Walter, who owned the local flower shop, paid us a visit we were discussing the possibility of going to the commissar to try to get a 'safe conduct' pass. But Frau Walter, a well-dressed woman in her late forties with a pale drawn face that would normally have looked attractive, seemed to know more about commissars than we did.

"Don't go near the man," she advised. "I went to his office at the kanslei this morning, one of at least a hundred, with complaints about the soldiers. But he seemed to have had orders not to help anyone. 'Sorry', he said. 'This is the army's business — not mine.' Besides, do you know what happened to the escaped English prisoner who was there yesterday — the tall one called Jerry? They interrogated him for two hours and now he's on his way back to England via Odessa, with a guard. That's two thousand kilometres away to the east when the British are only a hundred kilometres to the west. They've got some funny ways, the Russians."

So Jerry was on his way home — the long way round.

She turned to me.

"If they find you, they'll treat you the same. They'll never let you see Hilde again."

We listened to the wise words. She was right. 'Lie low', that was the answer, and get over to the British lines. The British would accept Hilde, after what she had done. But first we felt compelled to see my old friends — and enemies. Of course, I felt no vindictiveness, just a rather helpless sort of pity.

CHAPTER FOURTEEN

When the sun went down we managed to find a rug that we could lay on the floor but, as we waited for the raucous shouting down in the town to get nearer, sleep was impossible. Several times we heard screams and waited uncertainly; but luck was with us. Tonight the Russians were keeping their distance.

In the morning we made an early start and left to seek out some of the people I had worked for and with, on the way to Shaffendorf, where we had decided if possible to hide away from Russian protocol until the war was over. With the end of the war in sight, I had no intention of letting them separate us. At the end of hostilities the way would be open for a quick getaway to the British lines, already so near. Then it would be a matter of inventing some way of getting Hilde out. Luck would look after the rest.

After two hours, we had managed to get the house in quite good order, apart from the smashed-up or missing furniture. With the aid of a few screws and nails left in a drawer I got the front door back into place and was able to lock it. On our way to the Gartnerei we had a chance of seeing how the Russian women behaved. Apart from a few laughs and giggles coming from wherever the soldiers were barracked, we had had no sign of any Russian women since the smooth well-dressed member of the K.G.B. had welcomed us in Mattesdorf. She had been the 'swan': the one on point duty in the middle of the town was the ugly duckling.

Yet, ugly though she undoubtedly was she still was hoping to make herself beautiful with other women's clothes, in a pile beside her on the road. She showed no interest in us, but concentrated on the traffic, comprised of a staff car or two, the wagons of those farmers back at work and any likely-looking women on their own, who happened to be unfortunate enough to get near her.

With their dresses, jumpers and underclothes, she was probably passing away the time picturing the faces of any Russian soldier lover hankering after a Russian woman for a change, with her rolls of fat encased gloriously in real silk western anti-Marxist undies.

At the sight of her, Hilde shuddered:

"How did she get the undies?" she asked a woman standing near us.

Eager to recount all the details the woman explained:

"This morning she stopped poor Feisler Mitzi on her way to see if there was any flour left in any of the shops for her invalid mother, pointed her little pistol at her and made her take all her clothes off in front of everyone — men and all. She had to run to the nearest house naked, poor thing."

We left the policewoman with her shiny leather boots jaunty hat and pile of loot, and headed for the gasthaus. Many of the locals, recognising us, came up and spoke. Some even had time, between the sad stories they told about themselves, to be nosy, asking how we managed to be together, but few of them seemed to believe it when we told them the truth. As we walked through the massive gates into the forecourt of the gasthaus, I suddenly felt curiously conspicuous, struck by the thought of how unusual Hilde and I together must look to other people. But, seeing the forecourt empty and the way to the stables where I hoped to find Jan, clear, the thought of the surprise I was going to give him was uppermost. When we arrived at the entrance to the stables I was glad to find that everything was going according to plan. Jan, his back to the door, was so engrossed in his two horses that he failed to see us.

"Now, my 'curvar' beauties," he was saying stroking their velvety noses. "If you get the 'curvar' chance, don't forget to kick one of those 'curvar' Ruskis up their 'curvar' arses."

"You don't mean to say you don't like our friends either." The sound of my voice two yards away had the desired affect. With his mouth wide open, he turned, and seeing the two of us, stepped backwards into the same trough of 'beautiful horsepiss' that had claimed me on my first day. Hilde burst out laughing and, seeing Jan up to his knees in it, i was soon doubled up, the tears streaming down my face.

"B-But-but ... w-what are you doing here?" he gasped as he climbed out of the trough. Then, looking stupified at the sight of his old enemy.

"Fraulein Bayer. I-I can't believe..."

"It's all right, Jan," I said. "You're not dreaming. Aren't you glad to see us?"

"Glad to see you?" He showed his feelings by flinging his arms round my neck and kissing me on both cheeks. "And Fraulein Bayer ..." With a flourish he greeted her, in his fertile imagination already inventing fairy-tales. "So lucky you didn't let me go home. I was planning to stay there, you know — I can tell you now. In fact, my contacts were going to hide me and I was all set to disappear into the underground movement in Cracow. But if you had let me go home I would never have had the delight of this moment. Fraulein, I kiss your hand with great respect." His vast hands, channelled with dirt that would never come off, grasped her small one as if it was a horse's hoof. She smiled at him, wincing slightly.

"I'm sure you must have lots of stories to tell us," she said.

Jan hadn't lost his touch. While we told him enough details to keep his mind at rest, and his tongue quiet, he rummaged about under the hay, bringing out a bottle of wine and a few delicacies hidden there.

"Why still hide things?" I asked. "You're the master now." I looked dubiously at the cold pork. "Hey, you haven't chopped up Herr..." Hilde, have a piece of Herr Schneider. Jan promised he was going to chop him up in little bits as soon as he got the chance. What are you doing still working here, anyway?"

Jan looked sheepish, trying to make excuses:

"I love the horses. They're not Nazis and never did me any harm."

But he was not going to keep his pretence up for long. At that moment Herr Schneider came into the stable, checking himself at the sight of his former prisoner with the familiar girl from the labour exchange; but he didn't give away his emotions.

"Stooart," he said, stretching out a flabby hand. "Fraulein Bayer. Welcome. I see I have no need to offer you food and drink." In the smile he gave Jan as he looked at the remains of our feast, was the slightest trace of contempt.

After we had repeated our usual abridged version of the happenings of the last week, he seemed to sense that I was avoiding asking how he and his family had been faring with the Russians.

"We are very lucky," he said. "Jan has done so much for us. He is the great protector. Oh yes. I don't deny that Russian soldiers have been billeted in my hotel, nor that my family and I have been forced to live and sleep in the attic. But we are safe. Jan is as faithful as the old doberman I once had, and sleeps always on a mattress outside our door. No harm will come to us, I know that. I think he is grateful to me for being so good to him in the past. Aren't you, Jan?"

(And supplying him with so many delicacies without knowing it, as well as at least ten eggs a day, I thought.) Jan looked as near guilty as he ever would.

"Oh, Yes. Herr ... Yes, Yes." he gabbled.

"And Olga," continued Herr Schneider. "She helps my wife and daughter. She is even now in the town trying to get some flour and potatoes."

I thought it was time we left before I caught Jan's disease and prostrated myself before the great man — now a pale shadow of his former well-fed self. But I had no sympathy for him: if his right arm was getting flabby from lack of saluting, he would have to exercise it by doing a bit of work for a change. Still knuckling under to authority, Jan went off with the wagon and horses.

"I'll get the potatoes into the ground before the 'curvar' Ruski has them."

He wished me goodbye with a slap on the back nearly pitching me into the urine trough and squeezing Hilde's hand again as if he was trying to squeeze the juice out of a cocoanut. Then he cracked his whip at his two horses without touching them and disappeared quickly through the gates.

On his way to the fields Jan acted as an express messenger, spreading the news that we were around; and, wherever we went, we found ourselves raising the morale of the nosy ones by giving them something extra to talk about. When we finally arrived at the Gartnerei we were immediately surrounded by people. Up the path the 'Gaffer' was coming towards us his once jaunty hat, looking as if it had been used for mopping up the glasshouse after a watering session, pulled down straight over his head. Looking more like a clothes prop than a former Nazi 'Big Guy' he greeted us, explaining that he had already heard about us from Jan and asking us straightaway up to the house, where the 'Misery' shook hands, quite happy now that everyone else was in trouble. Over a glass of wine and a snack of bread and cucumber he told us his sad story.

"The Fuhrer might have been a fool over some things," he began, "but certainly not over the...communist problem." He could say what he liked about his worshipful master now — good or bad.

"He had the right idea: that Germany and England should join together to fight the Reds. Don't you think so?"

"I don't think anybody should join with anybody to fight anybody." exclaimed Hilde.

"You have the same idea as many, Fraulein. But when you hear my story you may change your mind."

"Please tell us, Herr Gruber, if you would like to," said Hilde. "But first, how is your wife? We have not seen her."

The 'Scratcher' must have been very ill indeed not to be down in the gardens, working.

"You will hear how my wife is." Brushing the tears from his red eyes he embarked on the most spectacular story we had heard so far.

"We had both gone to bed. That is to say, we were sitting fully clothed in our bedroom for the third time in three nights. We were very tired and hungry. The Russians had stolen most of our vegetables but we still had a few lettuce plants and we were eating those. In the early hours of the morning the streets were full of drunks, breaking into the houses and taking anything they wanted. I had barricaded the door, but one fellow smashed the window and got in. He wore a star, which showed He was a lieutenant, but this made no difference. He just got his revolver, stuck it in my stomach and forced me into a corner. Then he pushed my wife onto the bed, putting the gun on the side of the table where he could reach it."

As my former confident 'Partei' boss began to sob, I gave him a pat on the back. At that moment I couldn't help feeling sympathy even for someone who had climbed the ladder, using his fellow men and women as the rungs. The growth of stubble and the turkey neck helped to build up the image of a broken man. With a great effort, he pulled himself together and continued.

"When I saw him molesting her, dragging his sweaty hands over her body and flinging her clothes in a heap on the floor I dashed over, but he was too quick for me and waved me back into the corner with his gun. I thought it better to stay there. I would not have been any use dead either — and he would have killed me. Yes, he certainly would have killed me. She was screaming to me to help her, but what could I do?" He wiped the tears away again and continued haltingly. "There was a terrible noise of boots on the stairs and six of them, all common privates and all drunk, lurched into the room with machine pistols. One of them seemed to understand German, so I begged him to help my wife. He laughed and said: 'Yes, I think he has had enough. It is our turn now.' One of them kicked the officer off the bed before he could get his gun again and threw him down the stairs. Then..."

He paused, unable to speak clearly.

"Don't bother if you don't want to tell us," said Hilde lamely. But, wiping his eyes again he went on:

"Then your filthy allies raped my wife one after the other in front of my eyes ..." After he had blurted this out, he broke down completely, his head in his hands, his elbows on his knees.

I felt I had to say something, however weak.

"I didn't choose to fight in this rotten war. Nor did I have anything to do with the Russians being our allies." I looked hopelessly at Hilde.

"I am sorry for your wife — really sorry. Please tell her

this," she said.

"She's in hospital. She is lucky. There are so many who should be there and aren't." His voice was a monotone, devoid of emotion. "She slashed her wrists with some broken glass, but they got her just in time. She is still alive but doesn't know anyone — stares straight at the ceiling — always straight at the ceiling — doesn't recognise me, or anyone."

We left, feeling genuinely sorry for him and quite helpless. Outside the house we saw Auntie, beckoning to us from her favourite lettuce patch and looking none the worse for wear.

"I have heard about you two." Her hands, covered in earth, were grasping first Hilde's, then mine. "I am so delighted that you are together. What a brave girl you are, Fraulein Bayer." She told us that she had some Russians billeted in her house.

"I have to cook for them," she said. "They are really quite nice fellows." Her face was more like a shrewd little angel than ever. "They keep bringing me the food which they have stolen from all over the place. But it's all so silly, as I must be slowly eating my way through all my friends' larders. One of the boys is a very good cook. He says he used to watch his mother cooking nice meat dishes, until Comrade Stalin came along and took all the meat for the army." She gave one of her infectious little giggles. "You'll never believe this: the other day some of his comrades played a trick on him and he cooked Frau Doktor Bendel's cat, thinking it was a skinned rabbit. I knew about the joke and didn't eat any, but he and the other boys with me seemed to love it and kept smacking their lips, shouting 'Dobra' and swilling it down nicely with my last bottle of wine. I thought one of them 'miaowed' but he was only belching. Of course, I never told Frau Doktor Bendel. She only kept the cat to kill the mice anyway; and they've gone since the food ran out. Another time, he cooked some beautiful pork and, as I realised that only the Frau Burgomeister could have pork as good as that, I took what was left over back to her, telling her to hide it well. When they came back, I told them that some of their horrible friends had come and stolen it and, screaming and shouting with rage, they grabbed their guns and rushed out in search of their nasty comrades, who had done this horrible thing to their dear old

Auntie. They would kill them — kill them deader than the pig they had stolen. Of course, they never went back to look in the Burgomeister's house." She giggled again. "Poor Herr Gruber's marrows had more brains."

Her laughter was as good as a fresh breeze. Like Frau Bayer, she had found that the way past a Russian's tommy gun was through his stomach.

"Whatever happened to Frau Kempfer and Frau Tatt?" I asked.

"Oh, those two poor things," Auntie's voice was full of genuine sympathy. "Frau Kempfer is helping to dig the Russian defence line and Frau Tatt was sent off this morning to peel potatoes." She saw that we were puzzled. "Ah, you don't know: everyday our younger women are living in dread of being herded into parties and sent off to peel potatoes — the pregnant ones as well. They have to rely on their luck." She looked round her as if to make sure there were no Russians about, and whispered: "Some of the potato peelers haven't come back and we've heard that they have been taken on as prostitutes for the troops..."

"As if they needed any," exclaimed Hilde.

"We have heard that the girls have two alternatives," went on Auntie; "One to be willing and live, and the other to resist and get shot."

CHAPTER FIFTEEN

Sadly we left Auntie, the only worker left in an empty Gartnerei, holding the fort on her own, and made across the fields towards Shaffendorf in search of peace and security; away from the main road, overflowing with Russians, their guns full of bullets and their bellies full of 'fire-water'. Hilde, still padded out with four pairs of bloomers and wearing her grandmother's ill-fitting skirt, the old lace-up skating boots and a dingy-looking head scarf, still found all this ineffective against Russian gusto; attracting the few who had wandered off the main road into the woods, like pins to a magnet. As I had got used to a regular routine of simple persuasion I now found that I could convince all of them that I was English and that Hilde was my 'Zhena'. After a few slaps on the back and cries of "Zhena! Zhena! Dobra!" their interest in her would slip away like an old garment, and they would leave us alone again — alone, except for the dead horses. With an eye to the so-called superior intelligence of Man both sides had got rid of their dead soldiers, leaving the horses to contaminate the atmosphere and to provide the flies with a constant source of delight. We held our noses when we got anywhere near the sad, sometimes almost unrecognisable shapes, eaten away by the rapacious animals of the night and tried to avoid looking at their pitifully ineffectual bulk as they lay, often pushed unceremoniously out of the way into shell-holes. Now they were devoid at last of the splendour, which had made them the hardest-used, bravest and most beautiful fighting machines in history. Perhaps my father, if he had been there, would have suggested hopefully that somewhere, in a heaven reserved for animals, their souls (if animals had been blessed with such things) were grazing contentedly.

After picking our way through the woods for a mile or two, sitting down amongst the dried leaves and cones, we stared silently into the quiet shadow of the silver birches, dwarfed between the tall gently rustling fir trees. So far we had not experienced such peace and the promise of a haven away from the Russians, where we could sleep to our hearts' content, seemed not far off. On our way to the edge of the woods near Schaffendorf, disturbing a small doe a few yards away, we felt almost carefree again. There, impossibly near, its delicately sensitive nose twitching at the suspicion of a foreign scent, was a Bambi which could have jumped straight out of the Disney film.

How could the trees have warned us that also very near one of the nosiest people in Shaffendorf was watching, leaning on her rake amongst the trees probably doing nothing for the first time since I had last seen her?

"Stooart! Stooart! But...I don't believe it's you. How did you get free?"

All the time her eyes, full of curiosity, were resting on Hilde. Frau Tagmeier, drawn but healthy looking, was back at work in the fields, and wherever Frau Tagmeier was, I knew Heinrich would not be far away.

And there he was, standing in the middle of his neglected potato patch and getting the potatoes under the ground, like Jan, before the Russians got them; his two sad cows patiently waiting, one each side of the wagon-shaft, to get back to their sadder-than-ever evening meal of chopped-up straw and hard-to-see turnips. I soon realised that Heinrich, thinner and older-looking, had buried the hatchet as he grasped my hands, like a long-lost friend, and allowed his watery eyes to wander unchecked over Hilde's badly concealed curves; the corners of his mouth full of gold teeth and gaps, trying to spread round to his ears in a friendly smile. Sitting on the wagon, surrounded by the bare patches of untended earth, deserted by the terrified farmers, we recounted just enough of our story to cure the worst symptoms of Herr and Frau Tagmeier's curiosity.

So Heinrich's piggy bank was more important than his safety. With his wife, more terrified of him than of the Russians, he had decided that he was going to do his work and somehow keep alive.

"Has the village been left alone," I asked.

"Shaffendorf left alone by the Ruskis?" Heinrich's snarling grin greeted my suggestion that they had kept away from the little cul-de-sac village. "Not on your life, my friend. A commissar has taken over the burgomeister's bedroom as his office and is probably right now lying on the bed working on his papers, with his knees up and his boots on the eiderdown; if there's one left."

Suddenly his face became serious.

"My advice to you two is to get out of the village as soon as you can, if you want to keep together."

Was there never going to be a place where we could sit and think?

Balanced on the old wagon creaking and grinding its way back to the village, I noticed straightaway a change: the haughty geese and the friendly ducks were missing. Heinrich explained that they had one by one graced the tables of various official and unofficial Russian banquets.

"Where there's a commissar any animal fit to eat doesn't stay alive long."

Its streets deserted, the village was like a cemetery, with only one bright spot; the yard of Number Thirty-Five, where the food cooked by Frau Wagner and her daughter Anna was laid out on an upside-down four poster bed with the posts sawn off short acting as a table. As we passed the open gate we saw half a dozen Russians eating and drinking. One short glimpse was enough to show me how my old bosses were faring: Frau Wagner was struggling along with a huge dish of boiled potatoes in some sort of sauce; Grandfather Wagner was lost in the background keeping company with Frieda the owl, hopefully asleep under a black canopy. A Russian was sitting with one arm round Anna, pale and dishevelled, but still wearing her fixed wooden smile. The Russian was using his free hand like a mechanical shovel to fill his belly. Johann Wagner was leaning on a two-pronged fork with murder in his eyes.

We were not going to make the mistake of stopping to greet my old friends, in case some of the Russians might decide to tell the commissar: instead, we stayed on the wagon, drawn slowly towards the end of the village, where we could hear a group of soldiers approaching round the corner near Number Three, singing a boisterous, unmusical folksong.

"I think this is where we get off and hide." Hilde, though quite unperturbed, was taking no chances. "What are we going to do for somewhere to sleep?"

It's a problem all right," I said. "If only we could be alone, away from all the people who want 'protecting'."

We made our way along the road away from the singing Russians, watching the orange ball of the sun disappearing slowly behind the fir trees to the west, where the British would soon be waiting to help us to peace and freedom.

"Looks all right," I said. "As if no one's there."

At the same moment, the snarl coming from low down behind the gate and the black nose trying to push its way underneath in the dust, was enough to show us that at least a dog was there and that we weren't very popular.

"God! If it's not a Russian," I said, "it has to be some other sort of animal. When are we going to get some peace?"

"Stooart, come on in here."

I recognised the voice of Fred Bannister's 'Mrs' calling to me from a window of the farm next door. Frau Haffner, a pleasantly round woman in her forties, was calling over her shoulder into the house:

"It's Stooart...with..." She looked at Hilde, her eyes questioning.

"Fraulein Bayer." I introduced her and we were shown into a room full of women and girls, sitting round a table drinking coffee and eating a few skimpy scraps of food from a common dish in the centre.

As usual, I had to tell them how I came to be there — and with the girl who, (one of the women near to us was whispering, eagerly,) had been in charge at the Kurstenfeld Labour Exchange. The ritual over, we soon found out why they were all together in the one room.

"The Russian seems to lose his nerve when he sees so many women together. They are cowards, really." Frau Haffner looked concerned. "You are tired," she said. Why don't you go and sleep next door in Ida's house? It is empty. Ida has gone to her sister in Vienna. If we need you we'll shout, don't worry."

She smiled at me, as if she thought that a flick of my fingers could turn all Russians into angels.

"Fine," said Hilde. "But I don't believe the dog thinks the same as you do."

"Oh, Luchsi. Don't take any notice of him. He barks a bit, that's all, but he'd run away from a field mouse. He hasn't even stopped them stealing everything from the house, so naturally Ida didn't trust him to protect her. We're just feeding him, when we can, until she comes back. Just go in through the gate and take no notice."

It was pitch dark when we left them: the moon was new and the stars, unaffected by the madness of the tiny world so far away, twinkled serenely in the black depth of space.

Gingerly we made our way to the wicket gate, the savage snarls from the other side challenging us to open it if we dared.

"Luchsi, Luchsi. Good dog," cooed Hilde uncertainly, as the black mongrel leapt in the air, fangs dripping.

"He's only play-acting," I tried to convince myself.

But Hilde had brought a little piece of salami with her and within seconds the dog was grovelling at her feet, his tail wagging frantically.

Frau Haffner had told us where Ida had hidden some food; enough to revive our spirits and put an extra decibel or two on Luchsi's frightening snarls. Good friends with us now, he followed us round the cottage as we looked for somewhere to sleep. The only bed not smashed up was a double one in the corner of the front room, where a weak bulb hung from the centre of the ceiling over a table and four chairs. The bed, like a square shallow box with six inch sides, had a thin threadbare mattress, and no bedclothes — but we were tired enough to sleep anywhere. Sitting opposite each other, we spread out our little bits of food, while Luchsi, who had gobbled his small ration in three seconds, sat and stared hopefully up at Hilde, his dry black nose resting on her knee and his eyes full of sad reproach. In the room and over the whole surrounding district, an eerie silence hung like a heavy black curtain in the night; the only noise, when Luchsi opened his mouth, panted for a few seconds and shut it again. When we had finished, holding hands across the table we tried to plan our next move.

Hilde suggested the British lines, sixty kilometres to the west, but with the fighting still on we could well be shot as spies if we got too near the front.

"The war will be over soon. It must be," I said. "I just can't see why the Germans are holding out."

"Wouldn't England do the same, with the enemy on her own soil?"

Hilde was right, of course, but how long could things go on like this before the total collapse? How long would the ground in Shaffendorf shudder under the impact of bombs being dropped day and night on Graz, sixty kilometres away? What was the limit of human endurance?

"Come on," Hilde said. "We'd better get into this coffin." There was still no sound outside. "I don't trust the silence, but to hell with the Russians. I'm so tired I've got to sleep."

"We've got to be ready for them," I warned — but in five minutes we were stretched out on the thin mattress, with the light out, listening to Luchsi snoring in the corner, where he was lying on my jacket.

"Marriage might be a bit boring after all this," Hilde muttered with her eyes shut. She was nearly in dreamland.

But the heavenly peace wasn't to last for long. After about half an hour the front door shot open at the end of a thick boot. Before the intruder could get to the room, I leapt out and switched on the light. Luchsi was doing his best to appear dangerous - barking ferociously.

"Come on, boy, "I hissed." Get him! Get him!" But he didn't seem too keen on the idea and was content to go on barking at a distance. Hilde was awake by the time the man staggered into the room, obviously hopelessly drunk — grimy and carrying full kit, as if he had just come from the front. The markings on his uniform showed he was a lieutenant.

"Ang..." I was about to tell him I was English when I realised that be wasn't interested.

Luchsi had developed a continuous low snarl — his ears back and every hair along the top of his spine perpendicular. The Russian kicked out, catching him on the jaw and sending him squealing back to his corner. Bleary eyes threatening, the lieutenant turned his gun on us and we knew that the slightest wrong move would mean a bullet for one or both of us. He was glaring at Hilde.

"Essen!"

It sounded like his one word of German. He wanted food, not women — or at least, not yet.

He was shouting again:

"Schnapps!"

So he had another word. But things bad become difficult: we couldn't produce anything to drink.

"Poor old Luchsi,", whispered Hilde, reaching up to a shelf, high on the wall, where she had been keeping a few slices of salami, a chunk of bread and half a bottle of milk for all of us in the morning. But the lieutenant was paying no attention: pointing his rifle at the dog and shouting abuse in Russian he was taking aim.

"NO!" cried Hilde. "He hasn't done you any harm. Leave him alone."

The officer seemed to realise she was a woman for the first time and, looking her up and down, smiled. Then, scowling again, he shouted once more.

"Essen!"

Hilde laid out the breakfast she had saved on the table, avoiding the big map that the Russian had spread out with unsteady hands. Now that he had lowered his fur hood he was showing the familiar close-cropped head and slightly pockmarked skin of the Mongolian.

"There you are and I hope it chokes you," she said.

He towered over her suspiciously, hiccoughing in anger, but she just smiled at him without flinching. With a grunt he threw himself onto one of the chairs and, within five minutes, had pushed every scrap of food on the table and the milk down his throat, expressing his appreciation with a loud belch. For five minutes, he leant back in his chair, satisfied, his hands clasped across his stomach, staring at the wall, and taking no notice of Hilde and me, watching him from beside the bed where we stood. Then, as he slowly picked himself up from the chair we watched him reach for his gun which we had leant against the wall. I felt the chill of fear in my spine: for this man was as drunk as any I had seen and would stop at nothing.

Still sitting, he laid the gun on his knee, again staring at the wall: then he reached for his belt and slowly drew out a magazine of ammunition. The click, as he pushed it into position, sounded like the gates of hell closing, shutting us in with our fate. There was going to be no escape: to a man in his state the word 'Angleeski' would mean nothing. He got up, the gun in his hand, and turned slowly towards us, signalling us to get out of the way as he staggered over to the bed. Then surprisingly, first staring at us and then at the bed, he began to look almost human, a shadow of sympathy softening his features as unexpected as his next move. Pointing at the bed, he indicated that we should lie on it, and turned away with no more interest. Back in the bed, fully clothed and waiting for what was to happen I had soon given up trying to fathom out the reason for his behaviour. All I knew was that the unexpected was happening as he turned, lurched back to the other side of the room, took off his jacket and spread it out on the floor with his gun beside it. Within half a minute he was snoring and we were looking at each other as if the whole performance had been a pantomime act.

"We'd better think what we're going to do," I whispered. "Is it safe to stay here, d'you think, with the Russian? When he's sober he might not be so good-hearted."

I turned my face towards Hilde, six inches away. Her eyes were shut and she was fast asleep. Gingerly, I lifted myself up on my elbow, looking across at the curled up black ball that was Luchsi. The lieutenant lay on his hack, his gun beside him, where I could quite easily reach it: but, while I was making up my mind, he rolled over with a grunt on top of it. My eyes were heavy: my brain was not going to work much longer. Above everything, I had to sleep. The corner of the map, hanging over the edge of the table was the only thing at that moment keeping me awake. Something told me the map was important: the thin line, following an almost straight course from top to bottom, meant something. Carefully, I lifted myself out of bed and crept over to the table, terrified of waking the dog. On the large-scale map of Burgenland someone had drawn in red the border of what was obviously to be the Russian zone of Austria. Sadly, the fate of Kurstenfeld, seventeen kilometres to the east of the line, had already been sealed and was there, punching out at me from a flat uninteresting expanse of paper. I felt frustrated and inadequate: deep in the depth of hell I imagined Satan, sniggering, while the Burgenlanders were patiently waiting for their saviours to liberate them.

Down onto the map the light shone dimly, inviting me to fold it up and put it back in the officer's kit bag. Though I tried to persuade myself I was exaggerating, I couldn't help feeling that he might shoot us once he realised that we knew the top-secret he had carelessly passed on through being drunk, but there was just the chance that, giving us the benefit of the doubt, he might think, when he would find the map still open in the morning, that we hadn't bothered to look and, with this in mind, I left it where it was and let myself slowly back onto the hard mattress. Safer to be here than outside, I thought.

Nothing happened until seven o'clock in the morning when Luchsi, keen to get out and look for something like a lamp post, began to wander round the officer's leg, whining and sniffing as he washed himself in a basin full of cold water brought from a tap in the kitchen. Straightaway, noticing that he had taken away the map, I nudged Hilde, who had woken up but was keeping still.

"Keep your fingers crossed," I whispered. "I think the fellow's all right." I got up and let Luchsi out, waiting for some sort of comment from the officer. Instead, he busied himself packing his kit together, taking no notice of us, and holding his head, walked out without looking or saying a word.

Minutes later, there was a knock at the door and Frau Haffner let herself in. Without giving us time to ask how she and the other women had got on in the night, she cried breathlessly:

"Listen. The Tagmeier Heinrich met the Burgomeister

when he went out early this morning to pick mushrooms and he came running straight back. The Burgomeister told him that the commissar knows you're here. He's sending some soldiers round to get you. He says you've got to go back to England by way of Odessa — without Fraulein Bayer." She turned to Hilde. "He says he will give you a very special position, as you have been an Englishman's girlfriend."

"Very kind of him," said Hilde. "The position of his girlfriend, I suppose."

"You've got no time," exclaimed Frau Haffner, desperately. "You've got to ... "

There was a loud, official-sounding knock at the door — the next best thing to knocking it down completely. Luckily, our kit bag was packed and, grabbing it, I flew after Hilde through the back door and towards the woods a hundred yards away. A few deer, peeping out and grazing, disappeared as if they had springs in their legs. Reaching the trees, we didn't stop to look back, but, with a safe distance between us and the back of the farms, scrambled through the undergrowth until we both fell over, gasping.

That was the end of our visit to Shaffendorf, — one place I never wanted to set eyes on again. I knew now that the noose tied round Hilde's neck could be tightened by one false word or movement — or even by just a little bit of bad luck. Under cover of the woods, where the flies buzzed around merrily seeking out the dead horses, lying here and there among the trees stripped of their foliage by exploding shells, we found our way back to Kurstenfeld — and the Schneider gasthaus. Outside in the street stood Herr Schneider and Jan surrounded by Russian soldiers who stared at Hilde with watery eyes, shouting their usual friendly, "Dobra! Dobra! Zhena!" nudging each other when Hilde smiled at them and gabbling their endless unrecognisable jokes.

I was feeling that soon the dice were going to be thrown for or against us, when I first saw Alex approaching, the black curled hair hanging ever the dark skin of his forehead making him look more like a gypsy than ever. Here was a man whom everyone knew — who had become a 'character' in the town since he had first arrived from the Ukraine, with a batch of workers, and had gone straight into the hospital with an acute appendicitis. Recovering, he had left the ward and had been taken on the staff as a porter. That had been three years before and, during the ensuing time, he had grown to be respected by all and even feared by some, gradually gaining influence as a man who could lay his hands on anything which anyone might need, at any time, and at any price which would make it worth his while. As he came up to us he grasped the hand of the girl who would be his lifelong friend; for it was Hilde who, because of his undoubted efficiency, had got him the job in the hospital and helped to keep him there against a lot of opposition from the more jealous members of the staff.

"It's all very well those comrades shouting, 'Zhena'," he remarked aside to me, after she had introduced him. "But you two are going to be in trouble all along the line, unless you can prove that this lady is your wife."

"Wife?"

He took no notice of my astonishment.

"With a marriage certificate you'll be made. Your lives will change. No more dangers. Out of the cage, into the open." He didn't seem to notice my surprise. "Now, listen to me: we must see that you two get married."

You could almost hear his brain thinking it all out, as he turned to Hilde.

"Fraulein Bayer, you're going to get married." Giving her no time to answer he went on: "Many times I have offered you presents and you have always hurt my feelings by refusing them. Now," he looked triumphant, "you are not going to refuse. I am interpreter to the Kurstenfeld commissar and, if I tell him to, the commissar will marry you — Russian style."

I imagined vodka, like water pouring out of a tap, Hilde's hair bedecked in flowers and a cabaret of leg-slapping Cossacks.

"You have some very good ideas," said Hilde, half-joking.

"I have a very good brain." he was totally unabashed. "I use it and everything is easy. Don't forget, I am the Commissar's official interpreter and, on top of that, I have created my own personal position of 'official provider'. In other words, I get him what he wants - at a price, of course. The price today will be marrying you at three o'clock."

We went back to the house, ate a few scraps which, we had hidden away, and waited for the afternoon. With a marriage certificate, we had been told that we would not be separated and that nothing would happen to Hilde, so, as far as I was concerned, the sooner we got one the better.

Finally, in the commissar's office, we found Alex, wearing a pink shirt, with a primrose pinned on the front, and neatly creased blue trousers: beside him, the Burgomeister, with a clean apron and a beaming smile hidden behind his huge Hindenburg moustache and side whiskers. Also, the commissar and an orderly, both in plain uniforms and exuding the warmth of genuine welcome. After a glowing account from Alex, with embroidered details, of my escape, aided by Hilde and her family, the commissar, with the tail end of a hangover from some party the night before, wasted no time. Sitting himself at a table with a form printed in Russian, a pen, a bottle of ink and a clean sheet of blotting paper, he began to jabber at us in Russian.

"Don't take any notice of what he says," said Alex. "All you have to do is nod when I tell you."

During the rest of the proceedings we watched Alex and nodded at the commissar when Alex nodded at us, holding hands when we were told to and only realising we were married when the clerk stamped the form and handed it to us with Alex's witnessing signature. Then, thanking them all, especially Alex, highly delighted with his achievement, we left and made our way back to the house. Inside the front door, holding Hilde close, I said:

"What do you think could possibly happen to us now, a staid married couple?"

But she didn't answer. Instead, she went and sat on a chair in the front room, her chin supported on her hand with her elbow on her knee, staring at the wall. Then, suddenly jumping up, she exclaimed:

"We're not safe here." Her voice was quiet and earnest. "Let's go to Liefenstein — it's only twenty kilometres away."

"Liefenstein?"

"The castle — Liefenstein castle."

"What about the castle? You're not going to tell me we can get inside and hide in one of the dungeons."

"I don't know about the dungeons, but we can probably get inside."

"Whatever are you talking about?"

"The owner of the castle is Baron Von Halstedt. My father used to hunt with him when he was younger. They were great friends. I have never met him but I've heard he's very nice — and very handsome!" she added, enigmatically.

"Is that to the east?"

"Yes."

"Good, then we'll go west."

"You're jealous, and you haven't even seen him."

"Nothing you think up surprises me any more. Good, when do we go?"

I had put the marriage certificate on the table. As far as I was concerned, with all the Russian characters, it could have been a recipe for beef strogonoff, but to me it still meant security.

"If they're drunk they won't take any notice of that," she said with conviction. "Let's get away from here tomorrow."

CHAPTER SIXTEEN

After a reasonably peaceful night we set out once more across country away from the main road. In the woods and fields we came face to face with the hideous results of the fighting, picking our way past the shell holes, keeping as much distance as possible between our noses and the dead horses and avoiding masses of coiled barbed wire. Empty dugouts trees stripped from beauty to ugliness — everywhere the silence, like a muffling cloak over what had once been. Looking at the debris around us we heard the terrified screams of the wounded and smelt the smell of death still lingering.

At the entrance to a camouflaged pit, a gatepost served as a horizontal prop to hold up the roof. Hilde gasped:

"Look!"

We saw the crimson words scrawled from end to end. In its horror the plain message, rubbed on by a finger soaked in blood, shouted a frustrated soldier's last message to an insane world:

ALLES SCHWINDL (Everything a swindle.)

The man who had put his trust in the Austrian waif, Adolf Hitler, risen to the dizzy heights of mad power had finally died for him, disgusted and disillusioned.

Away from the trees we started to walk across a nearly-ploughed field, so even and clean that the god Mars must have decided to exempt a piece of land from the slaughter; and over it we walked with a sense of freedom now that we were away from the gory woods. And then, right in the middle, with a hundred yards of earth surrounding us on all sides, we nearly tripped over the first human corpse we had seen. Lying where the ground dipped into a shallow hole, steely blue eyes wide open and staring placidly straight at us, the young Russian soldier lay on his back, his mouth slightly open as if he had just remarked: "Oh, to be alive on a day like this!" — not a mark on him to show how he had been killed, not a scratch or a drop of blood.

"Look at his hands," breathed Hilde, almost reverently, as if we had suddenly entered a church.

With well-manicured nails, they were smooth, lying spread from his sides as if he was apologising, trying to say: "It's not my fault. I'm not here by choice, you know."

If a hand-grenade had not nipped my soldiering in the bud before I had had time to get 'tough' I would have thought nothing of emptying his pockets and turning him over to see what had happened; but I couldn't.

"We'd better leave the poor devil," I said.

"But he looks so...alive. So pathetic." Hilde stood still, staring down at him. "Shouldn't we bury him, or something?"

"They'll find him. Come on, let's go."

We set off again across the field.

"My God!" I suddenly realised what had happened to him. "Look over there." I gripped Hilde's arm. "Stop! Don't move!"

She looked across to where I was pointing. On a notice at the side of the field a hundred yards away, lettered large and red, were the words:

GEFAHR MINEN.(Danger land-mines)

No wonder they had left him there. In a hurry they must have wondered why they should risk the same fate. We stood stock still. A move in any direction and we might well join company with the dead man. We stared at each other uncertainly, and then at the smooth unruffled earth surrounding us. There was no answer to the situation: the spectre of death was watching, laughing at us.

("Take a chance. You've got to reach the other end of the field, anyway. If I hadn't been kind to you, Stuart, the hand-grenade would have killed you. And you, Hilde. How many times could I have had you shot? Now, perhaps, I have decided that your numbers are up. Who knows?")

Slowly, we moved one foot in front of the other, taking

longish strides and watching the ground for the slightest disturbance of the surface. Uncertainly, I told Hilde to follow me, putting her feet where mine had been. The temptation to run was almost unbearable.

"What about the woods? We — we just haven't been bothering." Hilde's tone was almost reproachful.

"Maybe we've been lucky, or maybe there weren't any mines. It doesn't matter. We've got away with it so far but we've got to look out from now on." I didn't feel like talking.

While we edged slowly towards the end of the field, I kept my mouth shut, concentrating; steering round a patch where the centre was darker, as if recently disarranged, until at last we had made it; and sat down a hundred yards from the dead man, where he lay peacefully contemplating the sky.

"Poor devil: we should have done something," muttered Hilde.

"Good God! You're lucky not to be in little bits."

My heart was still beating furiously — the realisation of what might have been was bringing me out in a cold sweat. And here was Hilde, feeling guilty about a dead Russian. My face must have shown my feelings.

"But we're all right," she said quietly. She put her arms round me. "Now, calm down."

An hour and a half later, towards the end of the afternoon, we reached Mariasdorf, a village on the way to Liesenstein.

"I've got friends here," said Hilde. "Herr and Frau Zimmerman. Let's go and see them."

We made for the farm, where the old man and his wife welcomed us with tears of relief.

"I can't believe it. I can't believe it," Frau Zimmerman kept repeating. "The Herr Gott is kind. Everything has been so horrible. Now we needn't worry any more."

When Hilde told them that we had to go on, they both begged us to stay for at least one night.

"It will be one night nearer the end of the war, and then all the filthy Russians will go, the British will come and we shall have peace at last," exclaimed Herr Zimmerman. "I will always be grateful."

I caught Hilde's glance: but how could we disillusion these hopeful people? Why should we upset them by telling them what we knew about the border?

So we agreed to stay with them and to start off early in the morning. Together we ate some of the spinach-like stew, which Frau Zimmerman had cooked from young stinging nettles, poured over what was left of our salami, trying to calm them and help them to forget their terror. But, before we went to bed, the two insisted that we barricade the doors front and back and settled themselves to sit bolt upright at the kitchen table, fully-clothed, in the way in which they said they had been spending the nights since the Russians had been in the village.

By ten o'clock we were settling down for the night. Hilde had been allocated the big bed in the front room and I was on an oak bench helping to prop up the barricade, my feet on my trousers which were hanging over the arm under a blanket and my head resting on a cushion the other end. We didn't have long to wait for the evening activity, which everyone had secretly been expecting. By eleven o'clock a boot had been pushed through the bottom panel of the door and, while a gun was held through pointing into the room a hand found the bolt and undid it. Now was the time to act quickly. It depended on Hilde's co-operation, and this time she must have been so surprised by the short sharp order that she didn't hesitate.

"Get out through the back window and hide. NOW!"

She wasted no time. As the flimsy barricade of furniture began to wobble and disintegrate, she disappeared. Three seconds later the barricade was pushed over completely and against the blackness of the night we were face to face with two objects which could have jumped straight out of 'The Arabian Nights' — Mongolians though they were — with high cheekbones, slanting eyes, cropped heads as hairless and shiny as mirrors, pock-marked faces, clean-shaven except for the six inch long wisps of hair twisted and dangling from the corners of their upper lips.

I understood enough Russian by this time to know what they were shouting as they barged from one room to another, opening cupboards and overturning any furniture which had been used in the barricades.

"Where's the woman?"

As they must have seen Frau Zimmermann in the kitchen they were obviously not referring to her; but must have sensed that there might be something younger. Both turned on me, threatening me with their deadly machine pistols, as they shouted the question again.

"What woman?" I asked in English, trying to sound calm, and adding: "Angleeski! Angleeski!"

One of them spat on the floor, the other gave me a jab in the ribs and, slinging his gun back over his shoulder, made a gesture describing the curves of a woman's body. Pushed about, punched and hindered by the fact that I was in my underpants, I tried to keep up the pretence of innocence by looking perplexed; but, when I went to get my trousers from the bed rail one of the soldiers grabbed them first, began to search in the pockets and found my 'AB Sixty-four' (the only evidence that I was in the British Army). With it was the marriage certificate, neatly tucked between two pages.

Like a sash, he tied my trousers round his waist, thrusting his face, clouding with anger, into mine and not noticing his bleary-eyed comrade who was taking gulps from a bottle tucked down his shirt front and eyeing the portly Frau Zimmermann as he would eye a comfortable mattress. Quickly, he showed that he was not going to be put off the scent by my poor acting and pulled back his safety catch. In the stark terror of the moment, quickly, unashamedly, I begged God to keep me alive.

"Once more," he shouted, "Where's the woman?" And once more, I managed to look dumb. Then, in disgust, he beckoned to his companion, who followed him, eyeing Frau Zimmermann disappointedly. Luckily, outside, they passed the house next door and staggered on further down the road, in search of young blood.

Immediately, Frau Zimmermann, looking scared but sighing with relief, came out with a pair of her husband's trousers, which she made me put on. Then I slipped round to the back door of the house next door, and knocked quietly.

"Don't worry, I'm English," I called out, in German.

I could hear the barricade being removed and, a moment later, the door was slowly opened and an old man peered out, suspiciously.

"Please, tell my wife it's all clear: she can come out now," I said.

In no time, Hilde was listening to the story of the missing marriage certificate — taking it all very philosophically. What could we do? It had happened. Shrugging our shoulders, we settled down to sleep, fitfully, until the first light of dawn slowly began to show up the tares in the blackout curtains. With typical Austrian hospitality, Frau Zimmermann spread out her hidden bits of food, including a large stale loaf, on the table and busied herself making coffee.

Finally, we wished the two of them goodbye and, determined to reach Liefenstein by the afternoon, walked out into the daylight, our morale boosted by the calm friendly rays of the spring sun.

Following deserted cart tracks, already overgrown with grass since the last wagon had passed, we sauntered through the woods under the tall pines, feet sinking deep into the cones and pine needles, which spread themselves away from us like a brown carpet as far as we could see. The air was full of their honey-scent, at last undisturbed by the stench of dead horses that we had grown used to. Finally, coming out of the woods into a kilometre wide clearing, we almost walked into a narrow stream of pearl-clear water, running between the fields down into a shallow valley. Here, we sat down to eat some of the bread and bierwurst which the farmer's wife had insisted we should take with us; but we soon found that, even in these peaceful surroundings, we had enemies. The mosquitoes, noiseless, meanly thin and almost invisible until seconds after they had dug in their long suckers, attacked us incessantly, until it was a relief to hear the occasional cow-fly approaching with the drone of a Stuka, and to be able to kill it before it could do any damage: but the bite of the odd one was as painful as the jab of a knife.

Lying back in the sultry sunshine, we listened to the rustling of the leaves until, exasperated at last, Hilde gasped:

"This heat is awful. I can't stand these bloomers any longer.

I'll keep one pair on but the rest are going for a six."

"You'll start getting a nice figure in a minute. I thought you were trying to look like a barrel."

"It's too hot to look like a barrel. Anyway, if I've got to run, I can run faster without them. Then, I somehow think they're not going to catch me."

When she started to peel off the offending garments, first the blue ones, then the red and the speckled grey, I warned her anxiously:

"Hey! Look out! These Russians have got binoculars. One look at this show you're putting on and they'll be over here like rockets."

But she took no notice, as unperturbed as ever.

"Can't be helped. The main thing is, I'm a whole lot cooler."

I looked across the stream at the silent woods, where the tall fir-trees, packed close together, could be concealing bloodthirsty murderers as well hares and deer. In their silence, the trees looked sultry and unnatural: at that moment, they seemed to conceal hundreds of prying eyes.

When we started to make our way across the fields, watching always for land-mines and carefully avoiding any suspicious-looking broken-up patches of ground, I felt relieved, convincing myself that the odds against getting killed were high. In the distance a meaningless shape amongst the trees was slowly turning into the fairy-tale castle of Liefenstein, growing in detail against a clear sky.

But could our luck last out?

It took us half an hour to reach the outskirts of the village, a small group of white thatched cottages in the middle of its surrounding rectangular fields. Here, everything had gone to seed, undisturbed by the hacking of hoes and scraping of rakes. No cows, no carts — nothing to take our eyes away from the grey towers of the fifteenth century fortress, hidden amongst the trees on a low hill, casting around it an aura of long-forgotten history. There wasn't a Russian in sight as we walked on through an avenue of trees to the drawbridge, covered in ivy, its rusty chains looking as if they hadn't been in actions for centuries. When we'd crossed over the dried-up moat, Hilde reached for the bell handle, high up at the side of the twelve-foot high oak doors, and pulled it.

"Surely, not even a giant could push these open," I said.

After a moments silence a man's voice was calling from the other side:

"Who are you?"

In a few words Hilde explained and the wicket gate in one of the doors was opened by a dark-haired smallish man, with just the right amount of elegant deference about him to be a servant but who was obviously trying to dress and act like a farmhand.

Politely he welcomed us in, eyeing us discretely and asking no questions. Then he silently led us through the courtyard, around which the castle with its ivy-clad walls, through the main entrance into a vast hall, where portraits of previous barons and baronesses surveyed us coolly. Here, he invited us to sit down, and left to inform the baron of our arrival.

Five minutes later Baron von Halstedt, smiling effusively, appeared. Looking appraisingly at Hilde he raised his eyebrows slightly then suavely kissed her hand, expressing how pleased he was to meet her and asking after her father whom he hadn't seen for sometime.

"Your father is a very fine gentleman and a great hunter," he said. He has taught me a great many things. I am looking forward to our next meeting: but this stupid war...One can't live naturally any more. One must forget the pleasures and think only of one's safety."

He was probably in his mid-forties; with a beard, which he seemed to be rather conscious of, clipped elegantly square for the benefit of the Russians.

"So far they don't know that I own the castle. If they did, I should have been shot or locked up long ago. No, my friends, they have been told that Baron von Halstedt, the rightful owner, put on his spurs and departed when Hitler came to power, and that the whole establishment had then been taken over by the Reich, converted to a museum and put under the directorship of Professor Wilhelm Graf — in other words, myself."

"It is like a museum," said Hilde. "Absolutely wonderful."

"Thank you, my dear. I see that you are discerning as well

as beautiful. Come, we will have tea."

Von Halstedt pressed a bell near the carved marble mantelpiece and, as if his whole life had been spent waiting for orders, the man who had first let us in appeared obediently from nowhere.

"Steiner, a pot of tea please and whatever you can find to go with it."

"Yes, Herr Baron."

Steiner was gone, but not for long. Coming back with a solid silver tray laden with exquisite bone china and plates with silver covers, he shuffled into the room, his baggy trousers and apron totally out of place.

"Frau Schmidt made some salami sandwiches with gherkins and soft cheese and has sent up also some little cakes left over from yesterday. She is sorry there is nothing else."

The baron nodded his approval and Steiner left the room.

"We shall be the last people round here to run out of food but if the war does not end soon our food supply certainly will," von Halstedt explained to us. "And, by the way, Steiner only wears those old clothes to be prepared: no Russian must ever think that I have a butler. It would be the end of us here. We have all been thoroughly socialist in our behaviour as far as they are concerned — working all together for the state — to them it doesn't matter what state — in order that the common people may gain from the culture of our museum."

In typical aristocratic style he asked Hilde to pour out the tea, waiting for me to take my first sip.

"Typhoo Tips," he said. "Do you recognise it? A tantalising taste of pre-war England (I could just taste the mould) from my hidden store cupboard."

During tea, the baron told us about himself.

"I was in England many times. I have many friends there. The late Rudyard Kipling visited this castle on his way to Italy, and there were many others. If the Russians were to get hold of my photographs they would pack me off to Siberia straightaway."

He laughed and, glancing round at a seventeenth century French clock on the mantelpiece, exclaimed:

"Good heavens, it's six o'clock. I promised to go and see my wife: she is hidden behind a bookcase in the library."

When he saw our looks of amazement, he apologised.

"Don't worry, I don't mean she's flat against the wall. There are two secret rooms in the castle which I know of and Magdelena and my mother are in one of them?"

"But supposing the Russians get in and find them," said Hilde.

"There is little chance of them being found. If you want to hide anything from a Russian soldier hide it behind some books."

"But why?"

"The Russian soldiers, my dear, are suspicious of books. They will not usually go near them for fear of having some spell cast over them. If you ask me, Stalin wants to keep them ignorant. A soldier with too much knowledge might decide to shoot him before the enemy."

" Now..." abruptly he brought the subject to a close... "You have the run of the castle and Steiner has orders to show you round. Later he will show you to your rooms."

Very tactfully he was using the plural. In fact, so far he hadn't even asked us how we knew each other or how we came to be together.

So his wife was about, even if she was behind a pile of books. After he'd left I tried to sound matter of fact, and said to Hilde:

"You like the baron, don't you? Even an amateur astronomer would recognise the stars in your eyes."

"He is the most handsome man I have ever met." She gave a long heartfelt sigh and, squeezing my hand, looked at me with the face of an angel. In spite of the trauma of life, I was beginning to feel jealous.

CHAPTER SEVENTEEN

In a few minutes Steiner arrived and soon we were following him around from room to room while he gave us the history of every object and piece of furniture which were part of the splendour of this typical mid-European, mediaeval castle: the bedrooms with their four-posters, heavily brocaded and curtains to match, the priceless tapestries, the forty-metre-long banqueting hall, with its quaint suits of armour, engraved with their family crests and mottos — all waiting to be smashed to bits by the first Russian soldiers who would get in.

When the tour was over, thoroughly wrapped up in the past, with mental pictures of swords, pistols, warming pans and jewellery, we found Baron von Halstedt waiting for us in the library. Ah! Now, I thought, he will press the button, the bookcase will open and we shall have the pleasure of meeting his relations. But he seemed to have no intention of introducing his wife and mother and, throughout the conversation it was embarrassing to think that they were only a few feet away. Like a backcloth dropped over a bird cage, the night descended over the castle, as the three of us sat by candlelight at a long table, eating a simple meal, prepared from what was available in the larders; with critical ancestors glowering at us, pale-faced and bubonic.

Afterwards, we chatted over a bottle of bourbon and smoked stale State Express 555 cigarettes. Pre-war cigarettes, brought from England in 1939 and saved for totally unexpected occasions such as this.

"Very smokable, don't you think?"

We nodded politely: four years of war had obviously dulled his senses. Encouraged by the bourbon, he turned the conversation at last to his wife.

"She's a cripple, I'm afraid," he apologised sadly. "Ten years ago she fell while horse-riding and has been in a wheelchair ever since. But she enjoys life and is still full of vitality, mentally — so much so that she got herself nearly killed by the Russians the other day."

On the wall his grandfather's face, surrounded by its elaborate frame, seemed to be getting longer.

"No," he said in answer to our questioning looks "she was not in her room, (he pointed at the book-cases). When 'your friends' arrived ...(I thought I saw a nasty little expression as he looked directly at me) ...I was a little optimistic after the first visit from the K.G.B. I don't know how to describe them..."

"Genial snakes in uniform?" suggested Hilde.

"And very smart uniforms too," said the Baron. Just plain blue with red here and there to keep up the communist image, and a silver star or two depending on the number of times they had said 'Yes, comrade' to the right man. Their patent leather boots were so shiny that one of my dogs stood and growled at itself, until it got a kick.

"It was my wife's idea to pretend that I was not the real von Halsdedt. She has a fair ration of woman's intuition. They celebrated their arrival by getting quite tipsy on some of my best wine. Then Steiner made the mistake of muttering: 'Stalin!' — a harmless enough word, except that he was making the motion of slitting his throat at the time. That rather upset them and I had to pretend he was a very good worker but slightly mentally deficient, with no knowledge of politics whatsoever. One of the women must have been an animal lover. She made a curious comment before she left. We were standing in the courtyard with my favourite peacocks strutting around at a safe distance, looking very capitalistic and well fed. She looked at them affectionately and said:

'If I were you, I should get them out of the way — hide them.' She gave no reason.

"I was not going to do what any communist woman suggested, which was unfortunate for the peacocks; nor was I wise enough to get my wife and mother out of the way. As a result, when the occupying troops turned up, not only did they have carte blanche shooting practice with the peacocks as targets but also, when my wife ventured to complain, real live capitalist women to insult, the sort which they had thought existed only under the Czars. The peacocks disappeared; plumes, feathers and all, hopefully to upset some greedy red stomachs. Luckily, my wife and mother did not, unlike some of the women in the village, who have not been seen for days. But they knocked my wife out of her wheelchair and pushed my mother about until she was black and blue.

"Immediately they had gone, I hid my wife and mother in the room behind the bookcase. Then I stormed down to the local H.Q. and complained to the only sober Russian I could find, a subaltern with a stomach ulcer. The next day a colonel in full regalia, with several subordinates, escorted us all down to the village square, where they lined up twenty men as near like each other as possible, whom they called 'prime suspects', and begged my wife to identify any concerned in the attack, promising to shoot them immediately if they preferred to have proof of Russia's honest intentions. My wife was wheeled up and down in front of the rank but was obviously unable to pick her attackers out. Lucky, I think: we all know what sort of revenge the intoxicated Russian soldiers would have taken. Anyway, the result was that the officer with the most understanding, and incidentally the most of my schnapps in him, actually advised me to keep the main gates locked and bolted. 'The Turks might have got in once upon a time but my lads won't; they're far too dim,' he guffawed."

The baron paused, lit another stale cigarette and went on:

"Now we are a little community on our own. I have to be hard-hearted, otherwise half the village would be squatting here. But wait, it is getting late and you must be tired."

In the shadowy light of the spluttering candles we got ready to go our separate ways. Hilde's bedroom was opposite mine somewhere in a wing on the third floor. Baron von Halstedt wished us a pleasant night and gallantly kissed Hilde's hand.

"Down in the village there may be some shouting tonight; but you need have no fear of Russians here. Get up when you want to: we have no rules."

Hearing this, and feeling safe at last, we said goodnight and went to our rooms.

In the eerie light of an oil lamp, I flung my clothes off, stretched out on a comfortable bed and, within minutes, was fast asleep. Hours later I woke from a dream in which I was surrounded by Cossacks in brilliant red uniforms: the sun was shining through a high window directly on my eyelids.

Dressed and feeling clean and refreshed for the first time in days, I crossed the passage and knocked at Hilde's door. The girl who opened it was a Hilde transformed. Instead of the old speckled skirt and skating boots she wore a close-fitting jumper, checked skirt and high-heeled shoes. Her hair was combed and curled outwards as if she'd just come out of Elizabeth Arden's.

"I found these clothes laid out on my bed last night. I suppose they belong to his wife. How do they look?

"Ravishing," I exclaimed. "If the baron's in anything like yesterday's mood, he's going to eat you, not just kiss your hand."

After we had something to eat, sitting at a little table on a concealed patio, we decided to visit the village and get the general lie of the land. To find out the state of the people under Russian occupation had become almost fascinating. In the village, the atmosphere was quite familiar: khaki-grey figures with machine pistols, singing, hanging around street corners, smoking aimlessly, laughing their unfriendly grating laughs and slowly topping themselves up in preparation for the evening games. We strolled among them, knowing the risk we were taking, listening to their curious growling dialects, as they tried to understand who we were.

"Angleeski prisoner," they kept repeating stupidly after me. Not one of them spoke German but at last we came across one who could speak a few words of French.

"When will the war end?" he asked four times before I understood what he was trying to say.

"About 1970 if your army doesn't get out and chase the Germans instead of staying here and chasing the women."

Luckily my French was as bad as his. Shrugging his shoulders he spat, just missing my toecap.

We felt elated. Alter all, the end of the war couldn't be far off. But how to get away from them to the west — this was the burning problem. If I had voiced my thoughts the Russians would have been flabbergasted: one of their great British allies, trying to get away from his comrades who had helped his country to win and were now squashing his enemies into the ground. Who cared about creeds and beliefs: comradeship was everything.

We sat down on some steps, hot in the brilliant sunshine. I had persuaded Hilde to slip on a dark raincoat over her bourgeoise get-up and put on a pair of walking shoes. In this way she was halfway towards looking unattractive. But with my worn battle-dress jacket and borrowed pinstriped trousers, I would have fitted in well among what Hitler had left of the gypsies. Sitting down waiting for something to happen, we were joined by a little soldier who grinned his way into our conversation. Like a child with a teddy bear, he nursed a big bottle of firewater. When I explained what I was, he looked at us admiringly, taking it for granted that Hilde was English too.

"Dobra! Angleeski!" he exclaimed, shrugging his shoulders as if to excuse himself for not speaking the language.

Within a few seconds he was showing me how to work his gun. This might be useful later, if there was going to be a 'later', I thought, peering dubiously down the barrel pointing at my left eye. Almost immediately he put the gun down, offering us a drink from his bottle and showing how sociable he was by drinking from it himself first with wet, slobbery lips.

Shaking her head with a smile, Hilde left the honour to me.

"Here goes, you nasty creature." I said to him, and he nodded and smiled happily.

I shut my eyes tightly and, putting the bottle to my firmly compressed lips, tried to appear to drink some of the fiery liquid, passing it back to him with an appreciative retch. Then I noticed that his happy smile had gone. On his face was a look of deep sadness: in his hand was his wallet. Slowly he pulled out some well-thumbed photographs and handed them across. Hilde was smiling almost sympathetically when she passed the first one to me — a rather tattered print of a dark-haired woman in her early thirties. She wore overalls and was leaning against a tractor. The second one was a portrait of quite a pretty girl of about ten, her hair plaited and wrapped round her head in a prim Ukrainian peasant style. Everything was black except for three red blobs, one on each cheek and one on her lips, all put on the photograph with a brush.

"Zhena! Zhena!" he shouted eagerly pointing to the woman with the tractor and then at the girl who must have been his daughter. After two more swigs from his bottle, he was crying like a baby, kissing the tractor instead of his wife and then each of his daughter's three red blobs in turn, at the same time mumbling Ukrainian words of love, which really should have been: 'I hope to be home, my darlings, just as soon as I have managed to rape another hundred or so defenceless Austrian women.'

His eyes lit up when one of his comrades, a tall knock-kneed fellow with a massive moustache and beard, arrived, full of backslapping, hand crushing bonhomie. When the other man pointed us out, explaining who we were, he shouted:

"Angleeski Angleeski. Dobra! England good. Good man. Good woman. Man. Wife. Zhena, yes? Good. Dobra. At last, here was a soldier from the Steppes who actually spoke a few words of English.

"Stefan Stefanovitch — beloved comrade!" shouted the little man, arms wide open and every decaying tooth in his wide-grinning mouth screaming for a filling.

Now, the firewater took over. Things moved fast. I could only guess at the meaning of the words tumbling over each other but could see that the attention of the men was on a house twenty yards away. With no warning, the smaller man threw his gun at me, indicating that I should look after it. Then, leaving his empty bottle on the steps, half staggered half ran over to the house and, smashing a front window, undid the latch and climbed in. His lanky comrade followed. After about a minute, screams and shouts came from inside the house and a man in his fifties was pushed out onto the road at the end of the lanky soldier's gun. While the little soldier raped the man's wife and daughter inside the house, with the pictures of his own wife and daughter in his pocket, the big one kept the father immobile, taking no notice of his tearful plea:

"My wife's pregnant — PLEASE, NOT HER! NOT HER!"

At that moment, could there have been a more bizarre tableau than this one? Two Austrian women being raped inside a house, the husband being held outside by a grinning Russian: leaving behind an Englishman armed with a Russian gun, whose only comment should have been, "Good luck to you, comrades, get on with it," and an anti-Nazi Austrian girl depending on the Englishman for safety from the Russians.

What was the answer? I had the gun, but shooting Russians would be shooting allies: and not shooting them would be condoning the rape of Hilde's countrywomen. The screams were not getting any softer. Five more Russians were queuing up outside the house. The husband was on his knees, blubbering. At that moment I would have thanked God for a thunderbolt on my head. Not waiting any longer Hilde grabbed me by the arm and dragged me away, as I threw down the gun in disgust.

Act Two was horrifying in its simplicity. It began just round the corner from the farm and ended a hundred yards away outside the surgery door of the only doctor in the district with any form of antidote for V.D. The queue comprised mainly women and girls of all ages and several boys just old enough to join the army where they could have been killed by nice clean bullets instead of being corrupted. As we watched, it broke up reluctantly. There was no antidote left. The Russians had produced the V.D. but not the antidote to go with it. Some of the unfortunate people had walked from villages twenty kilometres away; with the only present they would ever get from the Soviet Union. Wishing we could forget the scene, we turned and made our way back to the castle.

During the rest of the day, as the weather was warm and sunny, we lazed about in the gardens among the flowers and shrubs, relaxed in the knowledge that no Russian could kick his way through the oak doors or would be likely to try to scale an eighteen foot wall, and in this mood we joined Baron von Halstedt for the evening meal, a monotonous kraut and salami somehow made to taste palatable by Frau Schmidt. As we ate, the baron took us back a few hundred years, explaining how the Turks had stormed the original castle massacred all the inmates, plundered it and set it alight.

"So far, these Russians are not so bad, but basically I don't think time changes people or nations except for the worse. Surely communism is not going to work. The world will soon see how man's instinctive greed and ambition will destroy the Utopian ideal of sharing. What about the men at the top — the men in the Kremlin? You're not going to tell me that..."

The silence of the evening was shattered by a tremendous explosion. With our ears singing and our brains numbed we stared at each other as if hypnotised. A moment later Steiner rushed into the room without knocking, his face as white as the shirt hanging out from the back of his trousers. Though he seemed to want to speak, his lips stayed half open, trembling.

"Well, what is it, Steiner. What's happened?" Though tense, the baron showed no signs of panic.

"They've ... they've blown one of the gates off its hinges, Herr Baron: lifted it right up like a feather. " Baron von Halsdedt's face was grim, his lips set hard. In the steel-blue eyes was frustration and hatred. At that moment I felt sorry for the man whose priceless worldly goods handed down through generations were about to fall to the mercy of ignorance; but there was nothing he could do about it.

"It's no use," he said quietly. "We can't stop them unless you like the idea of being shot. Let them get on with it. With any luck they won't find the cider in the bath."

"The cider in the ...?"

"We've got to move fast," he broke in. "If they can blow up the main gates they will find the cellar door much easier. I have got about a hundred bottles of the oldest most potent wine in Burgenland down there. This has to be stopped."

He beckoned to his servant.

"Steiner, calm down now, man, and send for Frau Schmidt's son, Hans, to come and help us: we have a lot to do."

While Steiner was gone Baron von Halsdedt worked out his plan quickly.

"In the cellar are also two barrels of cider. We have quarter-filled one of the baths on the top floor already just in case of eventualities — so that we still have something to drink. The rest we must throw away. Perhaps they won't find this particular bathroom, and if they do and the cider doesn't kill them, it will at least knock them unconscious."

"Can't we hide some of the wine behind the books in the library?" said Hilde.

But the baron's mind was made up.

"There is no time. The wine must follow the cider down the lavatory." He pointed downwards with a grimace of disgust.

"It will be a final farewell to some of the rarest and most valuable wine in the country."

The whole operation started without delay. Steiner, the sixteen year old Hans, the baron, Hilde and I formed a relay team from the callers to the nearest lavatory. In this way it took very little time to get rid of thousands of pounds worth. Von Halsdedt, urging us on, was convinced that the Russians, now that they had a self-made entrance, would waste no time in using it. And he was right. The first contingent arrived five minutes after the last 'empty' had been stacked in a corner: three lusty Mongolians, guns strapped over their shoulders, sauntered in as if they had lived in the castle for years, acting as they probably imagined the Czars would have acted before the Bolsheviks' new improved detergent had arrived to wash away the stains of Russia's mucky capitalism. They took little notice of von Halstedt, who introduced himself as well as he could in sign language as the 'Direktor' of the museum and then wisely disappeared in the direction of the library.

Following them around at a safe distance, Hilde and I watched how they showed their appreciation of culture. Doors with seventeenth century brass handles, beautifully carved, were far too easy to open by hand. Legs as sturdy as theirs had to be kept in trim, so what better than to use the tough ox-leather boots encasing them to kick the doors open. When one of them discovered a light switch, he became so engrossed in pushing it up and down and watching the lights go on and off that his friends had to pull him away. Fascinated, we watched one of them squeeze an ample amount of toothpaste onto bread, spread it with his finger and eat it, a look of delight spreading across his pockmarked face. With great gusto they set alight to a two hundred year old four-poster bed, smothering the flames with a priceless eiderdown amidst roars of uncontrollable laughter.

In the meantime, one of the soldiers had crossed over to the dressing table where his roving eye had seen a bottle of eau de cologne. In utter amazement we watched him take the cap off and begin to drink it, smacking his lips with delight just as von Halstedt appeared in the doorway."

"That's it!" he said when he saw what was happening.

"I'm going to give these gentlemen the nicest present they have had in their miserable lives."

"Come!" he beckoned to the three soldiers, who lurched across the room after him, when he made the motion of drinking from an imaginary glass with his head thrown back. They followed him up a short flight of steps, while we kept in the background. We guessed he was going to show them the cider in the bath, a last long shot at getting them so drunk that they would be beyond doing more damage. When he came back, looking hopeful but at the same time apprehensive, we went with him down to the library: but it soon became obvious what a prodigious amount these Russians could drink when they lurched past the library on their way to the basement kitchens, looking for more drink and excitement. All the wine had gone down the toilet but the excitement was there in the form of Frau Shmidt, who was hiding in one of the larders. The baron looked at us, almost pleading.

"What are we going to do? They'll have that poor woman for certain. She's still quite attractive though she's getting on in years. And she's got that little bit of extra flesh — and you know as well as I do what that does to them."

In a moment we heard screams and ran to the window. Frau Schmidt was running into the vegetable garden pursued by two of the Russians, lurching but still conscious.

"It's all right," the baron assured us. "I think those two are only playful. The cider's made them happy, that's all."

He could have been right, if Frau Schmidt's sixteen-year-old son, Hans, hadn't seized a kitchen knife and raced down after them.

In spite of the knife, the bigger man of the two, laughing all the time, managed to grip the rather frail boy in a Siberian bear hug. But, when his mother went on screaming, Hans, with the strength of desperation, wrenched himself free and stabbed the big fellow in the arm. As he raced down the garden after his mother, who had broken loose and disappeared behind the glasshouse the bear began to roar and, lifting his gun, fired a few bursts in what he hoped was the direction of the boy. But Hans and the cider between them had done a good job, and the big Russian fell over in an alcoholic haze, only shattering some of the glass.

After we had locked ourselves in the library we kept silent, realising that the slightest noise could tip the balance between life and death, until the two Russians had left, dragging their unconscious comrades with them. Spilling out of their haversacks were all the priceless objects they had stolen.

That evening we watched a repair gang, mostly Poles from the village, fix the big door back in position.

"I hope that will keep them out until the end of the war."

The baron was keeping very calm considering all the damage done to his property.

As we sat eating bread and lard, the only food left, we discussed how and when the end of the war would come.

"Judging by what I have heard coming over on the British bulletins it simply cannot last more than a day or two," said von Halstedt. "At least, I hope not, because I have planned a 'goodbye' party to celebrate the departure of Adolf Hitler and his Third Reich. There is still some excellent Courvoisier behind the Encyclopaedia Britannica on shelf one."

When we went to bed, the uncertainty of what was going to happen to us, together with the exciting knowledge that the war would soon be over went to bed with us, creating a nightmare dilemma. Could it be possible that before long we would be behind the Union Jack, safe? But there was always the little crumb of doubt — the lurking knowledge that anything could still happen, good or bad.

The night was dark, with the thin edge of the moon just

showing in a clear black sky. Lying in my bed, with the blackout curtains drawn apart, staring up into the endless blackness I tried to count the pinpricks of light which were stars, hoping to sleep, but with the pessimism of the early morning hours, I saw the future as black as the heavens. How was I going to get this girl, who had stuck to me through the whole mad escapade, far away from the pitiful state of affairs which had driven our marriage licence into a drunk soldier's pocket. Under no circumstances would I leave her with the sadistic gang of uncultured peasants, which had swallowed up the peace of her country. Tossing and turning, I battled through a night of mental images until, as the dawn was breaking, frustration and aching limbs drove me out of bed into my clothes and out into the quiet gardens where the early morning mist lay like a soothing blanket over the greenness and the flowers, coating the webs of a million spiders with glistening dew. With the sun still behind the horizon I sat on a stone bench drinking in the fresh air. Then I noticed there was something different about the usual vague early morning noises and I could sense the excitement before I heard it. At last the Russians, with their hangovers, were up and about before breakfast, singing and cheering.

In that heavenly moment I knew the war in Europe was over.

As I listened, Hilde came out fully dressed and together we ran into the castle. The baron was standing against the mantle piece in the drawing room, still in his pyjamas, and a gold-coloured silk dressing gown that no Russian was ever going to steal. Up towards the high shadows of the ceiling the sadistic hours of the past weeks were disappearing in the smoke from his cigarette: on his face was the beaming smile of a little boy.

"We have heard that Hitler has reached Valhalla with the aid of his own gun and that the British have stopped about fifty kilometres away from here to the west."

I glanced at Hilde who shook her head quietly while the baron wasn't looking. Why tell them what we knew already? It wouldn't help now. They would soon find out that they were in the Russian zone fifty kilometres from commonsense and tolerance, and that they would have to make the best of it.

After the usual light breakfast, Hilde and I went down to the village, where we were immediately surrounded by cheering Russians, who seemed to have lost their antagonism and were waiting to be accepted as brothers into the fraternity.

Everywhere, we were greeted by smiles and laughter. On the surface, it seemed that Satan had at last gone on holiday; but lurking behind the general relaxed atmosphere was an unmistakable feeling that there was still time for nasty things to happen.

By midday we were back at the castle behind the gates, still locked for safety though the war was over. Baron von Halstedt was taking no chances, whatever trust he may have had in the Russians now completely shattered. In the evening Hilde went upstairs and came down looking radiant, to be greeted by the baron and myself, sitting waiting in the dining hall. In the centre of a silk Persian rug, looking pleasant but out of place on a small guilt Louis XV card table, together with several cut glasses, were two unopened bottles, one of Johnny Walker whisky and the other of Booth's gin.

"Ah! Fraulein Bayer. It is a pity the war can't finish every day, if it makes you look so attractive."

Where, oh where is his wife, I wondered.

CHAPTER EIGHTEEN

Aided by the baron's generosity with our drinks, over the next two hours we managed between us to solve most of Europe's future problems — economic and political; in fact create a whole new world which would never see a war again. This done, the baron and I shared Hilde, dancing on the smooth parquet floor to the music from the radiogram, much of which had been popular in England four years before. From this we were elevated to a lively Hungarian dance and, finally flattened, I had to throw in the sponge. As von Halstedt pulled Hilde down on the chaise longue and grasped her hands I saw, with no difficulty, the pointed horns protruding from his head. Prompted by this vision, I walked unsteadily over and pulled her away. He took a lingering look at her, relinquished her reluctantly and gave a whimsical smile.

"She is yours; take her away, you lucky fellow." He managed to pronounce with difficulty, before closing his eyes and going off to sleep.

It was then that Hilde, still more sober than us and certainly more tolerant, decided, on the spur of the moment, to venture out away from the castle with the excuse of getting some fresh air. Jolted into using my brains a bit more intelligently, I followed her, protesting:

"You always were a born optimist; but this takes the cake. Take it from me, you're not safe yet."

But, flushed and happy she took no notice, dragging me towards the bolted gates and wandering off into the night just as the clock on the village church was striking three. Like the night before, the sky was clear and black, glittering with tiny stars; the brilliant curved edge of the moon just showing. Undisturbed by the usual noise of the Russians playing their nightly games, nature had quietly taken over. All around us, impossibly close, was the continuous high-pitched whistle of millions of grasshoppers and crickets that, in their particular way, seemed to be celebrating the end of the war too. Just as Hilde was filling her lungs with the fresh uncontaminated air, we heard the Russians approaching and quickly started to make our way back to the castle, after I had somehow persuaded Hilde to take no chances.

But three of them caught up with us and waited by the oak doors, while I fumbled for the key. One of them was saying in broken German:

"We are friends now. Let us come in and we will drink to our victory."

With a friendly smile, he was holding out his hand, waiting for me to grasp it. But it was a hand that had probably dragged more than one girl like Hilde away from safety and into the woods, and in no way could I comply. Instead, I walked away, waiting for the curses and turning, watched him and his companions shrug their shoulders and walk off, taking their short-term memories with them.

Once more in the courtyard we slammed and bolted the gates behind us. Apart from blowing them off their hinges, an action that no Russian would dare to take again, there was no way in which they could get in.

In the morning, we knew it was time to go. The war was over the British lines not far away. Soon, some sort of bureaucracy would follow the shambles.

"How are you going to get over to your countrymen?" asked the baron, who seemed to have forgotten about the episode at the party.

Looking at Hilde, I had no answer; balanced on a razor's edge, never quite knowing what her real feelings were - would or would she not come with me?

Our marriage certificate, the only tie between us, was lost, and in any case had only been a questionable security. She was studying the ornaments on the mantle-piece, pretending she hadn't heard, and he didn't repeat his question, but just seemed full of regret that we were going.

"What shall I do without my charming friend and her devoted Englishman?" he exclaimed. "You would have been welcome to stay here for as long as you liked.

"I know," said Hilde. "And you are very kind. But we must see what has happened to my house and, of course, to my mother. She will have no idea where we are."

Frau Schmidt, Hans and Steiner also seemed genuinely sorry that we were going. Steiner bowed stiffly, but in his eyes was a look of cameraderie born of the recent events when for a while, he had at last forgotten his position as servant and had become a member of the bourgeoisie. Only the austere faces of the von Halstedt ancestors still showed their disapproval of our presence in their sacred home. Von Halsdedt himself, with his inscrutable enigmatic smile concealing the reason for not introducing his wife and mother, clicked his heels, kissed Hilde's hand and, patting her cheek paternally, gripped mine.

With no need to conceal ourselves and fewer suspicious Russians clamouring to find out who we were we decided to take a quicker route back along the main road to Kurstenfeld. Early in the morning we set out and walked all day along a route ten kilometres shorter than the roundabout way we had come, passing through one village and keeping out of sight of Russian staff cars and army lorries. In the village we found the people happy. "The Allies will be here soon. It will be goodbye to the dreadful Russians and good riddance."

One old farmer spat into his manure heap.

"Stalin, phew!" he exclaimed. "Give me Churchill, Roosevelt, Eisenhower, Montgomery."

To know all the names he must once have been risking his neck listening to the news from England.

As we had no intention of damping their good spirits, we told no one about the boundary but had to be content with just being sorry for them; nodding to everything they said. The remains of the broken Wehrmacht, German and Austrian soldiers, were everywhere, looking forward to throwing away their uniforms which some now felt ashamed to wear. Mixed up amongst them were the traitorous Vlasov troops; the Russian soldiers who had gone over to the Germans, led by General Vlasov, when Germany had appeared to be winning, and who would now rather walk around in their underpants than show themselves in German uniforms — giving themselves away by their high cheekbones and peculiar un-German language. Those who had enough control over their trembling nerves to keep their wits about them were begging for clothes without much success. Searched out by the K.G.B. they were running for safety, hiding wherever they could, avoiding their Russian brothers, the fear of the firing squad in their dark, despairing eyes.

"Please give us something to wear." Three of them had stopped a farmer and his wife and were almost in tears. "We are not like all the Russian comrades who have been plaguing you and stealing your belongings, but are good honest soldiers fighting to save your country from communism."

We left them almost on their knees and stared at by the villagers, torn between disgust and sympathy.

Late in the afternoon we arrived at the house in Kurstenfeld. Hilde's mother was overjoyed to see us and listen to our tales about the castle and its elegant owner. She had busied herself making the house suitable to live in and stocking up with as much food as possible. With our newfound and intoxicating freedom we chatted and laughed. But like a menacingly unseen figure, lurking always somewhere near, the problem of how, or for that matter whether to get away from it altogether was there waiting to be solved. Under the canopy of laughter I could sense how Frau Bayer was fighting her own little battle over her daughter's future, recognising what the alternatives of keeping and losing her would mean.

After a peacefully uneventful night, we woke in the middle of a rather cloudy morning. Again there seemed to be nothing to do but eat and discuss various plans while Frau Bayer kept discreetly out of it. The afternoon still found us uncertain about our next move. When her mother was not in the room Hilde spoke in whispers about her latest idea — that we should get as close to the border as possible, travelling through the night, and then wait for an opportune moment before making a dash for it.

"Our luck has held so far: just believe it will go on like that, and it will."

I couldn't believe what I was hearing.

"If you don't want to leave everything you know so well — if you don't want to leave your mother, your cousins, your sisters when they come home, your grandparents here in the Russian zone, you must tell me. But I won't leave you to the mercy of the Russians, however different they may be, unless you tell me to go."

Without thinking, I had pronounced sentence on myself. Gone was all my natural impatience to get home to see my lovingly forbidding father and my uncertain, worried mother — to be part of the system for which, four years before, I had nearly managed to get killed. I knew then that I would, if necessary, use every trick in the book to stay where I was. It would be up to Hilde. And it was then, while Frau Bayer was upstairs sorting out what the Russians had left, that the three breathless messengers arrived to sort our problems out for us. With no warning they crashed their small fists on the door, hardly waiting for Hilde to jump up and open it before they were in the room panting, staring excitedly; their young eyes full of the light of the adventure which they had been caught up in - three young boys, not one of them older than nine, all pulling at my sleeve together.

"Schnell! Schnell!" They were all three shouting at once. "The Englanders are down the road. You've got to go— QUICKLY."

"Just a minute." I tried to calm the most sensible looking of them. "Englanders? What Englanders?"

"English officer. English soldiers in a big truck," shouted the boy. "But they're going. THEY'RE GOING!" He was dancing about with excitement. "We told them you were here. The officer says you've got three minutes. IF YOUR'E NOT THERE, THEY'LL GO!"

There was no time to ask for 'Yes' or 'No'. Not even time to call Hilde's mother, still upstairs. Turning round, I looked at Hilde. During a second that was a lifetime, she seemed to hesitate: but the answer was there before the question was asked.

"Go quickly," she said calmly. "I will follow a few yards behind. No Russian must see us together."

As I ran out, the boys went on ahead. At the end of the road, near the main square, I could see two vehicles a three-ton open truck and a grey staff car. Beside the staff car stood two officers, a British lieutenant, looking anxiously at his watch, and a Russian colonel smiling at three girls standing at the other side of the road. Though I didn't look round, I knew that Hilde was following. When I caught up with the boys and ran up to the lieutenant, I saw a curious-looking bunch of men, most of them still in battledress, and two of them with corporal's stripes, staring at me from inside the truck, ready to greet me. As the lieutenant saluted, I realised that at least my jacket had made me recognisable as a British soldier and saluted back, feeling embarrassed. Somehow, I had forgotten that I was still in the army.

"Hallo, old man," The lieutenant looked relieved and glad to see me. "We were just going." I started to speak, but he raised his hand. "No time for formalities, old man. Jump in. By tonight, you'll be back in the British lines."

"But I..."

"Never mind. Naturally, you're surprised. Who wouldn't be? I bet you thought you'd never get home. The long and the short of it is we're here to get you chaps out."

Quickly, he introduced himself. "Control commission - Lieutenant Daniels."

Giving me no time to tell him my name or anything about myself, he went on:

"And lucky you are, too. It's the last journey they'll let us make. We've had a good few of you so far. You're about number thirty-six. O.K., jump in."

I hesitated, and he looked annoyed.

"I say, old man. Do you or don't you want to come? We haven't got all day. I've got a date tonight and I don't propose to miss it on your account."

He lowered his voice, leaning nearer, his head away from the colonel, who was still smiling at the girls. "From what we've been hearing of the Russians, only a nutter would want to stay with them, anyway. O.K. - jump in."

The back of the truck was down. They were waiting.

"Come on, mate," called one cockney, with the band of the R.A.S.C. on his shoulder. "First class accommodation at the front, second at the back. All the first seats taken, except the one next to me. The Fraulein can have that." He had seen Hilde and was grinning.

I looked desperately at her, standing with the three boys, near us. Then I pointed her out to the lieutenant and speaking softly, so that the colonel wouldn't hear, tried to explain my predicament.

"I can't go without my wife."

"Your wife?"

He was taken by surprise. His eyes, resting upon Hilde, showed his appreciation — but, for a moment, suspicion. The girls, who had been joined by two more, were still keeping the colonel busy.

"Good God, man. I can't do that." the lieutenant said, as loud as he dared. "I'd be court-martialled. What the hell did you want to get married for? What is she — Austrian, or what?" He gave me no time to answer. "You're in a spot now, aren't you? If you refuse to come, you're a deserter. You're still in the army, you know. Where's your A.B. Sixty-four? Let's have a look at it."

"Sorry, Sir. It's in some Russian's pocket."

"Look here, old man. I tell you what." Again, his eyes were on his watch. "Let's pretend I haven't seen you. You'll just have to stay and make your own way. I'm sorry, I've done my best."

By this time, the colonel had lost interest in the girls across the road and was looking at Hilde.

"Who is she?" he asked in halting English.

Quickly, and apparently without giving it a thought, Lieutenant Daniels answered:

"She is English — interned in a camp outside Vienna since 1939. Her name is Miss Smith."

For the first time since joining the British army, I saw one of its officers actually wearing a halo.

The colonel was delighted.

"Very nice Engleesh miss," he weedled, grabbing her hand before she could get it out of the way and licking, rather than kissing it. "Very nice name — Miss Smeeth."

"Yes," agreed the lieutenant, trying to pull her away towards the three-tonner. "Excuse me," he added, pronouncing the words slowly. "Time is running short. By nine o'clock, we have to be at the border. These were your orders, sir. Remember?"

"Ah yes, yes."

But the colonel's hand had shot out, grabbing Hilde by the arm.

"Engleesh miss," he faltered, obviously the worse for drink. "You come sit in auto with good Russian soldier. We have long talk. You tell comrade all about England."

"Yes," said Hilde, uncertainly.

It looked as if our fate was sealed. How could she last out with the only two words she knew? — 'Yes and 'No'?

But the lieutenant had all the answers. In his haversack was a bottle of whisky and, within two minutes a quarter of it was in the colonel's stomach. The rest — the Russian was clutching to him like a pampered child.

I pulled the lieutenant to one side.

"She has no clothes with her — nothing," I whispered. "Can we please call back at her house so that she can get some and say goodbye to her mother?"

"Absolutely not, old man. No more concessions. She either comes now or she stays."

The colonel had already settled the questions by pulling her down beside him in the back of the staff car. With no alternative, I jumped into the truck. As the motors started and the convoy moved away from the small group of inquisitive onlookers, gathering speed, I looked around for the three boys, hoping to shout goodbye, but they had disappeared up the road and must have been making for the house, just in time to tell Frau Bayer what was happening. As we sped past, I could see her leaning out of the window, crying and clutching a bundle of Hilde's clothes, which she threw down into the truck. Cut away from her mother's view, Hilde was sitting rigidly in the staff car beside the now thoroughly drunk colonel. In the truck, refusing to answer the questions from all sides about her, I was told I was 'bloody miserable' and left alone.

Scattering curious onlookers in every direction, we left Kurstenfeld at a hundred kilometres an hour. But Satan had been waiting long enough for a chuckle. Before we had covered ten kilometres, there was a tremendous explosion from the staff car, now well ahead, and we watched it swerve from side to side before slowly coming to a halt. The lieutenant jumped out looking annoyed and frustrated, and stared hopelessly at the nearside back wheel, which had only a few bits of tyre still clinging to it.

"That's jiggered it," he said. "No point in trying now."

"Don't worry sir. We'll fix it."

Before the corporal had finished the sentence, the jack was out and, in three minutes the wheel-change had been completed. In another two, the thick treads had dug themselves into the soft earth, the boots and most of the lower legs of the men in the three-toner, pushing, had dug themselves into the soft mud and the staff car was back on the road.

"We'll never do it now," said the lieutenant.

"We'll do it, sir." The corporal's tone was as soothing as a tranquillizer.

It was a good time to get Hilde away from the colonel's clutches and into the safety of the truck. The men welcomed her: this all added to the excitement. As one or two of them helped her up over the tailboard, there was a low cheer, and the colonel grunted in his sleep, stroking the empty bottle. The men had now taken on the challenge of getting this Austrian girl past the border to freedom. Not knowing who or what she was, they still respected their lieutenant's decision.

I soon found that they knew more or less as much about the Russians as I did, while Hilde, used to P.O.W. German and quite relaxed, soon became friendly with all of them and thankful for their concern about her. Now that she was with me again, with the border at Kierflach nearer each minute, I opened up to the others, explaining a few of the details about our original meeting and subsequent experiences; finding that all of them — British, Australians and New Zealanders alike — after escaping as we had, and knowing of Russia's plan to send them to England via

291

Odessa, had decided to wait their chance for a short cut. We listened to their stories about the Russian 'liberators', shouting above the noise of the motor, the banshee whine of the gearbox and the screech of tyres on well-tarmaced corners. Some had been locked up with captured German prisoners, others had spent much of their time at wild parties, with vodka and hooch flowing like water; and yet others had found themselves alternately 'protecting' families in this pro-Allied part of Austria and hiding away from Russian officialdom. Everyone had a different plan for getting Hilde across the border.

"She ought to make a run for it," suggested one sapper. They'll probably be so pissed they won't know which of her to fire at."

"Aye — bloody foony. An 'oo's to blame if they 'it right won' lad? You, yer great taiter. That's right stoopid idea."

The fellow from Burnley, whose sense of humour was not a strong point, spat out of the back of the truck.

After half an hour, a corporal from Clapham came up with the best answer.

"Dress 'er up, stick 'er dahn in a corner, cover 'er up and tell the bastards she's a soldier wots been taken sick."

The decision was taken. Everybody seemed to agree and, between them, they soon had Hilde looking more like an R.A.C. trooper than I did; in full battledress, boots, gaiters and black beret pulled well down, with her hair tucked under it, on top of her head.

Time was running desperately short, as the driver pumped at the accelerator, trying to catch up with the staff car, well ahead now that we had reached the winding, hilly roads nearer Graz. As, every now and then, the car waited for us, through the rear window we were able see the colonel contentedly hugging the army greatcoat that he thought was Hilde. Some of the most beautiful scenery in Austria went unnoticed as we clung onto the sides of the truck, skidding round hairpin bends up the hills near Graz, overlooking a carpet of scenery slowly fading into the uncertain light of the evening and, guided by the superlative driving of the grim-faced corporal, trying always to keep up with the staff car. This man knew how impossible the Russians would make it for the little convoy to get past the barrier, when their set time had run out.

"You won't get the bloody bloke through unless his bird goes with him," shouted one chap into the corporal's ear, through the flap in the canvas behind his head — and referring to me. "Best stop and let them piss off."

The corporal, glancing first at his watch and then at the rapidly darkening sky, just shouted back over his shoulder:

"Forget it — we'll do it," and left it at that.

Very suddenly, we were clouded in darkness by the quick drop of the Austrian night, but we had beaten the most difficult part of the journey, cleared the first hurdle and were bumping and swaying, with steam pouring from the bonnet and lights on full beam, towards Graz. After that, only few kilometres away, would be Kierflach and the border. I knew that the lieutenant in the staff car would have his eyes on his watch, no doubt thinking of the date which he still might be able to keep and silently cursing the sympathy which had allowed him to take an unknown girl with him into the British zone. But how could that British officer, knowing what he now knew, hand over to the Russians a girl who had risked her life for an Englishman?

The night had become pitch black, with no moon and not a star shining when suddenly, without warning, they were there — the two flags — one, a brilliant spot of light in the darkness — the flood-lit flag of the U.S.S.R., waving slowly above us in the slight breeze, whispering its warning to all those not prepared to abide by the rules it represented; and the other, across no-man's land, the friendly, welcoming Union Jack, emblem of security and freedom.

At two minutes to twenty-one exactly we pulled up under the red flag: the staff car in a cloud of dust, rising up like smoke and dulling the searing white brilliance of the arc-lights, with the truck only a few yards behind.

Within seconds, the driver of the staff car had jumped out and was already giving orders from the lieutenant to get Hilde into a corner and hide her. The colonel had come to just in time to see the entrance to the guard room and was in the arms of the officer in charge of the border guards, being held vertical and greeted in comradely style at the same time.

Here, under the glare of the lights, were the smartest soldiers we had yet seen. Beside them, Lieutenant Daniels looked like a weeping willow. The shine on their boots, matching their perfectly pressed uniforms, was almost painful to the eyes. The few badges and silver stars were unobtrusive: their friendly smiles were controlled by the importance of their position.

The officer of the border guards welcomed us all:

"Again, we have the brave Allied soldiers, escaped over to their friendly brothers and now about to join their dear ones." He addressed us in perfect English. "But," he continued, shaking Lieutenant Daniels by the hand, "there are papers to sign, formalities to go through, names and numbers to be checked, as you know. I feel that it is too late to perform these dull necessities: we should wave these proceedings until the morning. To-night..." he paused, not noticing the desperate looks on one or two faces..." To-night, you are our guests. All of you - the last fortunate men to be collected and sent home. You are invited to our party. We will eat Russian food, drink Russian vodka and wine and you will hear us sing our own happy Russian folk songs from the Caucasus and the Steppes. Today never ends. Tomorrow never comes. Remember that, my friends, and live always for the moment. Long live our two great states."

"Three, sir," interrupted another English-speaking officer. "You have forgotten America." His superior scowled at him and said nothing.

Lieutenant Daniels, who had been trying to get a word in, managed at last.

"I can't do it, sir. Got to get back. Orders."

"Orders? " the Russian repeated with a touch of sarcasm.

"The war is over." Then he looked a little more understanding. "Don't worry, I shall personally take all responsibility. Now, leave your vehicles and come and join us."

The lieutenant played his last card.

"Impossible, I'm afraid; though we are very grateful for your hospitality. But we have a sick man in the truck. We must get him across to the M.O. with all speed."

"But my dear fellow," said the Russian. "We have a doctor here — a very skilled one. Allow me to let him examine your invalid."

"It would not be wise, I'm afraid. My seniors would not approve. In my mind he has the symptoms of typhoid."

His intuition had worked. The officer's mood suddenly changed.

"Right, we shall not waste time." He called to the sergeant. "Kailovitch, check the truck. Take all the names and numbers quickly. Look for contraband: we are only letting through soldiers — nothing and nobody else. Don't touch the sick man."

The big test was on now: the efficiency of his men against the acting ability of ours. The only part of Hilde showing above the army greatcoat and blankets and below the edge of her black beret was her nose, which, even in the shadows, couldn't easily pass off as masculine. The Russian sergeant was approaching, holding a torch. Quickly I bent down and squeezed Hilde's hand, pushing it back out of sight.

"If they get you, I'll get away and wait for you," I whispered. If they get me, they won't hold onto me. I'll get back somehow, sometime. Good luck."

The sergeant pushed aside the coverings. The torch was shining on the hands — the face, lighting it up like the moon. The game seemed to be up: but instead he was looking puzzled, shrugging his shoulders. Never had he seen anything so effeminate in the Russian army. So this was what they had been told about. The decadent British, even calling up the homosexuals to help populate their mobile brothels. Here was one of them. Fancy, a homosexual having the guts to escape. With the Russian officer chivvying him from outside the truck, he quickly took the names and numbers of the others, speaking English and leaving Hilde out.

"The sick man," called the officer suspiciously. "How sick is he, then?"

"Very sick, sir." But the sergeant wasn't referring to any physical state.

Within half an hour, an almost triumphant Lieutenant Daniels had signed the necessary papers. It was then only a matter of a few half-hearted handshakes, followed by an official salute, and slowly, as the barrier was raised, the wheels of the staff car and the truck began to turn. Everything was going too smoothly: it simply had to end in a fiasco.

The rear of the truck had passed under the barrier and the Russian soldiers were waving goodbye when a red-faced and watery-eyed colonel catapulted from the guardroom. Over the noise of the urgently revving engines we could just hear his despairing wail.

"My lovely Miss Smeeth; she had deserted me!"

But, with the two vehicles now fifty yards into no-man's-land, it was too late. The guards officer stood under the brilliant arc-light, glaring at us as he argued with the stupefied colonel. Along the road, through the blackness we sped towards the Union Jack.

In the distance, ever smaller, we could see just a few of the raised fists of the U.S.S.R. shaking furiously at their future enemies.